AF317028

An American Saga

The Tale of the Kolkers, Browns, Wievels, and Wooldridges

With an autobiography of Charles J. Kolker, Jr.

Charles Kolker

ISBN: 979-8-9892911-0-6

Published OCTOBER 2023

Forward and Acknowledgements

It should be known that this family history is imperfect. It is meant to be a starting point for future generations to correct and add information. Genealogical research is part guessing game. Census takers, priests, relatives, and other record keepers weren't always accurate. Many names were spelled a variety of ways. Birth and other dates differed in the records. I did my best to confirm important dates by cross-referencing to other sources. Also, I mostly used photos of family that are seriously outdated, many dating to my mother's funeral in 1997.

I was intrigued early on by the idea that we're all, somehow or the other, related to royalty. Adam Rutherford, who wrote A Brief History of Everyone Who Ever Lived, wrote, "Most people don't have a coat of arms, but I can say with absolute confidence that if you're vaguely of European extraction.... you are descended from Charlemagne..." (page 160). So, congratulations on being royal! Of course, Charlemagne helped out by siring "at least eighteen children by motley wives and concubines, including nine by his second wife, Hildegard of Vinzgau." (page 158.)

This definitely has been an adventure. It started in 2018 when I thought it would take a year to complete. But it's 2023!

It is my hope to create a Volume 2, which would devote much more space to my wife, children, and travels around the world. Here's hoping for a long life!

There are many to thank for this effort. My brother Bob is the much more likely family genealogist. He has been helpful in numerous ways throughout this task. His research is thorough and hopefully, he will be able to read this family history without too much wailing.

My siblings contributed their own accounts of their lives and provided photos and tales of growing up that provide authenticity. Thanks to all of them.

This account would be much less informative had not my Dad, Charles (Carliss) Kolker, agreed to a sit-down interview. Likewise, my aunt, Anna Lee Brown Schlitt, cooperated in granting a series of long interviews that provided insights into the lives of our family. Her identification of people in old photos contributed much to believability.

Over the course of this effort Audrey Hoisington, formerly of 2Nimble.com, and Dina Klarisse Dugar, also formerly of 2Nimble, provided encouragement, undeserved praise and lots of editing help. Later, they were joined by Angela Huff, index magician among other terrific talents. Thanks, Audrey, Angela, Dina, and Lantern Author Services!

Charles J. Kolker, Jr.
August 2023

TABLE OF CONTENTS

Book III - Laura Drews

VOL. 1

BOOK I – 1770s to 2021

Chapter 1

The Kolker Ancestors and the Kingdom of Hanover

The territory of Hanover (sometimes spelled with two ns) had once been a principality of the Holy Roman Empire until it was elevated to an electorate in 1708. Hanover later became part of a "personal union" with Great Britain, meaning that there was a combination of Hanover with Great Britain, each retaining its own boundaries, laws, and interests, but with the same person as the head of state. This happened because the Hanoverian Duke Ernst August became the First Elector of Hanover and then he married Sophie, the granddaughter of James I of England, bringing the succession of the English throne to Georg Ludwig (George I) in 1714. From that time until 1837, with a brief interlude in the Napoleonic period, the same ruler governed England and Hanover. In 1803, the French and Prussian armies conquered the "Kolker area" in Hanover in the Napoleonic Wars, with Napoleon's youngest brother, Jérôme, being named the ruler in 1807[1] . Great-great-great-grandfather, Johann Gerhard Henrich Kolker, was a young man in his 20s when the French, Prussians, and others swept through his neighborhood.

Johann was born on July 22, 1779, in Merzen, Osnabrück, Niedersachsen (the latter being known in English as Lower Saxony), Germany, at a time of revolution in France and one ending in America.

1

The map above shows the modern-day District of Osnabrück, within Lower Saxony, Germany. Note that the places identified with our Kolker ancestors, Merzen and Fürstenau, are in the northwestern part of that District. Maps are devilish things, though, and especially so in "Germany"/Kingdom of Hannover, as "Germany" was, at the time, a hodge-podge of fragmented kingdoms, bishoprics, and other sovereign pieces, not a unified state.

However, the Prince-Bishopric of Osnabrück , identified in the map above of the Kingdom of Hannover until 1866 (and had been so since the "personal union" with Great Britain ended in 1837), is roughly the same area as shown in the map on the previous page, so our Kolker ancestry's place in what is now known as Germany is nailed.

So, what was happening then in our "New World"? Just a few days before Johann's birth, General Anthony Wayne led his Americans to a victory over the British by capturing Stony Point, New York. In the same year, while Johann was still a gurgling baby, John Paul Jones while losing his ship, the Bonhomme Richard, was able to claim victory leading his Americans to take the British ship, Serapis.

We know that Johann married Margarethe Adelheid von der Benken, although we're not sure when. One of his children was great-great-grandfather, Eberhart Kolker. And, just to make things more confusing, there's information out there that a "Margaretha Adelheid Kolker" was married to Bernard Heinrich Kolker, and thus was the mother of Johann G H Kolker, not his spouse. Further research, though, seems to confirm Margarethe as Johann G H's spouse, not mother. This kind of confusion is not uncommon in genealogy, as research sources sometimes differ as to the origins, name spellings, ages, and other aspects of an ancestor.

It is hard to imagine the living conditions and exact circumstances in which Johann existed. Bishops were rulers as any other noblemen, and most of them, clergy or not, were not all that sympathetic to the underclasses. There is no reason to believe that Johann was anything but in the underclass, a farmer.

In most of Germany, farming was handled by tenant farmers who paid rents and obligatory services to the landlord, who was typically a nobleman. Peasant leaders supervised the fields and ditches and grazing rights, maintained public order and morals, and supported a village court which handled minor offenses. Inside the family the patriarch made all the decisions and tried to arrange advantageous marriages for his children. Much of the villages' communal life centered around church services and holy days.[2]

Merzen was a small village in the northern part of what is now the District of Osnabrück in Lower Saxony. The Netherlands borders Lower Saxony to the west. According to the Encyclopedia Britannica that part of Germany is, and was then, dominated by "the great North German Plain". Much of that northern part consisted of sandy lowlands of heath, bog, and polder, interspersed with scattered forests. According to Britannica, "Lower Saxony's climate offers mild winters, moderately warm summers, and a steady year-round rainfall ranging from 24 to 35 inches per year."[3]

Added to Johann's woes as a lowly farmer would have been the armies of the competing powers roaming across the place where he lived. Much of the rest of the world was in turmoil as well. The United Kingdom fought the United States from June 1812 until February 1815. The U.K., along with other allies, fought Napoleon's armies from May 18, 1803, to June 22, 1815, when, on that later date, Napoleon famously met his Waterloo. Present-day Kolkers are lucky to be here; Johann could have perished from French, English, German, Austrian, or Prussian weapons. And those weren't the only combatants; it seemed as though every European country joined one side or the other, pursuing after or retreating from opposing armies. Waterloo, then part of the Netherlands, was and is about 120 miles southwest of Merzen, but many of the armies passed through before they got to Waterloo.

French control of Hannover lasted eight years until the territory of great-great-great-grandfather Johann was overrun by Russian Cossacks. Then it was the French. Eventually, treaties ended French control and the Electorate was restored to the House of Hanover. In fact, the 1814 Congress of Vienna elevated Hanover to an independent kingdom with its Prince-Elector, George III of Great Britain, as King of Hanover. When Queen Victoria took the

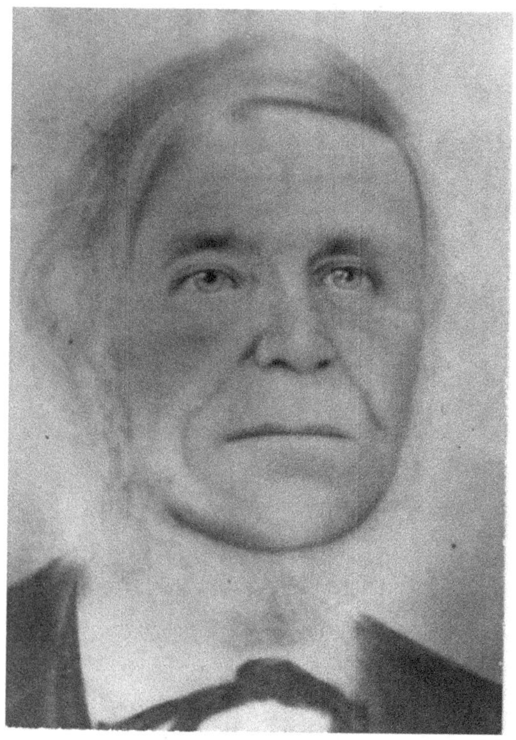

Johann Eberhard (or Eberhardt) Kolker, born September 16, 1818, in Hanover, Germany; died December 7, 1905, Mt. Carmel, Iowa.

British throne in 1837, the 123-year "personal union" of Great Britain and Hanover ended. There's a detailed analysis of this "personal union" translated from German, at the European History Online: Personal Union and Transfer: Great Britain and Hanover, 1714–1837 — EGO (ieg-ego.eu)

Again, according to the above article from the Encyclopedia Britannica, "The population of Lower Saxony regards itself as Low German, linked by a common ancient Saxon origin and the use of the Low German dialect know as Plattdeutsch. The latter, a dialect closely related to Dutch, Frisian, and English, is quite distinct from the official High German." Low German would have been the dialect spoken by Johann and his family.

Johann Eberhart Kolker, a son of Johann G H Kolker, was born on September 16, 1818[4], in the Kingdom of Hanover; he was 19 years old when Queen Victoria took the British throne. That must have been exciting to him, as Victoria was born May 24, 1819, just a few months later than he, and, therefore, she was his contemporary when she took the throne. He also would have been vibrantly alive and aware of the great, historic events happening to his homeland and all over Europe.

Semi-Salic law prevailed in the Kingdom of Hanover, which excluded accession to the throne by a female while any male of the dynasty survived, meaning that Victoria's uncle, Ernest Augustus, of the House of Hanover, took over as Ernest Augustus I of Hanover.

Events were about to directly affect great-great-grandfather Eberhart. The 1840s were years of upheaval in Europe, including Germany. There were street demonstrations of workers and artisans in Paris from February 22 through 24, 1848, causing the abdication of King Louis Phillipe of France, and sending him into exile in Britain. Revolutions spread throughout Europe. They erupted in Austria and Germany, beginning with large demonstrations on March 13, 1848, in Vienna, resulting in the resignation of Prince von Metternich as chief minister to Emperor Ferdinand I of Austria. Metternich joined the growing crowd of exiles in Britain.[5]

The revolutionaries demanded freedom of the press, freedom of assembly, written constitutions, arming of the people, and a parliament.

Metternich's resignation and exile didn't satisfy the crowds. Feeble efforts by Ferdinand I to reform were not enough, and he fled Vienna on October 7, 1848, abdicating in favor of his nephew, Franz Joseph.[6]

Turmoil spread throughout the German states in 1848: Baden, the Palatinate (then part of the Kingdom of Bavaria), Prussia, Saxony, the Rhineland, Bavaria, and Greater Poland (even though the latter was not technically a German state). Ultimately, however, these revolutions largely failed. Many of these people who wanted reform were terribly disappointed and left for the United States. Notable among the leavers were Carl Schurz, Franz Sigel, and Friedrich Hecker. These emigrants became known as "the Forty-Eighters". Great-great-grandpa Eberhart was almost certainly in this exodus of the disappointed, although we know that his brother, Georg, left in January 1846, while the ferment of revolution was in the air. We know that as early as the Hambacher Fest of May 27-30, 1832, that there was growing unrest in face of heavy taxation and political censorship. While the Hambacher Festival was at Hambach Castle near Neustadt an der Haardt in what is now Rhineland-Palatinate, Germany, it was a harbinger of what was to come for the entirety of Europe. In January 1832 a number of journalists established a democratic association for freedom of speech and the press, which was almost immediately banned by the state government. This resulted in the so-called fair, or fest, at Hambach Castle, where 20,000 to 30,000 showed up to protest. It didn't come to much, but it stirred revolutionary thinking and that kind of unrest sparked a cascade of events up to the 1848 revolutions. [7]

According to Family Search, a genealogical website maintained by The Church of Jesus Christ of Latter-Day Saints, "in the 19th and 20th century, from 1820 to 1930 Hannover (Lower Saxony) lost approximately 700,000 people due to emigration....Between 1832 and 1886 the Kingdom or Provinz of Hannover lost officially 183,355 inhabitants to emigration. Most emigrated to the United States of America and Osnabrück supplied 42% of emigrants, or 77, 056 people. Emigration occurred in three phases. In the 1840s a crop failure initiated an emigration wave of the under stratum. After the American Civil War emigration from Hannover increased again because of the Homestead Act of 1862 promising emigrants 160 acres of farmland, practically free of cost. The last wave of emigrants to the United States was in the 1880s. The emigration from Hannover proves that gainful employment in Hannover throughout the 19th century was not very promising."

One of the Kolker family historians, Robert (Bob) Kolker, the second oldest son of C.J. (Carliss) Kolker, who spoke some German, traveled to Germany in the late 1990s to research our family history. He then sent his older brother, Charles John Kolker, Jr., a letter in December 2010, stating: "[O]riginally, the only information we had was that our great-great-uncle, Georg Kolker, came from Fürstenau, Hannover, Germany." Bob then attempted to find the birth records or any records for Georg but discovered that there were three cities named Fürstenau. Bob discovered a map of the area during the time of Georg's birth. He also discovered that the Hanover which was referred to was most probably the Kingdom of Hanover and the only Fürstenau in the old Kingdom of Hanover was one about 20 km (about 12 ½ miles) northwest of Osnabruck, which is in northwest Germany, about 70 km (about 43 ½ miles) from the present Dutch border.

During the Napoleonic wars, Fürstenau was a Protestant town and Catholics couldn't go to church there and probably couldn't live there either; therefore, they lived and attended church in small towns surrounding the bigger cities. Bob found that the birth records for all those little villages were kept in the bishopric offices in Osnabrück. Bob determined that our Kolkers were descended from those in the Merzen area. The earliest birth record the Osnabrück bishopric found showed a Johann Gerhard Henrich Kolker, our great-great-grandfather, being born on July 22, 1779, in Merzen.

We have been unable to find where our great-great-grandfather landed when he came to this country, but we have found a source that states he emigrated from Germany to the United States in 1852.[8] Thanks to Lois Kolker Glennan[9], a daughter of my Dad's oldest brother, Reynold Kolker, (whose research and writing dated July 6, 1985, is quoted nearly verbatim for most of the following history in this chapter), there is a record which shows that the ship Meta landed in New Orleans on January 8, 1846, with the brother, Johan Georg Kolker, of great-great-grandfather Johann. This brother, Georg, who was born April 5, 1825, enlisted in the U.S. Army on October 26, 1846, in Milwaukee, Wisconsin to serve five years in the military, including the Mexican American War of 1846-48. (There is some dispute about Georg's birth date, as the Holy Cross Catholic Cemetery record, in Dubuque County, Iowa, has a photo of his burial plaque, giving his birth date as April 26, 1823, and death as November 30, 1858. He is buried in Section B, Row 3, Plot 4.) He was in Mexico from June 1847 to July 1848, where his Company K, 6th Regiment, U.S. Infantry, fought in the battles at Churubusco, Molino Del Ray, and Chapultepec, among others. It's entertaining to think of this German-speaking young man in Mexico with a unit of English-speaking Americans fighting Spanish speakers.

His discharge papers showed that he was born in Fürstenau, Hanover, Germany, and that he was a tailor in Germany. In those papers, he is described as being 5'6" tall, fair complexion, light hair, and blue eyes. Among the interesting experiences he had in the Army after his service in Mexico was a stint camping on the Iowa River near Marengo, serving under Samuel Woods, tasked with persuading Chief Poweshiek and his tribe to move from there to Fort Dodge, Iowa. He was discharged from the military service as a Corporal on October 26, 1851, at Fort Dodge and filed for bounty land on October 30, 1851, seeking 160 acres. However, the records indicate that he got only 40 acres of bounty land to which he added 165 acres that he bought for $1650. He married Amelia Graybill, a 17-year-old neighbor who accompanied him to record his claim, at her home in Millville Township, Iowa, on January 10, 1852.[10] As of about 1990, there were still Kolker descendants from that brother, Georg, living in Gutenberg, Iowa.

Georg became a US citizen in Clayton County, Iowa on October 25, 1854. On August 4, 1852, he sold part of his acreage to his brother, Johann Eberhart Kolker, our great-great-grandfather. We'll just call him Eberhart from now on, although the name is variously spelled as Eberhard and Eberhardt in the records.

Georg died on November 30, 1858, of cancer.[11] He is buried in the Catholic cemetery at Holy Cross, Iowa, along with a Gearhart (also spelled Geerhart) Kolker, who died at the age of 81, and the father of Georg and Eberhart. The 1860 Iowa Census shows Geerhart Kolker, age 81, living with Eberhart Kolker and his family. This "Geerhart" was our great-great-great-grandfather, Johann Gerhard Henrich Kolker. Doing the math, Geerhart must have died in the year of the 1860 census; subtracting 81 from 1860 gets us back to his birth year, 1779.

Eberhart Kolker was born on September 16, 1818[12], in Hanover, Germany, according to Lois Kolker. He married Maria Elizabeth Goedken (also spelled Gottken, or Gödken, in some records) in March or April 1853, in Iowa. Maria Elizabeth was born in Hannover, Stadt Hannover, Niedersachsen, Germany, on Dec. 28, 1830. Thanks to tremendous passenger list information, we know that Maria Elizabeth Goedken left the port of Bremen, Germany with her mother, Gertrud, age 44, and her little sister, Anna, age 10, and landed in New Orleans on or about December 15, 1845, on the three-masted, 658 nm ton, ship Leontine, which, having been launched on April 19, 1844, was a relatively new ship. It was originally engaged in the packet trade between Bremen and New Orleans before its voyage with the Godkens and others. She and Eberhart had six children: John, Bernhard (Barney), Maria, Julie Katerina, Maria Elizabeth, and Herman. John and Barney moved to Washington State in about 1883 where John drowned while doing construction work on a bridge.[13] Barney settled on a fruit ranch along the Spokane River with his wife, Emma, and three daughters. Maria, the daughter, born in 1859, died at Mount Carmel, Iowa, in 1880, of tuberculosis at only 21, according to Lois Kolker. Julie Katerina married

Joseph Waldman in Mount Carmel on April 6, 1880, and died on July 26, 1881. She and Maria are both buried in the Eberhart Kolker section in Mt. Carmel Cemetery in Iowa. Maria Elizabeth, the daughter, married Frank Hagen on April 26, 1881, and they had nine children, one of whom, Anna Regina Hagen, became a nun, Sr. Mary Arthur, who furnished Lois Kolker with some of the information herein.

Maria Elizabeth Hagan died in 1945. Herman, the youngest child of Eberhart and Maria, died shortly after birth, possibly at the same time as his mother, Elizabeth Goedken Kolker, who died on May 14, 1866.[14]

Eberhart didn't wait too long to find another wife, marrying Mary Ann (shown in several records as "Mariam") Roesner on June 25, 1867, according to Iowa State Marriages Index at St. Boniface Church, New Vienna, Dubuque, Iowa, (Lois Kolker believed the records show that marriage in March or April 1868, probably in Millville Township, Iowa. In my opinion, the official records should be believed.) Mary Ann was born August 16, 1837, in Aldenburg, Germany, now called Oldenburg, which is located at the Rivers Hunte and Haaren, in the northwestern part of Germany between Bremen and the Netherlands city of Groningen.

They had four children: Anna, born in Luxemburg, Iowa on January 23, 1869 (which may put conception on their wedding night.) However, Anna died as an infant. Louis John was born on March 6, 1870, in Millville Township, Iowa; Joseph Henry, my grandpa, was born on May 1, 1873, at Mt. Carmel, Iowa; and Anna Agnes, born on October 13, 1874, at Mt. Carmel.

Thanks to the incredible research of my brother, Robert, we know quite a bit about the marital life of Louis John Kolker. Following is the relevant text from an email sent to me by Bob in August 2017:

He married Theresia "Tess" Berger in Iowa on 5 Oct 1894, and moved to Oregon in summer 1903 (according to Lois Glennon's account). Tess died 22 Feb 1916. He then married a well-to-do widow named Laura B. Paine, who was the widow of a well-known medical doctor and banker in Eugene named Dr. Dewitt Alonzo Paine. She was about seven years older than John Louis. They married 14 Feb 1919 (Valentine's Day!). He must have been doing a little "gold digging". In May 1921, she filed for divorce, saying he left her 5 Mar 1920 "and has contributed little to my support". The divorce was final 31 Mar 1924, and she had her previous name, Laura B. Paine, restored. On 2 Nov 1926 Louis married another Tess, Teresa Elizabeth O'Brien, 22 years his senior. After his death in 1946, she married a man named Eric Eastman (in 1949).

In the spring of 1868, when Eberhart was excited over Mary Ann, Lambert Kniest, of Dubuque, Iowa, organized a Catholic colony for the Germans in the area. The I. Blair Land and Townlot Company appointed Kniest the exclusive agent for the entire township of what was then wild prairie land, giving him the exclusive right to select and sell tracts to practical Catholics in good standing. Bishop John Hennessey of Dubuque approved of this plan.

Eberhart and Jacob Wiewel, father of Elizabeth Wiewel (later, Kolker), were among the 70 good Catholic families that struck out in horse-drawn wagons in July 1868 to look for suitable settling sites in the Catholic township. Apparently, there were many excellent, choice sites, making it difficult to decide on the best place. But Lois Kolker's account relates:

Finally, an elevated plateau was reached; there they rested and were admiring the magnificent scenery—the waving grass in the rich valley and sloping uplands on every side. This, they decided, was the place! The stake or pole was taken from the wagon, having been brought as a marker for the chosen spot and they set it firmly in the ground, while they consecrated the land to God in pious prayers, and their eyes were dimmed with tears of joy. What name shall we give this new colony or parish? Looking up the date in the almanac, they found it was July 16th, the Feast of Our Blessed Lady of Mt. Carmel, providing the name selected.[15]

Eberhart didn't stay long at his newly claimed land, as on February 12, 1872, he and Mary Ann sold 165 acres in Millville Township to Charles T. Hall, and as best determined, moved to Mt. Carmel with his family.[16]

Endnotes

BOOK I

Chapter 1

[1] Wikipedia contributors. "Kingdom of Hanover." Wikipedia, The Free Encyclopedia. Wikipedia, The Free Encyclopedia, 1 Jun. 2017. Web. 1 Jun. 2017. For more on Jérôme Bonaparte, an interesting character and a sometime thorn in the side of his Emperor brother, see Glenn J. Lamar, Jérôme Bonaparte: The War Years, 1800-1815, Westport CT: Greenwood Press, 2000, p. 176. Jérôme married an American, Elizabeth Patterson, but was pressured by Napoleon to dump her; he then married a princess, Catherine of Würtenberg. It was through Jérôme that the Bonaparte line extended into the United States. His eldest son, Jerome, grew up in Maryland with his American mother. Jerome's son, Charles Joseph Bonaparte, graduated from Harvard in 1871 and Harvard Law School in 1874. He was a Republican presidential elector for Maryland in 1904 and in 1905 was appointed Secretary of the Navy. President Teddy Roosevelt appointed him as Attorney General of the U.S. in 1906 and he held that office until March 4, 1909. He died near Baltimore on June 28, 1921. (Info on Charles Bonaparte excerpted from U.S. Dept. of Justice website.)

[2] Wikipedia Contributors. "18th-century history of Germany." Sagarra, Eda (1977). A Social History of Germany: 1648-1914, pp. 140-154. For more on farmers in that space, see Bernd Kratz, "Jans Stauffer: A Farmer in Germany before his Emigration to Pennsylvania", Genealogist, Fall 2008, Vol. 22 Issue 2, pp. 130-169.

[3] Britannica, The Editors of Encyclopaedia. "Lower Saxony". Encyclopedia Britannica, 17 Jul. 2013, https://www.britannica.com/place/Lower-Saxony. Accessed 15 June 2021.

[4] See endnote below, giving a birthdate of September 29, 1819, for Eberhard. If the 1819 date is correct, he was a very few months younger than Queen Victoria.

[5] Wikipedia contributors. "Revolutions of 1848." Wikipedia, The Free Encyclopedia. Wikipedia, The Free Encyclopedia, 1 Jun. 2017. Web. 1 Jun. 2017. For more see Dill, Marshall (1970). Germany: A Modern History. University of Michigan Press. ISBN 0-472-07101-7 (p. 106)

[6] Wikipedia "Ferdinand I of Austria." Wikipedia, The Free Encyclopedia. Wikipedia, The Free Encyclopedia, 30 Apr. 2017. Web. 1 Jun. 2017.

For more see Dill, Marshall (1970). Germany: A Modern History. University of Michigan Press. ISBN 0-472-07101-7. (p. 106 et seq)

[7] Wikipedia contributors. "Hambach Festival." Wikipedia, The Free Encyclopedia. Wikipedia, The Free Encyclopedia, 15 May. 2017. Web. 1 Jun. 2017. Additional information on the Hambach Festival see: Koerner, Gustave (1909). "Chapter VIII. The Hambach Festival."

[8] Source: 1899 Biography of Eberhard Kolker, found in the German language newspaper, Der Carroll Democrat, in a special 25th anniversary edition on Friday, September 20, 1899, and translated by David Reineke and posted on-line on January 13, 2006. That same source said he emigrated to the United States in 1852.

[9] Lois Catherine Kolker (1922-1995), was the second child of Reynold E. Kolker (1898-1960), who was the first child of Joseph Henry Kolker, (1872-1939), who was a son of Johann Eberhard Kolker (1818-1905) and his wife, Mary Ann Roesner (1834-1904). Her married name was Glennan.

[10] 1984 History of Clayton County, pub. 1984 by Clayton County Genealogical Society, Elkader, Iowa, "John (Johan) George and Amelia Graybill Kolker", at page 403. Amelia remarried after Georg died, and details of her life after Georg can be found at pp. 1014-16 of the 1882 History of Clayton County (Iowa) and History of Clayton County.

[11] Amelia, the widow of Georg, re-married on June 9, 1862, to Charles James, of Staffordshire, England. Charles, born April 5, 1827, emigrated to the U.S. landing in New York in 1831 as a young boy, then was moved to Ohio where he lived 18 years, later relocating to Chicago and then to Dubuque, Iowa, where he lived until 1861, when he came to Clayton County, Iowa, settling in Section 68 of Millville Township. He farmed and was also in the marble business. From the 1882 History of Clayton County, page 1016.

[12] A contrary birth date is found in the 1899 Biography Of Eberhard Kolker, cited below: "Mr. Eberhard Kolker was born on 29 September 1819 in the District of Fürstenau, Province of Hanover, Germany." Confused yet?

[13] A newspaper article in the Spokane Falls, Washington, on May 13 of that year, stated: "News has been received here of the drowning of John Kolker at Fetler's Ferry, on the Little Spokane, under peculiar circumstances. Kolker and two other men had gone out in a small boat to repair a cable. One of the oars was lost, and Kolker becoming frightened, grabbed the cable as the boat swept under it. The boat

was carried on downstream by the swift current. Kolker then tried to gain the shore by working his way hand over hand, but when within fifty feet of the bank he gave out and fell in the river."

[14] Source: 1899 Biography of Eberhard Kolker, found in the German language newspaper, Der Carroll Democrat, in a special 25th anniversary edition on Friday, September 20, 1899, and translated by David Reineke and posted on-line on January 13, 2006. However, the paper was wrong in one regard: Eberhard and Maria Elizabeth Gottken had six children, not five.

[15] Mt. Carmel, Carroll County, Iowa.

[16] 1984 History of Clayton County, pub. 1984 by Clayton County Genealogical Society, Elkader, Iowa, "Johann Eberhard Kolker", at p. 402.

Chapter 2

THE WIEWELS (continuing with the story as told by Lois Kolker Glennan, a daughter of my Dad's oldest brother, Reynold)

Eberhart's pioneering buddy, Jacob Wiewel, was born November 17, 1842, in Bavaria, to Joseph Wiewel, born November 22, 1808, and who died March 7, 1888, and Anna Maria Fall, or Voll, (or even Pall, in some records) both of whom are buried in the Mt. Carmel Cemetery. Jacob would have been only 30 years old to Eberhart's 54 when they did their staking out in Iowa. It's not clear how they knew each other. The 1900 census shows Jacob emigrated to the U.S. in 1867. Jacob had at least two brothers: Joseph and John and one known sister, Helena.

Jacob married Mary Helena Schulte on February 16, 1871, at Mt. Carmel. They had four children: Mary, born October 23, 1873, died 1949, who married Henry Scheidel (1873-1956); Matthias, born October 10, 1874, who married Anna Agnes Wiewel (Joseph's sister); our grandmother, Elizabeth (Lizzie), born May 3, 1876; and one child named Anna who died as an infant.[17] Baby Anna does not appear on the 1880 census, but there is a Henry and Mary Gottlobe living in the same household with Jacob and his children. Mary Gottlobe may have been Jacob's sister. When the Gottlobes moved, they took Lizzie with them. They later moved to Texas (probably Muenster, Cooke County) where Henry Gottlobe had a saloon, and the family in Iowa lost track of Lizzie. She had a hard life with this Texas family and was even mistreated at times. (By the way, one of the census records showed that the highest grade attained by Grandma Elizabeth was the third grade.)

According to research done by my sister, Deborah Ann (Kolker) Roll, Jacob Wiewel, while in Mt. Carmel, started a shoemaking business as well as a tavern, "Zum Bayerischen Hof" (The Bavarian Inn), which he operated until his death in 1900. My brother, Robert, found, in the 1882 Iowa State Gazetteer and Business Directory, that at that time Mt. Carmel was a village of 75, with a Catholic priest, Rev. J. Anler, a church and school, a brewery, and two saloons. This makes me wonder, as Joseph Henry Kolker was also supposedly running a saloon there as well. Could it be that both the paternal and maternal sides monopolized the Mt. Carmel booze business? The same Gazetteer entry explained that from Mt. Carmel there were tri-weekly mail stages to Carroll City and Grant City, for a fare of fifty cents each trip.

Meanwhile, Jacob Wiewel, after Mary Schulte's death, married Catharine Disher on April 26, 1881, in Mt. Carmel. Jacob was 35 years old at this marriage and Catharine was 25. They had nine children: Helena, who married Michael Lodes; Bernadine, who married John Lodes; John, who married Catherine Stieferman; Theresa, who died at birth; Mary Catherine (Kate), who married Henry Lodes; Clara, who married Leonard Hoebing; August (Gus) Frank, who married Cornelius Stieferman; Philomena (Minnie), who married Joseph Williams and later Edward J. Werndy. It looks suspiciously like there was a lot of intermarriage. The Lodes family was a large presence in the Catholic community in Elgin, Oklahoma when I was growing up there. The John Lodes home, on what is now Tony Creek Road in Elgin, still stands as this is written.

About 1893 or 1894, Mary Wiewel, Lizzie's sister, located her in Texas with the Gottlobe family. Mary went to Texas and returned Lizzie to Iowa and her family. It surely must have been a joyful occasion to meet all her family after all those years.

Lois Kolker continued:

> Remember, Mt. Carmel was a very close-knit farming community with the church at the center of it. There was a band that played at various functions and Joseph and Louis Kolker played in the band. It was probably at one of these gatherings that Joseph and Lizzie met. She was a new girl in the community, so surely all the young men were looking her over and vice versa; although shyly on her part I'm sure.

Here, view a photo of "Lizzie", born Elizabeth Wievel, or Grandma Kolker, as she was known to me, in her later years while living with her daughter, Bea Shaw, and her husband, Dewey, in Lawton, OK.

On April 27, 1897, Lizzie and Joseph were joined in holy matrimony, becoming our putative grandparents. Their first four children: Reynold, Laura, Bertha (Bea), and Clara were all born in Mt. Carmel. The next three were born in Okarche, Oklahoma: Walter, born February 14, 1907; Francis (Frank), born August 8, 1910; Marie Catherine, born August 10, 1911; the last and eighth was my Dad, Charles John Kolker, born January 10, 1914, in Oklahoma City, while the family lived in Elgin, OK.

This is the wedding photo of Joseph Henry Kolker and Elizabeth "Lizzie" Wiewel, married on April 27, 1897, at Mt. Carmel, Iowa.

Also on April 27, 1897, Joseph's sister, Anna Agnes, and Matthias Wiewel, Lizzie's brother, were married, so it must've been quite a celebration.

On December 8, 1897, Eberhart divided his property and sold or gave it to his two sons, our paternal grandpa, Joseph, and his brother, Louis. In the summer of 1903, Louis moved his wife, Theresa Berger Kolker, born June 24, 1869, and two daughters, Mabel and Myrtle, to Oregon. The move was made because Theresa had tuberculosis. Louis opened a small grocery store in Eugene, Oregon, and kept it until his retirement. His wife, Theresa, died on February 22, 1916, in Eugene, Oregon. Louis later married Laura Payne (twice), then Tess O'Brien, who survived him. Lois Kolker located Shirley Norris, a granddaughter of Louis, in Portland, Oregon. Lois found Shirley Norris to be a "very warm, charming person and interested in the Kolker relatives". Louis died on August 19, 1946.

Grandpa Joseph's mother, Mary Ann, died on December 18, 1904. Eberhart died December 7, 1905. In December 1906, Joseph sold his farm to Henry Bruning and moved his family to Okarche, Oklahoma. In 1912 or 1913 our Grandpa Joseph and Grandma Elizabeth moved to the Elgin, Oklahoma, area where my dad was born.

Above are photos of "the Old Kolker Place" where Joseph and Elizabeth Kolker lived with their brood. Of course, these photos were taken long, long after Joseph and Elizabeth were gone. These buildings are now completely gone, having been burned because they were safety hazards, and there is now a subdivision of homes in that area.

The Jacob Wiewel family moved to Okarche in about 1903. Jacob died on April 19, 1924, and he and his second wife, Catharine, are both buried in the Holy Trinity Cemetery at Okarche, Oklahoma.

Endnotes

BOOK I

Chapter 2

[17] Actually, according to brother Bob, Baby Anna was listed as six months old as of the census of June 29th, 1880, so she must have been born late in 1879 or very early 1880. Her mother, Helena Schulte Wiewel, died of "Child Bed" in February 1880, attended by Dr. Feenstra.

CHAPTER 3

THE BROWNS

Okay, we've learned about the Kolkers and the Wievels, now it's time to discuss the maternal grand lineage.

We'll start with the Browns, who originated in the Alsace region on the ever-shifting border between Germany and France. This region became the soccer ball that was kicked back and forth between the Germans and the French as each side took turns conquering the region and adding it to its territory. This shifting back and forth caused spelling changes to our Brown ancestors' family name. When the territory was French the name became "Brun"; when German, the name was "Braun". Of course, on arrival in the United States, the name was Brown. All this has made the family genealogists more focused.

To make it just a little more interesting, our Brun/Braun/ Brown predecessors really, really liked the name "Francois Antoine". Fathers, sons, deceased male babies, and brothers could all be named Francois Antoine. No such niceties as "Jr." or "the III" were used to distinguish one from the other. So, there was a Francois Antoine Braun born in 1778, 1812, 1838, and 1842. The 1838 model died in 1839. This name became Frank Anthony in the United States. Apparently, this love affair with Francois Antoine extended to the whole town of Valff, so it was safe to greet every male with the same name. [18]

We shouldn't ignore the history of the region. By 1500 BC, Celts began to settle in Alsace, attracted by the rich fertility of the soil, which partly explains why Alsace was so attractive to invade. The Celts/Gauls occupied the area and were there when Caesar conquered it around 58 BC. With some interruptions, Rome governed the area until the Roman Empire began to collapse after 400 A.D. The Germanic migrations began about 300 A.D., and these invaders occupied the region. Between 486 and 614 A.D. the Franks conquered Alsace. Charlemagne reigned over the Frankish Empire, including Alsace, from 795-814 A.D. On Charlemagne's death in 814 A.D., there began a series of divisions of the Frankish Empire, so that the treaty of Verdun of 843 gave Alsace and Lotharingia (later Lorraine) to Lothar I (one of the grandsons of Charlemagne) part of the Carolingian Empire for the period between 847 and 870 A.D., followed by the Treaty of Mersen, which gave Alsace to East Francia, a German kingdom of the Carolingian Empire. The Holy Roman Empire "ruled" the area during much of the following centuries. We know that in the 12th and 13th centuries, Alsace prospered, probably because of better governance under the Hohenstaufen emperors, and rulers in the Holy Roman Empire during those centuries, but the good times ended in the 14th century due to harsh winters, bad harvests, and the Black Death. Prosperity returned to Alsace under the Habsburg administration during the Renaissance.[19]

As the Holy Roman Empire declined, the French began expansion. In 1299, the French proposed a marriage alliance between Philip IV of France's sister Blanche and Albert I of Germany's son Rudolf, with Alsace as the dowry. This would have been at least peaceful, but the deal fell apart. France was then involved in the Hundred Years' War. The Hundred Years' War was a series of conflicts waged from 1337 to 1453 by the House of Plantagenet, rulers of the Kingdom of England, against the House of Valois, rulers of the Kingdom of France, over the succession of the French throne. Each side drew many allies into the war. It was one of the most notable conflicts of the Middle Ages, in which five generations of kings from two rival dynasties fought for the throne of the largest kingdom in Western Europe. The war marked both the height of chivalry and its subsequent decline, and the development of strong national identities in both countries[20], which period of conflicts kept France busy and unable to do a lot of annexing and conquering, but in 1444 a French army arrived in Alsace and Lorraine, demanding submission. "Ownership" of Alsace bounced around among the Duke of Burgundy, the Holy Roman Empire, and the Habsburg family.

By the time of the Protestant Revolution in the 16th century, the inhabitants around Strasbourg were prosperous and becoming Protestant, but not without resistance by the Catholic Habsburgs, who tried to eradicate "heresy" in Upper Alsace. Alsace became a mixture of Protestant and Catholic.

From 1618-1674 Louis XIII annexed portions of Alsace during the Thirty Years War and Louis XIV completed the job during the Franco-Dutch War of 1672-1678, and subsequent territory grabs were confirmed by various treaties through 1697. But French rule wasn't to last forever. The Franco-Prussian War of 1871 caused Alsace to be ceded to the German Empire, only to be ceded back to France by the Treaty of Versailles at the end of World War I. But Nazi Germany conquered the area in 1940 and once again it was German. The end of World War II brought Alsace back home to France, where it remains today.

True to form, the Alsatians were divided during the Revolution, with some opposing the revolutionaries. Thousands fled to Russia when the revolutionary armies marched into Alsace. Since Francois Antoine isn't traced to Russia, it is assumed that he was not a counterrevolutionary that fled, although family legend has it that he was destined for the guillotine more than once during the Reign of Terror and somehow wiggled out of it. In fact, Howard Brown, oldest son of James Lafayette Brown, visited Vallf, France in 1991, and discovered that "F. A. Brown...bought [his] life for $18,000 the third time during the Reign of Terror (1791). His name was on the list for the fourth time when Robespierre was put out of power." The questions are, of course, why was he important enough to be put on such a list, and, where the heck did he get all that money? Unfortunately, Uncle Howard Brown is now deceased, and he took with him the knowledge behind these intriguing morsels of information.

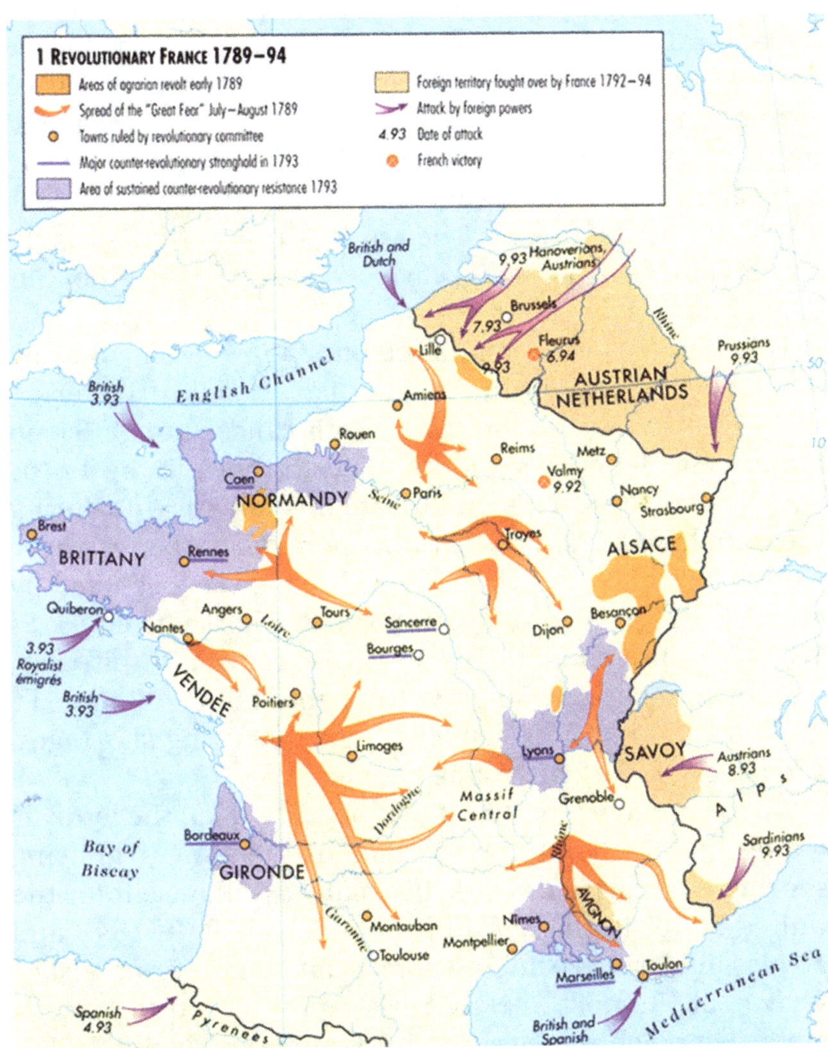

The orange-brown splotches on the above map show that
Alsace was an early joiner in the French Revolution, so
our French Alsatian ancestors had a front-row seat to that
Revolution.

During the French Revolution "La Marseillaise" became its inspirational song. Various tales of how and where it arose are out there, but one has it coming from the Alsace region. There, where there were many German speakers, there was even a German version: "Auf, Bruder, auf dem Tag entgegen", in case you want to break out with it during your next bout at the tavern. The truth is it was first sung by a raw volunteer named Francois Vireur, in Marseille. But enough of this deviation.

The French Revolution fizzled out by 1799, only to bring on Napoleon, who in turn finally fizzled out at Waterloo in 1815, destined to die of stomach cancer at age 51 on faraway St. Helena island. Our ancestor born in the 1770s would have been in his mid to late 30s to early 40s during the Napoleonic era. The Bas-Rhin portion of Alsace, where Valff is and was and where he was from, was occupied by over 280,000 foreign soldiers and 90,000 horses from 1815-1818, causing economic turmoil in the region. Despite this, the Alsatian population grew from about 800,000 in 1814 to 1,067,000 in 1846, causing hunger, housing shortages, and a lack of work for young people.

We don't know whether it was because of all the leftover horses, the many foreign soldiers, or the hunger, housing shortages, and lack of work, but many Alsatians left for the United States in the period from 1840-1850. In 1843 and 1844, sailing ships bringing immigrant families from Alsace arrived at the port of New York. Some settled in Illinois, many to farm or to seek success in commercial ventures. For example, the sailing ships Sully (in May 1843) and Iowa (in June 1844) brought families who set up homes in northern Illinois and northern Indiana.[21]

Lest we forget, Francois Antoine Brown, born in 1778, married Marie Ursule Muller. Marie was born in 1774 and died in 1841 in Goxwiller, Bas-Rhin, Alsace. As our great-great-great-grandmother, she bore a son, who follows:

Our great-great-grandpa, Francois Antoine (naturally) Braun, was born in Alsace in 1812 (the same year the barely minted Americans started fighting the British, again), and came to America in 1852, settling in Hamilton, Ohio, which is now part of the northern Cincinnati metropolitan area. Its neighborhood of Lindenwald was settled by German immigrants in the mid-19th century and later.[22] Hamilton, OH is approximately 25 miles northwest of Dover, IN, where he died in 1889. Dover is perhaps 10 miles from the Ohio border, close to Cincinnati and southeast of present-day Indianapolis. Francois Antoine Braun married Anna Marie Schehrer in Valff on April 19, 1837. Her parents were listed on the marriage certificate as Blaise Schehrer and Veronique Kormann. Witnesses were Francois Antoine Schehrer, Anna Marie's brother, Francois Antoine Saas, Francois Matheis Hirtz, and George Mosher.

My brother Bob, the epitome of a family genealogist without whom this history would be nothing, wrote me on November 21, 2021, with a new find:

...after Anne Marie Schehrer died Francois Antoine (of 1812 vintage) married a widow, Margaretha Zimmerman. Both she and her first husband, Georg Bauch, were from Bavaria. Bob sent copies of the 'temporary passports' that they were issued to come to North America. On hers, she is described as a shoemaker's daughter and he as a shepherd's son. Embarrassingly for them, those documents supply blunt details: she 'had a pointed, saddle-nose and a bulging forehead'. He had a 'low forehead and a pointed chin'.

In one of the many diversions in searching family history, a hand-written deed was found conveying 32+ acres to Stephen Horn in Hamilton County, Ohio (for Eight Hundred Dollars), signed by Anthony Brown (I finally figured out that this was Francois Antoine Brown, our great-great-grandpa) and his wife, Anna Marie Brown, on September 25, 1865. The Civil War had ended only five months before. Anne Marie died two years later about 25-35 miles west of Hamilton County, Ohio, in Dover, Dearborn County, Indiana. Great-great-grandpa, the other deed signer, died on May 12, 1889, so he remained behind while his son traveled westward to Illinois.

His son, Great-grandpa Francois Antoine Brown, was born on October 16, 1843, in Valff and died on December 29, 1922, in Comanche County, Oklahoma. He was 25 years old when his mother, Anne Marie, died in 1867, the same year he married Magdalene (also known as Mattie and Martha) Weakley (or Weekly) in Dover, Indiana, on August 12. At some point, this 1843 version of Francois Antoine Brown struck out for Illinois.

Francois Antoine Braun, photo above, born October 16, 1843, Valff, Alsace, France; died on December 29, 1922, and is buried in the Catholic Cemetery in Elgin, Oklahoma.

His son, our maternal grandpa, James Lafayette (Lafe) Brown (along with his twin, George Washington Brown) was born July 3, 1879, at Whitley Point in Whitley Township, Moultrie County, Illinois, which is east of Terre Haute, Indiana, about nine miles northwest of Mattoon, Illinois, and south of Champaign, Illinois. Lafe died in Elgin, Oklahoma, on January 18, 1962, and is also buried, near his father, at the Catholic Cemetery in Elgin. It's a remarkable westward migration of the family.

Grandpa Lafe also had an older sister, Mary Josephine Brown. She was born two years before Grandpa on March 30, 1877, and died Monday, January 6, 1958, age 81, at Fort Supply, Oklahoma, where she had been institutionalized because of mental health issues. She is buried at the Elgin Catholic Cemetery. Her funeral took place at St. Ann's Catholic Church in Elgin, with Rev. M.P. Gans, pastor, officiating.

I wanted to confirm that Grandpa was actually born in Illinois, so, after camping with friends at Litchfield, Illinois during most of Labor Day weekend 2019, I drove to Sullivan, the county seat of Moultrie County in central Illinois, to search the records. On Tuesday, September 3, the very helpful staff in the County Clerk's office in the courthouse searched records for me. There was a typed Index of births that included 1879, but there was no mention of Frank Anthony Brown or Grandpa. The original, hand-written version turned up the birth date and "MM" for twin boys, born to Frank Anthony and Martha Brown. But I wanted the actual birth certificate. They drug out dusty old books filled, in no particular order, with birth certificates encased in plasticized coverings. Since they were neither arranged alphabetically nor chronologically, it took some leafing through many pages before we struck "gold". There it was: a "double birth certificate" for the twins! I got certified copies for my records.

The newborns are listed as the "third and fourth (twin boys)." We know that, at the time of the twins' birth, there were Mary Josephine, George, and Lafe, the twins, but also the oldest, Charles (known as Charley) Noah Brown, born January 3, 1874, in Illinois, and died in Elgin, Oklahoma in 1928). Martha is described as "German, age 31" (although the writing makes "31" look like "81", which, for a moment at least, made me think that maybe our family had produced a child-bearing miracle, like Old Testament Sarah.) The father, Frank Anthony Brown, age 37, is shown as being born in "Strasburg, France", with his occupation listed as "farmer". The delivering doctor's name is hard to decipher but looks like "D. D. Euer". The certificate is dated on the twins' birth date at Whitley Point (a part of Whitley Township, Moultrie County, at the time). Of course, Grandpa's siblings didn't end with the four of them listed above who were still living in Whitley Township, Moultrie County, Illinois when the 1880 census rolled around. But the last sibling would be the baby boy that Martha was carrying in her arms when they made their way from Comanche County, Kansas to the Oklahoma Land Rush of 1889. Born in Kansas about a month before the trip, on March 6, 1889, was little brother Frank Anthony Brown, who died a tragic, early death, on September 13, 1912, as described in a newspaper article:

Frank Brown, 23, a young farmer residing near Fletcher, is dead, the victim of a simple fall from tripping in the pasture path. The accident occurred two weeks ago. When Brown fell, he struck the back of his head on a bucket he was carrying. The fall wrenched his spine and although his injury was not considered serious it resulted in complete paralysis.

Above is a selection from the newspaper. It reads, "Frank Brown, 23, a young farmer residing near Fletcher, is dead, the victim of a simple fall from tripping in the pasture path. The accident occurred two weeks ago. When Brown fell, he struck the back of his head on a bucket he was carrying. The fall wrenched his spine and although his injury was not considered serious it resulted in complete paralysis."

But the tragedy of the young Frank Brown's death was magnified by this fact: He was married on February 12, 1912, in Noble, Oklahoma, just a few months before his accident. The bride, Cora May Horn, became a very young widow, (she was only 17, requiring the consent of her mother when she married Frank). Frank's estate was probated in Muskogee on October 14, 1912.

I wanted to get a flavor of what it was like in his area around the time of Grandpa's birth. I found, in the library in Sullivan, a reference to the Moultrie County Historical and Genealogical Society's "Century I, Notes on Sullivan, Illinois, 1845-1872-1972" which had a trove of information, some of which follows.

Interestingly, the first courthouse in Moultrie County hosted Abraham Lincoln on several occasions as he tried cases there while riding the circuit between 1849-1852.

Sullivan, just a few miles from Whitley Point, circa 1853, was described as:

"At that time the village had no policemen and some of the rougher elements that usually gets out as soon as civilization becomes established still remained in the county. This part of the population, when in town, made the saloon their headquarters. They at times indulged in fist fights and other disorderly conduct, as a result of which the north side of the square was called then and for a long time subsequent, 'sodcorn row.'" Century I, Notes on Sullivan, Illinois, 1845-1872-1972"

Apparently, though, the area settled down a little in the 1870s after a city marshal, James Taylor, brought his firmly-held temperance views to town. We often forget how primitive conditions were in those times. Much of the county was unsettled prairie around the time of the Civil War. Health problems occurred because of undrained prairie swamp-like land. By the time Frank Anthony and Martha arrived the area had been drained and most of the land had been sold and began to be farmed. The railroad finally arrived nearby by 1872, only seven years before Grandpa was born. In fact, Sullivan was not incorporated as a city until December of that year. By the early 1880s multi-story office buildings were on the town square, so progress was rapid. When Grandpa was one year old, Sullivan, the nearest town to him, had activity enough to be described vividly:

"A pedestrian on the east side of the east side of the square in about 1880 encountered a mixture of sights and smells. The meat market, besides selling meat, bought hides and pelts. The market's smell of fresh blood and saw dust mingled with the heavy aroma of oiled leather, the distinctive smell of the harness shop next door. At the sign of the boot, Mat Layman was working at his cobbler's bench. From the open door of Brosam Bros. Bakery came mouth-watering aromas of fresh-baked goodies. Several customers were in John R. McClure's grocery, indicating that his 23-year-old business was in much better condition than his two-story building. Several slabs of marble were lying in the street in front of Fred Sona's Marble Shop, waiting to become grave markers through the skillful blows of his chisel. Above the hardware at the end of the block was the law office of I. J. Mouser, with whom young Albert J. Beveridge, a future U. S. Senator, spent many long hours learning about law and politics. Across the street south a few men had stopped to visit in front of Mayer's Dry Goods Emporium while on their way to pick up their mail at the post office next door." Century I, Notes on Sullivan, Illinois, 1845-1872-1972".

Since Sullivan was the only close place to do business when Frank Anthony and Martha lived nearby, it is wholly reasonable to expect that they would have been in many of the places mentioned.

"Sullivan's citizens slopped around the square in the mud or ate its dust until 1894." Century I, Notes on Sullivan, Illinois, 1845-1872-1972.

Above, photo of Sullivan, Moultrie County, Illinois, c. 1879, at the time Great-grandpa, Frank Anthony Brown, would have trod these very streets.

R. Eden Martin wrote The Whitley Point Record Book. He was still living while I was in Sullivan, but I was unable to reach him to get even more specific information about Whitley Point. [23]

Endnotes

BOOK I

Chapter 3

[18] We have a copy of the birth certificate, in French, from the Mayor's Office in Valff, Alsace, France, recording the birth of Francois Antoine Braun in Valff , on August 4, 1838, at 10 A.M., the father being Francois Antoine Braun, age 26 and mother Marie Anne Shehrer, age 36 years. Witnesses were Francois Antoine Schehrer, and Francois Antoine Hirtz.

[19] Wikipedia contributors. "Alsace." *Wikipedia, The Free Encyclopedia.* Wikipedia, The Free Encyclopedia, 23 Jun. 2017. Web. 28 Jun. 2017. Most of the historical materials in this chapter are from this source. .

[20.] Wikipedia contributors. "Hundred Years' War." *Wikipedia, the Free Encyclopedia.* Wikipedia, the Free Encyclopedia. 27 Jun. 2017. Web. 28 Jun. 2017.

[21.] Wikipedia contributors. "Alsace." *Wikipedia, The Free Encyclopedia.* Wikipedia, The Free Encyclopedia, 23 Jun. 2017. Web. 30 Jun. 2017.

[22.] Wikipedia contributors. "Hamilton, Ohio." *Wikipedia, The Free Encyclopedia.* Wikipedia, The Free Encyclopedia, 25 Jun. 2017. Web. 6 Jul. 2017.

[23.] For those willing to dig more, here's a link: http://edenmartin.com/newsite2/index.php/shelby-a-moultrie/books/the-whitley-point-record-book, (The Whitley Point Record Book, by R. Eden Martin, copyrighted in 1996).

Chapter 4

The Oklahoma Land Run

We've so far been unable to trace F.A. Brown's family from Illinois to Kansas, but we know they landed in or near Coldwater, Comanche County, Kansas, and from there they later made their trek into Oklahoma for the April 1889 Land Run.

A little background is helpful to understand the context of the Land Run. After the Civil War, there was a "hole" in the middle of Indian Territory, simply called "unassigned land." This "hole" was caused by the Creek and Seminole Nations having to cede part of their lands to the U.S. Government because they were on the wrong side in the Civil War. (In fact, the victorious Union decided that because the Five Civilized Tribes allied with the South, they had to forfeit all their annuities and half their land.)[24]

Above is a map of the land that was opened for the 1889 Land Rush.

President Rutherford Hayes issued a proclamation on April 26, 1879, forbidding trespass into the land, but many were pressuring Congress and the President to open the land for settlement. These pro-settlement folks were known as "Boomers", who made illegal excursions into the land to make settlement a fait accompli. Thus, in late April 1879 Boomers showed up in Coffeeville, Kansas led by Colonel C. C. Carpenter, and he assembled a large group of people just north of the Kansas/Indian Territory border. By May they had progressed to the North Canadian River, were found by U.S. troops, and sent scurrying back. This didn't discourage repeated attempts to settle in the prohibited land, which was surrounded by large allotments to Native American tribes, notably Chickasaws to the south, Creek, and Choctaw to the east and southeast, and Cherokee and Osage to the north of the unassigned land.

But the pressure was building in Congress. On February 27, 1889, Illinois representative William M. Springer added a section to the Indian Appropriation bill which gave the President the right to issue a proclamation opening the unassigned land. Original "settlers" were to be kicked off that land, which was to then be opened to land-run settlement. President Grover Cleveland signed a law doing so on March 2, 1889. Cleveland's first term ended one day later on March 3, so it was President Benjamin Harrison who actually issued the proclamation on March 23, 1889. (Cleveland has the distinction of being the only president who served two non-consecutive terms.) The proclamation opened 1,887,796 acres for settlement by land run. Each eligible person could claim 160 acres.

The April 1889 Land Run opened all or part of the current counties of Canadian, Cleveland, Kingfisher, Logan, and Oklahoma.

All this information whetted the appetite of many, including Great-grandpa F.A. Brown, who was in his early 40s and strong enough to make the journey. As you will see his wife, Magdalene (also known as Mattie or Martha), who was about 39-40 years old at the time, was no wimp, either.

Endnotes

BOOK I

Chapter 4

24. The anger against the Five Civilized Tribes abated over time. All five had fought for the Confederacy, but some were divided. There was a large segment of the Cherokees, for example, that fought for the Union. But the Unionists decided that because parts of the Five Civilized Tribes fought for the South, the whole of those tribes should be punished. Originally, the fervor was for making them forfeit all their lands in the Indian Territory, but gradually that was reduced to partial losses and some payment for the losses. Some of the compensation was pretty pitiful. For example, The Seminole Tribe ceded all their land to the federal government but got only 15 cents an acre. To add insult to injury the Seminoles then had to purchase back the same land for 50 cents an acre. William D. Pennington, "Reconstruction Treaties", The Encyclopedia of Oklahoma History and Culture, https://www.okhistory.org/publications/enc/entry.php?entry=RE001.

Chapter 5

Lafe Brown's Account of the Land Run

Grandpa Lafe (short for his middle name, Lafayette) Brown, one of the sons of F.A. and Magdalene (aka Martha), wrote an account of his family's journey from Kansas to the site of the Oklahoma Run of 1889. Following is that account:

[Titled by him as "Life on the Western Frontier"]

My father owned in Comanche County, Kansas, what was known as a timber claim, where you could plant as much as 10 acres of some kinds of timber and thereby get a deed to the land. My father did a great deal of hauling before the railroad was built through Comanche County, of which Coldwater was the county seat.

[Note: Coldwater, Kansas, is about 173 miles north by the present-day highway from Elgin, Oklahoma. Comanche Co., Kansas is centered on the southern edge of Kansas, just across the border from Indian Territory. Interestingly, the Cimarron River, which Grandpa mentions, was, and is, at the southwestern edge of Comanche Co., Kansas. They could have followed its course, which angled southeast into Indian Territory and led very close to the site of the Land Run. Instead, Grandpa's account indicates they followed the North Canadian River, which runs parallel to the Cimarron River and south of it.]

He would haul merchandise for the stores. Also flour from Saratoga Mill to the stores in Coldwater. He used three horses until he lost all three from exposure to bad weather. Then he used oxen which could pull heavier loads and stand more exposure in bad weather. He kept 2 yokes of oxen. One of the bulls and one of the steers (Long Horns). He would haul hard cedar posts from the cedar canyons and salt from the salt plains in the Cimarron River in the Indian Territory that laid south of the Kansas line. No one in there but cattlemen and Indians unless it was freighters. He sold fence posts and salt to the settlers in Kansas who kept cattle. He would even get out on prairies and gather wagon loads of cattle and buffalo bones and sell them to be shipped to factories to be used in making sugar.

Along about 1889 the government made a treaty with some small tribes of Indians right in the middle of Indian territory to open settlements for the whites. So President Cleveland issued a proclamation to open for settlement land comprised of 4 counties: Oklahoma County, Logan County, Canadian County, and Kingfisher County.

The date of the opening was set at 12 o'clock noon April 22, 1889. To open with a run. My father had a mortgage on his timber claim, so he borrowed $200 more on it. He let the loan co. have it. So we up and left for Okla., the promised land. We started on our long journey April 2, 1889. With our little belongings loaded in a covered wagon with an overjet on it. We had a good yoke of steers to it which was pretty good travelers. A neighbor, Nick Smith, and his family went from Kansas with us. He had five wagons pretty well loaded—one ox team and one *horse team. It was pretty slow going. Even at that, we reached the Cimarron River the second day about noon. The river here is 4 miles wide at the salt plains crossing. Smith got stuck with his horse team. The grown girl was driving them and let them stop in a water channel where there was quicksand and the wagon went down. So we put our oxen to it and pulled it out. We were from noon until dark getting across 4 miles to the other side, where we camped for the night.*

The next morning one of our dogs got poisoned from poison put out by cattlemen for coyotes. We tried to save him by pouring milk down him but to no avail. He died. We hated to lose him; he was a greyhound. Mr. Smith had a milk cow he was taking with him that provided the family with milk. We still had a bulldog left.

From the Cimarron River on the south was a level plain country for miles and miles, where great herds of longhorn cattle roamed. Where we traveled was a winding trail across the shortgrass prairie. (Mostly shortgrass) with no creeks or streams of any kind, so our waterkegs on the side of our wagons were a long time empty. Near the middle of April, the weather was getting hot and dry. The men took a waterkeg and went about ½ mile off the trail where they saw some trees in hopes they might find a stream of water, but no luck. At last, about dark we came to a nice little creek with clear water. But when we tasted of it we found it was salt water. We camped anyway. We made coffee from it by boiling it and pouring it off but it wasn't very good.

We came near having a fire in our wagon. One night, the lantern that was hanging right over a bed on an overjet got knocked down on the bed and turned over. Luckily Mr. Clevenger saw it in time and jumped in and threw the blazing lantern out before it did any damage to speak of. My brother, [this would have been Frank A. (what else?) Brown, born March 6, 1889, and died September 13, 1912] about 4 or 5 weeks old, was sleeping in the bed. It did not even wake him up.

We traveled along the North Canadian River for miles. There were lots of wild turkey and deer. We saw one black bear. One night we camped near Camp Supply (Freighters supply), now called Ft Supply. Smith's team of horses was about played out. So we left one wagon at Supply.

Mr. Marc Clevenger was an unmarried man who was going with us. He was a good singer. He would sing evenings around the campfire. Mr. Clevenger was a school teacher not long from the east. He hadn't seen much of the hardships of the Western frontier.

We did not have any feed with us for our teams. The oxen did very well on grass at night and a long noon to graze, but Nick Smith's horses couldn't stand it. They got weak.

We traveled for days down a winding trail toward the border of the country to be opened at 12 o'clock April 22, 1889. There were covered wagons as far as you could see back and in front on the trail going toward the promised land—lots of ox teams besides ours. At last we reached the border. By then the wagons were pretty well scattered down the line. There were soldiers on horses riding up and down the line to keep out sooners. We arrived on the line April 21st—the day before the opening.

At noon on April 22 at 12 o'clock noon, the soldiers fired guns all down the line. My father and Mr. Smith and Mr. Clevenger ran on foot about 2 ½ miles. Each carried a spade and a stake with a red handkerchief on it. They ran for bottom land on Johns Creek. When they made their mounds and put a flag on it they found that all that bottom land had been soonered. They came out of the brush from nowhere. Slipped in the night before. Some had 2 or more sooners on it. In some cases, there were shootings over that bottom land. We followed up with wagons, camped all night there. The next day we hunted some good upland that was run over and not taken. We stopped about a mile from the creek. My father and Nick Smith got places joining.

[Thus ends Grandpa Brown's handwritten account.]

There are many things that stand out in his account. First of all, he was only 9-10 years old when he wrote it and experienced the events he recounted. Obviously, a 10-year-old then had maturity beyond what we expect today. The entire account, written in Grandpa Lafe's own hand, was preserved by my mother and made available to the family. But the part that astonishes me is that Lafe's mother was holding a baby through all this oxen-driven wagon trip! Imagine traveling all those miles, including crossing a four-mile-wide river in this bone-rattling, heavy vehicle carrying a tiny baby, let alone caring for that child through his very young life. I weep that we don't know more about this remarkable woman.

As best this amateur historian can determine, Johns Creek, where Grandpa Brown and his family first settled during the April 22, 1889, Land Run, runs roughly from Kingfisher to Okarche, Oklahoma, east and somewhat parallel to what is now U.S. Highway 81. It's west of Guthrie, where we believe the land claim was registered. It's also been described as "north of El Reno".

The Oklahoma Land Run of April 22, 1889, caused quite a hullabaloo across the country and even the world. There was a lengthy article in The New York Times headlined "Into Oklahoma at Last", subtitled "Thousands Wildly Dashing in for Homes". It's a pretty breathless account of the run and the instant towns, including Guthrie, Oklahoma City, and others that sprung up in its wake. Its dateline was Purcell, Indian Territory, on April 22. The article describes U.S. Army troopers, headed by Lt. Samuel E. Adair of the Fifth Cavalry, maintaining the line and heading off those who wanted to cross early, being only partially successful. Gunshots were heard as people squabbled over claims. A body of an unidentified man was found across the line "...lying in the sand....a youth of not more than twenty years. He was poorly clad and his eyes, his ears, and his nostrils were filled with sand." Such tragedies were part of the frenzy of the run.

So the Brown family staked out upland near Johns Creek, north of El Reno, but later traded a team of horses for a farm that the seller had claimed from the Cherokee Strip Run of 1893. That farm was described in an article in the Oklahoma Territory newspaper out of Guthrie, the Oklahoma Review, written on March 15, 1901:

The Brown Farm...four miles west of Waukomis is the F.A. Brown farm, noted for its completeness as an ideal farm. This is a model farm because the industry of Mr. Brown and his sons have made it so. Of course the farm is productive, but not more so than other farms where the same energy and good judgement have been displayed. Mr. Brown settled on the farm in 1894, having traded a team for the claim. If ever a man began at the bottom, Mr. Brown did, having absolutely nothing, not even teams to work the land. Everything we now find there was produced on the farm. The writer found there six good teams, four good wagons, five sulky plows, two binders and a header and other machines too numerous to mention. Speaking of wheat, Mr. Brown produced the figures showing that in 1897 he raised 1,182 bushels; 1898, 2,589 bushels; 1899, 4,340 bushels; 1900, 5,333 bushels. His oat crop has been proportionately large, getting 75 bushels per acre. The largest wheat yield being 38 bushels per acre. He has raised good crops of corn every year. The fruit grown on the farm is most remarkable for variety, quality and quantity. No sooner was the wild nature of the land subdued than Mr. Brown and his sons began to plant orchards and vineyards. To obtain the trees was the greatest task. The boys worked out at 40 cents per day to buy the trees to plant, many of the finest varieties costing 90 cents per tree, making many of the trees cost over two days of hard work, but persevered. They planted only the best budded varieties in great quantities. They are now reaping their rewards in the great quantities of excellent apples, peaches, plums, apricots, crabs, quinces, cherries and nectarines. Their Elberta peaches weigh ½ pound each; plums were 6 ½ inches around and the finest apples ever seen in the country. The vineyard around the house produced three tons of grapes in 1898 and four tons each year for the last two years. Last year Mr. Brown made about 250 gallons of wine. Grapes sell at two and a half cents or three cents per pound at the vineyard. The family home pictured in the Guthrie Review of 1901 was two-story, eight rooms with two dormer windows on each side of the roof. Mr. Brown and his industrious sons have done Oklahoma a world of good by proving that this country is adapted to the successful growth of all kinds of fruit, which has an excellent influence in bringing a desirable class of settlers to the country.

My brother David located the precise location of Grandpa Lafe's Waukomis farm:
36°15'39.7"N97°58'05.6"W, being one mile south of Waukomis, OK, 4 ¼ miles east, north side, on E5020 Rd. (W. Flynn Rd.), Garfield County. Enid is the county seat.
David did some marvelous research finding the above-quoted article, and he followed that with this statement:

About 1903 or so F.A. Brown was offered so much for the successful farm near Waukomis that he did not feel like he could turn it down. With a considerable sum of money in his hands combined with low land prices in Comanche County near Elgin and Fletcher, F.A. Brown purchased a farm for himself and each of his children. Apparently, F. A. Brown felt his family had worked as hard as he had, so he shared the wealth.[25]

Endnotes

BOOK I

Chapter 5

[25.] David tracked the farms purchased, as follows:
- For Frank A. (F.A.) Brown (the father) dob: 1842   dod: 1922
- NE 1/4, Section 23, T-4-N, R-10-W, Comanche County, Oklahoma

- For Charles N. Brown (son) dob: 1874 dod: 1928
- SE ¼, Section 17, T-4-N, R-10-W, Comanche County, Oklahoma

- For Mary Josephine Brown (daughter) dob: 1877 dod: 1958
- SW ¼, Section 16, T-4-N, R-10-W, Comanche County, Oklahoma

- For James Lafayette (Lafe) Brown (twin son) dob: 1879 dod: 1962
- NW ¼, Section 24, T-4-N, R—11-W, Comanche County, Oklahoma
  - This farm was purchased from a man who received it in the land lottery (drawing) that took place in Lawton. Lafe later purchased the NE ¼ of the same section giving him the whole north ½ section. David Kolker, Lafe's grandson, later purchased this half section on December 5, 1995 from Lafe Brown's heirs. About half of this land is now Country Aire Estates, filled with homes David developed or built.

- For George Washington Brown (twin son)   dob: 1879   dod: 1960
- SW ¼ , Section 14, T-4-N, R-11-W, Comanche County, Oklahoma
  - This farm is "catty corner" across the intersection from Lafe's quarter section. It's now owned by the City of Lawton for Lake Ellsworth.

- For Frank A. Brown (son) dob: 1889 dod: 1912
  - Frank Jr. died at the age of 23 in Fletcher, OK, paralyzed from a fall, dying two weeks afterward.

More on Grandpa Lafe

I was a young boy when we moved across the road (now 13786 NE 75th St. in Elgin, OK) from Grandpa and Grandma Brown. Grandpa was a lean, wiry man with thinning hair. (The thinning hair part I inherited). He couldn't hear worth a damn, but he could see a hawk in the pasture a half-mile away. He was definitely not a whiner. I don't think I ever heard him complain or cry out in pain from the many blows he must have taken from life and cantankerous farm machinery. Grandpa was a farmer, a strong Roosevelt Democrat, and a man who had ideas far ahead of his neighbors. He belonged to the Farmers Union, which was an insurance cooperative, but he argued extensively for the actual unionization of farmers. He was frustrated that his neighbor farmers, who so treasured their "independence" that they'd go bankrupt before uniting to help themselves.

Grandpa was an adventurer. He rode his horse from Oklahoma to the 1904 World's Fair in St. Louis, which was held from April 30 to December 1. This was several years before Oklahoma was a state, so there would have been no Interstates from southwest Oklahoma to St. Louis. Having made that trip the lazy way by Interstate highway, going back and forth from St. Louis University to our home in Elgin, I can tell you that there are the Ozark Mountains, deep valleys, intimidating rivers, lots of trees, and rough terrain. Research of the history of the Frisco Railroad revealed that a railroad line was completed from St. Louis to Lawton, Oklahoma in 1883. Presumably, he would have followed this railroad. Even so, his trip had to be a heart-thumping experience. He was 25 years old.

Grandpa was an inventor, probably out of necessity. When a piece of machinery broke, he found a scrap of metal lying around that he could weld in the place of the wrecked part. He could pound on metal framework until it conformed to his idea of where it ought to be. He had a shop behind the house in which he tinkered for hours, sometimes with a noisy, nosy grandkid, me, watching intently.

Grandpa also owned a 1950 Nash automobile, which looked like an inverted bathtub and which he drove across the pastures like it was a Sherman tank, not slowing for terraces, but roaring across them, landing on the other side with a whoomp that testified to the spongey-ness of the springs. It was an adventure riding with Grandpa, better than any roller coaster. Although these rides were breathtaking, there was never the slightest hint of exhilaration on his part….this was just a kind of observational farming. The thought of slowing down never entered his mind.

Grandma, unlike Grandpa, was "big-boned". She came from Kentucky, being born in Elizabethtown, Grayson County, where she lived until she was about 16 years of age and her family moved to Oklahoma. Her memories of Kentucky included storing butter in a "spring house", which was a cellar-like place with a spring running through it. She had an eighth-grade education.

My memories of her included her frustrations with Grandpa, as he would turn off his hearing aids when Grandma was talking. She would continue her "discussions" with him until she realized that he wasn't responding and hadn't heard a word of what she'd said.

Long before the hearing aid episodes, Lafe had been a bachelor in his early thirties living "on the west place," the wooden two-story house he'd built west of the final home on the top of the hill about a half-mile from there, when he got to thinking about girls. A good resource was the nearby Wooldridge place where the family had several eligible daughters. His eye fell on Lillie, who he dated, but who wasn't as keen on him as he was on her. Bluntly put, she dumped him. I guess he moped around a little until he got a penny postcard from Ida, Lillie's little sister, who wrote, "Just because you're not seeing Lillie anymore doesn't mean you should stop coming over here." Lafe was swift enough to revisit the Wooldridges to scout this out. The rest is history, as they say. Lafe and Ida were married on January 11, 1911, in Apache, Oklahoma.

James Lafayette (Lafe) Brown, left, age 26
Ida Elizabeth (Wooldridge) Brown, right, age 16

Grandma home-schooled Howard, the oldest of the Brown kids, when he was small, after which he went to Midway School, walking there from the old Brown place. Anna Lee had a special place in her heart for Howard, remembering him as a kind of protector. She recalled Howard as one constantly inquisitive and learning. He learned drafting, using a T-square in the upstairs room above the carport. He was a master carver of canes, wooden puzzlebox toys, and many other things. He could play the saxophone as well. Anna Lee was sensitive about her other brother, Frank, who dealt with many problems throughout his life.

Grandma had a brother, Tom Wooldridge, who lived in California. In the age when writing letters was the tool of communication, Tom would write Grandma, passing on news of the California family, but nearly always adding his own very conservative views of politics, as he was a staunch Republican. Grandma would stride down the driveway from her house to ours to talk about Tom's letters and we would gather around the dining room table to analyze Tom's epistles. Grandma was distinctly not a Republican. Tom's letters would cause Grandma's blood to boil when he descended into Republican talk. She had very strong, and adverse, reactions to his political thoughts, especially if he denigrated FDR. At that time my parents were also Democrats, so Grandma had sympathetic ears.

Grandpa and Grandma had four children: James Howard; Frank Nathan; my mother, Rose Mary; and the baby, Anna Lee[26]. The photo above was taken probably at Christmastime, 1922, as Anna Lee was obviously a young baby. They are, left to right: Anna Lee, born Nov. 7, 1922; James Howard, born October 22, 1911; Rose Mary, born December 8, 1915; and Frank Nathan, born September 27, 1913.

Anna Lee Brown c.1942

L-R: Rick and David Kolker; Anna Lee Brown Schlitt, c. late 1990s

I was fortunate enough during the lifetime of Anna Lee to sit down with her, in December 2006 and February 2007 and interview her about her life and parents. Those interviews are on discs and are too long to be set forth here in detail. But the following are paraphrased excerpts from those interviews:

After Grandpa made it to Comanche County, Oklahoma he built a two-story house with his own hands northwest of Elgin and west of the eventual home on the top of the hill across from where I lived as a boy. This house burned when Anna Lee was about three years old. For a time they lived in a tent, afterward moving to a garage building which exists to this day behind the final Brown home site. An imposing home was built, with Grandpa doing much of the work, as he was a carpenter/framer of sorts. John Lodes did the stucco work, also plastering the basement.

This two-story house, with an attic, was built in 1925-26. The house was built on solid rock, with the ever-talented Grandpa doing dynamite work to fashion a "root cellar" beneath it. Cedar trees were dug out from the Wichita Mountains and hauled to the home site on a Ford Model-T truck. Those trees, meant to be a windbreak, lived for nearly ninety years in two rows to the north of the house, but have gradually died out, leaving only a few stragglers.

This magnificent house stands on the top of a hill overlooking a long valley, which, when the house was built, was occupied by nothing other than coyotes, hawks, grass, and open land. Grandpa owned the northern half of the section on which the house was located and farmed much of that land to the south, north, and west within that section. The house stands today looking as stately as it did almost a hundred years ago. For its time it was a marvel and still is architecturally remarkable. But the interior reflects the times in which it was built. It had only one, very small bathroom and two bedrooms, on the first floor, also small. It had and has a large combination living room/dining room. Above the "portico" was a bedroom with no electricity, so it was not heated or air-conditioned. The portico is so narrow that a modern car won't fit; we have photos of a Model T parked there decades ago. Unusually for a home in Oklahoma, it has a basement, hewn out of rock dynamited by Grandpa. I can remember that there was also a clothes chute that went from the first floor to the basement, so one could deposit clothes that would drop down to the lower floor for washing. Little boys could also drop down that chute into the laundry basket. Adventure is so easy for little guys.

The photo above is unusual in that it apparently was creased to eliminate the barn which was to the south of the house (left on the photo). There are several photos of the home without the barn. It's mysterious as to why it was cut off later, but there you have it.

The Brown children walked two and a half miles to school in Elgin. Anna Lee revealed that my mother, Rose Mary, sometimes walked with a boyfriend, "Socks" Hefner.

The house across the road from Grandpa's was occupied by the Herndon family for years while Anna Lee was growing up, but at some point, Mrs. Herndon was injured in a tragic auto accident and paralyzed. Grandma took care of Mrs. Herndon, spending much of her day providing it.

Later the Comstocks replaced the Herndons. Mrs. Comstock was Irish to the bone, and they had a gang of kids that the Brown siblings could play with: Margaret, the oldest; Helen, Josephine, Frank, John, and Bessie, the youngest—even younger than Anna Lee.

Grandma was a very caring person. Anna Lee remembered her mom would snuggle with her in bed, calling Anna Lee her "little stove". For ten years, Grandma's mother, Frances Anne Gatton Wooldridge, lived with Grandma and Grandpa with Grandma as her constant caretaker. Frances Gatton Wooldridge, despite being an invalid, lived to age 83, dying on September 7, 1939. While she was living at the Brown house Grandpa gave up his bedroom on the first floor so that his mother-in-law could live there.

But while Grandma was "very caring", she was also the family disciplinarian, and she was "strict". She used a yard-long hickory stick for enforcement. Grandpa apparently was an easy touch and didn't do the discipline of the children.

Grandma did "tatting"—lacing/edging (like a doily), plus embroidery and quilting. Cloth things were sometimes different than today's selections: for example, bed sheets were muslin, sewn together to be large enough to cover a bed. Pillows were stuffed with goose down, from the family's own geese. Grandma and my mom were expert clothesmakers; Anna Lee remembers dresses made for her.

Grandpa, typical of his time, was not demonstrably affectionate and didn't talk a lot, either. Anna Lee couldn't remember him showing a sense of humor, seeing him as a person that was "all business". He was a farmer, but during the Depression, he also was an office worker and worker recruiter for a Franklin D. Roosevelt program: the REA (Rural Electrification Act of 1936). That job originally entailed work in Lawton but he was later able to conduct that business from the basement of the home.

He was also a Farmers Union agent later in his life. That business later went to my Dad, who continued selling that insurance for much of his life.

The Great Depression meant conserving. Cows were raised for beef and when butchered the meat was stored in the home's basement until it could be canned. That was some busy basement because when I was a boy, Grandpa would make and store beer there.

Grandpa's twin brother, George Washington Brown, originally had a farm nearby his brother, but he later sold and moved to Apache, where he would see Grandma and Grandpa at the Catholic Church there on Sundays. George married Mary Margaret (Mamie) Cunningham on November 14, 1907.

George's eldest son, Edwin, fought and died at the Battle of the Bulge in World War II. Other children of George's included Joe, Florence, Agnes, and Marjorie, the latter being close to Anna Lee's age so that the two of them could play together.

Grandpa had a close friend: Harry Roll, father of John Roll and grandfather of Mike Roll, my sister, Debbie's, now-deceased husband.

When I asked Anna Lee about what the family did for entertainment, she fondly remembered her father singing a cappella on the front porch during the summer evenings. He had a great voice and memory for pioneer lyrics, some of which he learned on the trip to the Land Run. One of the songs she remembered him singing was "My Little Old Sod Shanty". Just for fun, I captured the first three verses so I could imagine Grandpa singing them:

> I am looking rather seedy now while holding down my claim,
> And my victuals are not always served the best;
> And the mice play shyly round me as I nestle down to rest
> In my little old sod shanty on my claim.
>
> The hinges are of leather and the windows have no glass,
> While the board roof lets the howling blizzards in,
> And I hear the hungry coyote as he slinks up through the grass
> Round the little old sod shanty on my claim.
>
> Yet, I rather like the novelty of living in this way,
> Though my bill of fare is always rather tame,
> But I'm happy as a clam on the land of Uncle Sam
> In the little old sod shanty on my claim.

The family would go sometimes go to the Elgin Catholic Church hall for "pitch parties", where couples would form small groups to play cards. A wind-up phonograph would play music such as "Shuffle Off To Buffalo".

Anna Lee remembered making rope together with her father. Rope, of course, had a myriad of uses on a farm with horses and cows, so lots of rope was needed. She also remembered turning a wheel on a grinder used to sharpen the blades on the horse-drawn scythe. These memories with her father were precious to Anna Lee; she took them as his way of showing her love and affection.

Apparently, Great-grandpa Francois Antoine Brown (or Braun), born October 16, 1843, in Vallf, France, and died December 29, 1922, (about seven weeks after Anna Lee was born) in Elgin, Oklahoma, handed down to his family the strong impression that he didn't like Germans, who he felt "ran him out" of France. Anna Lee thought this was an additional inspiration to change Braun to Brown on reaching American shores.

Sometimes in this genealogical adventure one stumbles upon a factual goldmine. This time it was another discovery by brother Bob. I had always wondered if we had anyone in the family tree who was engaged in battle during the American Civil War. Well, our second great-grandfather (our great-great-grandfather) on the maternal side, who was born on October 1, 1821, in Baden-Württemberg, Germany, fits the bill perfectly. First, a little family background for Andrew. He was born to Cornelius Wiegele (this became "Weekly" in America), when Cornelius was 37 and his wife, Wolberga was 24. Andrew married Mary A. Fagen and they had five children together, including Magdalene Weekly, Grandpa Lafe's mother and the strong woman who carried the tiny baby across the Cimarron River along the way to the Oklahoma Land Rush of 1889. After Mary died, Andrew then married Catherine Hilberg and they had four children together. He died on October 3, 1902, in Kelso, Indiana at age 81.

Andrew enlisted in the Union army, the 83rd Infantry Regiment Indiana, a unit that was organized on September 4, 1862, and fought many savage battles during the Civil War.

For example, his regiment fought at:

- Chickasaw Bayou, MS on December 28, 1862;
- Arkansas Post on January 11, 1863;
- Ford Farm, MS on March 25, 1863;
- Vicksburg in battles on May 16, May 19, May 22, and May 28, 1863, while in Ulysses Grant's army;
- Dallas, GA on May 29, and May 30, 1864;
- Kenesaw Mountain, GA; on June 27, 1864;
- Atlanta, GA on July 28, and August 26, 1864;
- Jonesboro, GA on August 31 and September 1, 1864;
- Macon, GA on November 22, 1864.
- Memphis, to Chattanooga, and Missionary Ridge. With General Sherman;
- The famed "March to the Sea" with Sherman, from November 15, 1864, to December 21, 1864.

The list of armed struggles is actually longer, but you get the picture.

The original strength of his regiment was 973. It lost 56 enlisted and five officers killed or died by mortal wounds. 116 were unaccounted for. Many died from disease or accident: 220. The unit mustered out on June 3, 1865, so that Andrew could go home to his family, which included Magdalene Weekly.

Great-grandma, Andrew Weekly's daughter, Magdalene (aka Mattie, or Martha) Weekly, born November 1, 1846, in Dover, Indiana, and died in Elgin, Oklahoma in April 1938, was a tall and slim woman, (much like my mother, Rose Mary Brown Kolker, according to Anna Lee). Mattie was still living when Anna Lee was a young girl, and was "stone deaf", causing her to stay silent most of the time. The family moved from Garfield County, Oklahoma to the southeast of Fletcher, Oklahoma, at some point, and raised concord grapes for eating, grape jelly, grape juice, and wine.

Later, Grandpa and his twin brother, George Washington Brown, bought fruit trees for 70 cents each and planted an orchard at the "old Brown place" down the hill and west of where Grandpa ultimately settled. He also built a huge storm/fruit cellar there and a two-story wooden house at that "old place".

Grandpa Lafe had an older brother, Charles (known as Charley) Noah Brown, born January 3, 1874, in Illinois, and died in Elgin in 1928, who lived near Fletcher—on a hill as seemed to be the preference for all the Browns. Charley died at only 54 years old, probably of food poisoning.

Lafe also had an older sister, Mary Josephine, who was born on March 30, 1877, in Illinois, and died on January 6, 1958, in Elgin. Mary, unfortunately, had a mental illness that later caused her to be institutionalized. She also lived near Fletcher. Lafe, of course, had a twin brother, George Washington, who lived in Apache, Oklahoma, and died there on February 12, 1960, and a younger brother, Frank Anthony Brown, who was born on March 6, 1889, in Comanche County, Kansas, and died September 12, 1912, in Elgin. This younger brother had a remarkable history: he was the tiny baby carried in the arms of his mother, Mattie Weekly, as the family made its way from Kansas to the Oklahoma Run of April 1889. Unfortunately, he died young, at age 23.

Grandpa Lafe only had an eighth-grade education but learned the English language well enough to write his history of the Oklahoma Run in a manner beyond what many eighth-graders might be expected to do.

I asked Anna Lee if she had any memories of being around the family table when she was a young girl. At a time when she was a devotee of Santa Claus, her older brothers, Howard and Frank, announced, as the family was finishing dinner on Christmas Eve that they were going "to shoot Santa Claus" while carrying shotguns. This dramatic declaration sent Anna Lee into a screaming, anguished cry that she remembered vividly at the time of my interview of her, decades later. I did not do a good job of maintaining a proper somber attitude.

Anna Lee remembered her father as a good eater, and one who ate butter "like it was going out of style". His "dessert" was often a large piece of homemade bread slathered with fresh butter and liberally sprinkled with sugar. He enjoyed breaded tomatoes, mashed potatoes and gravy, and fried chicken. Yet grandpa was "skinny as a rail" all his life. This must have been the French in him.

Grandpa also made his own beer, which he kept in his basement, where it was cool. He enjoyed a bottle of that beer on a hot day but limited himself to just one. Grandma was even more temperate than that: a sip would "go to her head", so she'd stop at that.

Apparently, this alcohol self-limiting was passed down to my mother, Rose Mary, as well. Anna Lee recounted that Bud Lodes, a buddy of Dad's, had proposed to Mom and she refused him because of his level of beer drinking. When Dad entered the competition he was told that the Lodes level of drinking wouldn't be acceptable. Dad accepted this ruling and from that point onward was a limited drinker of alcohol. I guess that worked or we wouldn't be here.

Some other memories of the times while Anna Lee was growing up included the men of the family putting a large black iron pot in the backyard over a large fire and putting large slabs of pork fat into it, which was boiled down to lard, used in cooking. The fried chicken Grandpa liked so much was cooked in that lard. Maybe it was that good cooking that made Grandpa the quiet, even-tempered man that he was…and it carried over to Grandma, too. Fried chicken was part of a typical meal. Grandma would put out chicken feed, the chickens would gather to eat it, and she would hook one with a wire hook until she could grab it by the neck, which became a handle so the chicken could be whirled around until the head separated from its body. Of course, I got to see this execution as a boy and was fascinated that the chicken body could run around headless for a while before dropping. That chicken would take all morning to prepare. Water was boiled; the chicken was dropped into the water so the feathers could be plucked. There were remaining little pinfeathers, which were singed off over a fire. Finally, the chicken was cooked, and that which didn't make it to the table was canned and stored in the cool basement.

While Grandpa was, indeed, a "quiet, even-tempered" man, there was one exception. When I was a young boy, Grandpa would venture out with his rifle to take his vengeance on crows, which he hated with a passion. There was a tree not far from our present house in Elgin where the crows would land in large numbers, caw-cawing in a way that Grandpa deemed to be brazen defiance. Approaching this crow-filled tree meant stealthy, careful steps with the gun behind him so the crows couldn't see it. But crows are smart. They would let him get just outside of decent rifle range and then fly off together with wicked grins on their faces, or so Grandpa thought. When he didn't have a rifle he could get as close as underneath that tree—close enough that he'd get bird droppings. They must have enjoyed every minute of this. But Grandpa wasn't to be denied. He had used dynamite before, to blow out the rock beneath the ground level of the new house he was building. So he wrapped several sticks of it together and lodged it high in the "crow tree", stringing a line far enough away so he could detonate it from a distance.

You can imagine the tremendous explosion this caused. Did it kill a single crow? No.

I had always thought Grandpa's unsatisfied vengeance on crows was unique to him, particularly the dynamite method. But in the April 15, 2021 issue of The Chronicle, a local weekly newspaper, there was a column by Debi DeSilver entitled, "Controlling Crows by 'Bombing' Their Roosts". She was citing a March 1946 issue of "Oklahoma Game and Fish News", on "...efforts by officials to attempt crow control by using a dynamite bomb system..." That 1946 article called Oklahoma the "crow center of the United States". It described the "tremendous damage to crops and other wildlife...and they are a menace to the nests of waterfowl by robbing eggs." No wonder Grandpa hated them! Apparently in 1933 officials in Oklahoma noted the number of crows wintering in the state was "increasing at an alarming rate and spreading over a much larger area." Unofficial attempts to "bomb" the crows were made using "chat" (crushed limestone) placed atop seven sticks of dynamite. This worked to eliminate several hundred crows in Beckham County in 1934-35. Game rangers joined in with the crow bombing, using the method in Blanchard, Okemah, Shawnee, Willow, Oklahoma City, and Anadarko, killing about 60,000 crows. Grandpa must have been insanely jealous. Anyway, this effort grew to the point that even the state legislature appropriated money to pay for materials, so that in 11 seasons from 1934-35 through 1944-45 over three million crows were done away with. Texas sportsmen even joined in, killing over 70,000 birds. Kansas, too, blew up over 75,000 crows. Debi's article stated that "An article at crowbusters.com noted that the last crow roost bombing was in Stafford County, Kansas in 1952."

But when not hunting the devious crows, there was food gathering to be done. Fresh corn was gathered from the garden, as well as green beans and peas. Potatoes were dug from the ground and some were stored in the basement. Butchered pigs provided sausage, other pork meat, and bacon, the latter being salted and hung out. When the beef was killed, everybody had a job. (Beef dropped to about 2 cents a pound during the Depression, to the point that government programs caused cattle to be killed to drive up the price.) The butchered beef was hung between boards that were placed across a U-shaped section of the basement, covered with tarp and ice was brought in and put on the floor beneath the hanging beef.

Anna Lee also remembered the critters that lived around the family home: lots of jackrabbits, horned toads, opossums, skunks, and coyotes, the latter howling in the night-time.

I was curious if Anna Lee could recall discussions of her father or mother indicating feelings of prejudice toward blacks or Native Americans. She couldn't remember her father expressing such sentiments, but "sensed" her mother was prejudiced against Native Americans. I'm not sure that my Kentucky grandmother didn't have similar prejudice against blacks, but time has made specifics impossible to resurrect these thoughts. My reasons for suspecting my dear grandmother of possible racism are admittedly based solely on her Southern origins. That's not a really good reason to attribute such a negative perspective to my grandmother, but I felt I just had to ask Anna Lee about this issue.

Photos above were taken in January 1961. Left, James Lafayette ("Lafe") Brown, approx. 80 years old. Right, Ida Elizabeth and James Lafayette Brown, c. 1961.

One thing Anna Lee was sure of was the politics of her mother and father, who were both strong Democrats—Franklin Roosevelt Democrats. Anna Lee vividly remembered their Depression struggles, and the blame put firmly at the feet of the Republicans. It was FDR who set up the REA (Rural Electrification Administration, enacted in 1935) that gave farmers help in industrializing farming. Grandpa Lafe also got a job through the AAA (Agriculture Adjustment Act of May 1933) Program during the depression which paid him $4.00 per day, doing office work, as he was intelligent and a good writer despite only an eighth-grade education. The family lived on its own, raised chickens, gathered their eggs, milked the cows, and took eggs and cream to town to trade for groceries, which they bought at Kolker's Groceries in Elgin. Her brother Howard sold encyclopedias in Kansas to help pay his way through school.

We also talked of the sickness and death of her parents. Grandpa died of prostate cancer, insisting at the end to leave the hospital and go home, where he died. Grandma also died of cancer—colon cancer, which she thought had been removed earlier but returned more lethally. When Anna Lee was a teenager, her father almost died from a black widow spider bite. For medical events such as this, Elgin had its own doctor, Doctor Chesley M. Martin, a country doctor if there ever was one, as he'd come to the sick person's home to treat if necessary or assist in a birth. Doc Martin's office in Elgin was part of his "medical complex" because he also owned the pharmacy, where he'd mix his own drugs. Doc Martin was born in South Carolina on June 11, 1889, and died on April 27, 1966, but spent his professional life centered in Elgin, where he was also a dominant force on the school board and in town politics for decades.

One last crumb on Grandpa Lafe. There's a family story that Grandpa at one time was a neighbor of Frank James, the brother of the infamous outlaw, Jesse James. Trying to track this down led to a story in The Oklahoman, dated July 25, 1909:

James and his wife moved to a farm near Fletcher in southwestern Oklahoma in 1906. There they raised corn and chickens on 100 acres of land....Mr. and Mrs. James attended church and social gatherings in Fletcher, and Mr. James is ranked as one of the foremost men in that part of Oklahoma.

The article located the James farm as being one and a half miles north of Fletcher. It further states that James lived there until about 1911, shortly after his mother died. The family story would have had Grandpa living as a neighbor to Frank James. What we do know is that Grandpa and/or his father did own land north of Fletcher at the time. Grandpa, having been born in 1879, would have been 27 years old in 1906. Of course, it might be possible that it refers to Grandpa's father. I've searched everywhere I know to look for a photo supposedly taken of Grandpa with a horse bought from Frank James to no avail. So at this point, this story is not solidly confirmed, but we all like it, anyway.

Endnotes

BOOK I

Chapter 6

26. A summary of the Lafe/Ida Brown immediate family:

James Lafayette (Lafe) Brown
DoB: July 3, 1879, Whitley Pt., Moultrie Co., IL
DoD: January 18, 1962, buried Elgin, OK
Ida Elizabeth Brown
DoD: December 24, 1976, buried Elgin, OK
DoB: October 10, 1889, Clarkson, Grayson Co., KY
   Married: January 11, 1911, Apache, OK by Rev. Frederick Vanderaa

Children:
James Howard Brown
DoB: October 22, 1911, Elgin, OK
DoD: October 19, 2006, La Canada, CA
Married: Catherine Cecilia Tuttle, September 1, 1939
   Six children: James Howard, Jr., born June 15, 1939; Lawrence Earl (deceased), born Sept. 16, 1942; Mary Catherine, born Oct. 29, 1943; Anita Elizabeth, born Apr. 21, 1946; Paul Anthony, born March 30, 1949; and Irene Louise, born July 31, 1954.

Francis (Frank) Nathan Brown
DoB: September 27, 1913, Elgin, OK
DoD: December 24, 1982, Oklahoma City, OK
Married: Irene Lodes, November 1937
   Six children: Charles Joseph, born Nov. 10, 1938; Mary Frances, born Nov. 19, 1939; John Francis (Frankie), born May 9, 1941; Elizabeth (Betty) Ann, born Aug. 11, 1942; James Paul, born Aug. 26, 1947; Donald Richard, born January 19, 1952.

Rose Mary Brown
DoB: December 8, 1915, Elgin, OK
DoD: January 16, 1997, Lawton, OK
Married: Charles John Kolker (Sr.), April 27, 1938, Elgin, OK
  Six children: Charles John(Jr.), born Nov. 8, 1940; Robert Paul, born Jan.
  22, 1946; David Alan, born Oct. 10, 1948; Deborah Ann, born Oct. 7,
  1953; James Michael, born Dec. 21, 1956; Richard Joseph, born Nov.
  30, 1959.

Anna Lee Brown
DoB: November 7, 1922
DoD: September 2, 2014, Lawton, OK
Married: John Edward Schlitt, September 4,1948, Elgin, OK
  One adopted daughter: Roberta Ellen Lemmon Kirby, born Jan. 2, 1946.

Chapter 7

The Wooldridges

Tackling the huge Wooldridge family lineage is intimidating. Grandma Ida Brown was a Wooldridge, and there were, and are, hordes of Wooldridges. For those Biblical scholars familiar with the "begats" in the 5th Chapter of Genesis and the 1st Chapter of Matthew, this Chapter may seem too detailed, but, hey, this is part of our matriarchal lineage.

Grandma Brown's father was Nathan Gaither Wooldridge, born August 26, 1850, in Grayson Co., Kentucky, who died June 6, 1927, in Fletcher, Oklahoma; her mother was Frances Ann Gatton, born July 12, 1856, in the same Grayson Co., and who died September 7, 1939, in Elgin, Oklahoma. Her obituary stated, "Mrs. N. G. Wooldridge, 83, died at 5:30 a.m. Thursday in the home of her daughter, Mrs. J.L. Brown, two miles north of Elgin. Mrs. Wooldridge, a resident of that community since 1906, had been an invalid for several years. Her husband died 12 years ago." Nathan and Frances were married in Grayson Co. on November 12, 1871.

Photo of Nathan Gaither ("N.G.") Wooldridge, with his wife, Frances Ann Gatton, and first child, Annie Belle Wooldridge. Taken about 1870.

The ancestry of Great-grandma Frances Ann Gatton is deep and fascinating. Let us go backward in time.

Frances was the daughter of Sylvester Otho Gatton, our second great-grandfather, who was born January 20, 1821, in Grayson, Kentucky, and died January 20, 1915, in Louisville, Jefferson Co., Kentucky. He married Lydia Frances Wellington on February 22, 1841.

Our third great-grandfather, James William Gatton, Sylvester Otho's father, was born in 1795 in St. Mary's, St. Mary's County, Maryland. He died on April 5, 1837, when his son, Sylvester, shot and killed him in a hunting accident while in Sunfish, Edmonson, Kentucky. James William married Mary Newton.

Our fourth Great-Grandfather, Sylvestor G. Gatton, born in 1755 in Frederick County, Maryland, died in Kentucky in 1820. He married Anna Robey on September 29, 1786, also in Frederick Co., Maryland. Sylvestor G. enlisted in the Revolutionary Army during the American Revolutionary War, on June 10, 1778, and was discharged on November 1, 1780—but he had been a prisoner of war who was exchanged in a prisoner swap on October 2, 1780. He had served as a private in the Maryland 1st Regiment.

Our fifth Great-Grandfather, Richard E. Gatton, Jr., was born in 1736 in Montgomery, Montgomery County, Maryland, and he died in 1822. He married Jemima Vetch on July 1, 1785. Remarkably, he enlisted to fight in the American Revolutionary War on the same day as his son, Sylvester G. Gatton, that is, on June 10, 1778, and was also discharged on November 1, 1780.

In 1777, all Maryland voters were required to take the Oath of Fidelity and Support. This was an oath swearing allegiance to the state of Maryland and denying allegiance and obedience to Great Britain. As enacted by the Maryland

General Assembly in 1777, all persons holding any office of profit or trust, including attorneys at law, and all voters were required to take the oath no later than March 1, 1778. It was signed by 3,136 residents of Montgomery and Washington counties.[27]

Our sixth great-grandfather, Richard Gatton, Sr., was born in 1717 in Frederick, British Colonial America, Maryland. He died on February 19, 1768, also in Frederick.

Our seventh great-grandfather, Thomas Gatton, was born on May 21, 1676, in Richmond, Surrey, England, and died in 1772 in Prince Geo, Maryland. He married Mary Clagett in 1729. She was born in 1713 and died in 1792.

Our eighth great-grandfather, John Gatten Gatton, was born in 1641 or 1646 in Richmond, Surrey, England, and died in Richmond on July 25, 1676. He married Dorothy Vause, on July 18, 1666, at St. Mary Magdalen, Richmond, Surrey, England.

Our ninth great-grandfather, Edward Gatton, was born September 14, 1617, in Shere, Surrey, England, and died at Gatton Parish, Surrey, England on July 25, 1641. He married Ann Gurnet, on July 8, 1640. It was a short marriage for Edward, but Ann, born in 1617, lived until 1709.

If one really wants to go back, the Gatton family is the one to pick. The earliest of the name on record appears to be GATONE (without surname) who was listed as a tenant in the Domesday Book of 1086. Surnames derived from place names are divided into two broad categories: topographic names and habitation names. Topographic names are derived from general descriptive references to someone who lived near a physical feature such as an oak tree, a hill, a stream, or a church. Habitation names are derived from pre-existing names denoting towns, villages, and farmsteads. Other classes of local names include those derived from the names of rivers, individual houses with signs on them, regions, and whole countries. Later records of the name include Hamo de GATTUNE, who was documented in 1273, County Kent, and Robert de GATTON appears in Sussex in 1279. Alicia de Gatton of Yorkshire was listed in the Yorkshire Poll Tax of 1379. In the Middle Ages heraldry came into use as a practical matter. It originated in the devices used to distinguish the armored warriors in tournaments and war and was also placed on seals as marks of identity. As far as records show, true heraldry began in the middle of the twelfth century and appeared almost simultaneously in several countries of Western Europe. Later instances of the name mention Thomas Gill and Elizabeth Gatton, who were married in London in 1591 (no church given), and Francis Gatton and Susanna Smith were wed at St. James's, Clerkenwell, London in the year 1669. When the first immigrants from Europe went to America, the only names current in the new land were Indian names which did not appeal to Europeans vocally, and the Indian names did not influence the surnames or Christian names already possessed by the immigrants. Mostly the immigrant could not read or write and had little or no knowledge as to the proper spelling, and their names suffered at the hands of the government officials.

The early town records are full of these misspelled names, most of which gradually changed back to a more conventional spelling as education progressed.[28]

The Gatton family crest, or Coat of Arms, in England.

Grandma Ida Wooldridge Brown, a descendant of the aforementioned Gattons on her mother's side, had a sizeable number of siblings. Hopefully, the following list of the children of Nathan and Frances is complete and in the correct birth order:

Annie Bell Wooldridge, born November 1, 1872, in Clarkson, Greyson Co., Kentucky; died August 2, 1962, in Chattanooga, Comanche Co. Oklahoma. She married William John Murphy, who was born July 1, 1856, in Frampton, Quebec, Canada. He died in 1937. Annie and William Murphy were the parents of Fr. Joseph (Fr. Joe) Murphy, who was born Francis Aloysius Murphy on December 1, 1910, in Chattanooga, Oklahoma, and died on October 19, 1989, in Pomona, California. He was an occasional visitor at our family home in Elgin, always full of numerous, well-told stories. He was ordained as a priest on May 31, 1936. He earned a Ph.D. from the University of Oklahoma in 1961 and was the author of two published books: Tenacious Monks (a history of St. Gregory's Abbey in Shawnee, OK) and Potawatomie Indians of the West. He was an adopted Potawatomi by action of that tribe's business council on August 27, 1985. Fr. Murphy had one sister and possibly six brothers, but the problem is that Annie Bell was wife number three, so a bunch of these siblings are half-brothers/sisters. Annie and William are buried in Highland Cemetery on Ft. Sill Blvd., Lawton, OK.

Mary Joseph (known as Josie) Wooldridge, was born November 8, 1874, and died July 11, 1965, in Elgin. She married Bruno Sabinas Thomas (1880-1978) in 1903 at St. Ann's Catholic Church in Elgin, Oklahoma. Many of my siblings probably remember the Thomas family as they sat in St. Ann's in Elgin when we attended. Mary's middle name is a small mystery, as it's chiseled into her gravestone as

"Joseph" but appears as "Josephine" in other family records. Both Josie and Bruno are buried at the Catholic cemetery in Elgin. They had six children:

Bernard Nathan, born March 11, 1905, and died June 1, 1986. He married Nona Belle Littlefield on October 30, 1930, in Oklahoma City; they had no children;

Genrose (Rose) Annett, born December 22, 1906, died September 17, 1990. She remained single;

Mary Frances, born July 16, 1908, died February 5, 2009. She also remained single;

Sarah Katherine, born March 2, 1910, died January 16, 2000, also remained single;

Helen Elizabeth Thomas Nelson, born August 28, 1912, died July 10, 2000, and married Charles Nelson. They had five children: Mary Ann, Betty Jean, Charlene, Frank, and Barbara;

Jesse Peter Thomas, born June 25, 1916, and died September 28, 1977. He married Pauline Nelson in Apache and they had twelve children: Katherine Roberta, Terese Mae, Arnold Gerard, Ann Geraldine, James Howard, Lawrence Alen, Martin Eugene, Janet Marcella, John Joseph, Mary Beverly, and Donald Jesse, thereby making up for all the single siblings.

Francis Lee Wooldridge was born on January 31, 1877, in Clarkson, Greyson Co., Kentucky, and died on April 13, 1946, in Apache, Oklahoma. Her first name is sometimes spelled "Frances". She married John Joseph Clancy in Apache in February 1911; she and John are buried at the Apache, Oklahoma cemetery. They had six children:

Mary Allene, born in Pratt, Kansas on November 19, 1911, died December 12, 2007, and who married Valery Vapp on April 10, 1940, in Apache. They had one child: James Edward Vapp;

Lawrence Emmitt Clancy, born December 20, 1912, in Fayetteville, Arkansas, died December 6, 1999. (Lawrence was a lifelong bachelor. I stayed with him one summer during college and worked with him at a grain elevator near Dodge City, KS. He drove a Cadillac at top speed and would fall asleep while driving, an experience I'll never forget.);

Francis Joseph Clancy, born January 5, 1914, in Fayetteville, Arkansas, died September 17, 1991. He married Frederica ("Freddie") Massad, on July 6, 1953, in Dodge City, Kansas. They had three children: Frank, Antoinette, and Paul. Frank was in the Air Force during WWII. He was buried with military honors at Copeland Cemetery, Copeland, Kansas;

Catherine Ida, born July 2, 1915, and died November 12, 1973. She remained single, and is buried in Apache;

Helen Elizabeth, born in Fayetteville, Arkansas on April 11, 1917, died July 10, 2000;

James Nathan, born August 17, 1921, died March 16, 2001, and married to Lena Trent on July 27, 1952, in

Atoka, Oklahoma. James and Lena had two children: Patricia and Michael. James was married a second time to Gerri Bramlage on June 19, 1987, in Maryville, Kansas.

John Allen Wooldridge was born December 3, 1879, in Clarkson, Greyson Co., Kentucky, and died September 26, 1923, in Holtville, Imperial Co., California. He married Lottie Gatton in Pawnee, Illinois. They had seven children: Marion, born in 1907; Joseph; Margaret Thayer; Rose; Frank; Donald and Dorothy.

James Richard Wooldridge was born May 15, 1881, in Clarkson and died on October 14, 1896, in the same town and county. Grandma Ida wrote, "Jim died Oct. 4, 1896, at the age of 15. Died suddenly of a heart ailment and a congestive chill." I'm not sure why the day of death is different.

William Preston Wooldridge was born August 1, 1883, and died only a day-old on August 2, 1883, in Clarkson.

Ida Elizabeth Wooldridge, our grandma, was seventh in line, born October 10, 1884, in Clarkson, and died in Elgin, Oklahoma on December 24, 1976. I remember her death vividly as I was at her deathbed at the Comanche Co. Memorial Hospital in Lawton, Oklahoma when it occurred. The family was at home for Christmas Eve doings. Her death, of course, considerably dampened the holiday.

Lillian (Lillie) Catherine Wooldridge was the sister of Ida who jilted Grandpa Lafe. She was born in Clarkson on July 25, 1885, and died on November 17, 1964, in Colorado. She married Frederick Harris Doering (1869-1947). They had two children: Fred and Helen.

Sylvester (Vess) Charles Wooldridge was born on February 9, 1887, in Clarkson, and died on July 18, 1967, in Elgin. He married Anna Marie Logsdon (1897-1988) on August 26, 1914, at Fancy Farm, KY. They had six children:

James Walter (1915-2004), Thomas Nathan (1918-1994), Sylvester Charles (1922-1923), Dorothy Marie (1924-1989), Sylvester Edward (1926-2017), and Beatrice Agnes (1927-1943). One of the reasons for listing these children is to highlight the numerous Sylvesters. My siblings and I knew Sylvester Edward, as he was a common fixture at St. Ann's, so we'd see him and his wife, Myrtle, at church. He was blunt-spoken. On one of my visits with my parents, we attended St. Ann's for Mass. After church when the congregants would gather outside the building gossiping and greeting one another, Sylvester approached me with these words, "Gee, you've gotten fat." That was it. No hello, no further comment. (I was all of 180 lbs. at 5'11", but that was "fat" for Sylvester.) Sylvester Edward and his wife, Myrtle Theresa Schettler, had a trove of children, some of whom were good friends with my brothers, especially brother Jimmy: Charles Edward, Jo Ann, Albert Andrew, Lee Arnold, Rose Mary, Paul Joseph, Robert Mathew, and Catherine Marie. Vess is buried at the Catholic cemetery in Elgin, as are Sylvester Edward and his wife, Myrtle.

Francis (Frank) Edward Wooldridge was born on January 29, 1892, in Clarkson, and died on February 23, 1923, in Elgin, Oklahoma. He married Anna Marie Ida Hotter. Confusedly, some family records show her as "Anna Zemple". Frank and Anna had two children: Mary Gertrude Multhauf, who lived for a time in Jefferson, Wisconsin, and Francis N. Wooldridge, who lived in El Paso, Texas. The elder Frank is buried at the Catholic cemetery in Elgin.

Thomas Gregory Wooldridge was the "Uncle Tom" who used to send his conservative, political letters to Grandma and rile her up. He was born February 16, 1895, in Clarkson and died January 21, 1976, in Redondo Beach, Los Angeles County, California. He married Agnes C. Hall on August

18, 1928, in Los Angeles. They had four children: Thomas Wooldridge; Rosemary Wooldridge-Plue, who married Ronald Plue. Rosemary may be our family's claim to fame, as she won the James Beard award as a top pastry chef. Sue and I had the privilege of tasting some of Rosemary's famous desserts at a restaurant in California while we were with brother Bob and his wife, Joy. They had, at last knowledge, five children: Mike, Nicole, Chris, Shelly, and Eric; John Wooldridge, who has three children: Chris, Steve, and Mark; and Dorothy Wooldridge, married to Bill Gram. No children are recorded in the records I have.

Martin Leo Wooldridge, number 12, was the last of Grandma's siblings. He was born on August 12, 1899, in Clarkson and died on December 25, 1918, in Elgin. He's buried in St. Ann's Catholic Cemetery in Elgin. Grandma Ida wrote that "Martin died with "flu" and pneumonia early Christmas morning 1918 at the age of 19 years."

Oddly, I don't remember mention of any of Grandma Ida Brown's siblings except "Vess" and "Uncle Tom". The times of our grandparents and even our parents were different. There was no Facebook or iPhones to make communication easy. Once family members left the birthplace they seemed to disappear from mention.

Hopefully, no brother or sister of Grandma Ida was missed. It would be interesting to have a photo of the family home where this herd lived in Clarkson, KY, where they all were born. When they put the homestead up for sale in Clarkson, the Notice of Sale stated: "A farm for sale in grayson county. One mile to railroad, two miles to grayson springs five miles to county seat. Mills, school, churches all handy. Grayson public road good outlet. Well-watered. Plenty of timber. One hundred and thirty acres in cultivation. Good buildings, good fencing. For further particulars and price/address, contact N.G. Wooldridge."

When the family moved to Oklahoma in January 1906, they lived on a farm near Fletcher, Oklahoma until Nathan Gaither Wooldridge died there on June 6, 1927. His widow, Frances Ann, then lived with her daughter and son-in-law, Ida Elizabeth and James "Lafe" Brown in Elgin until her death in 1939. There is no attempt here to extend the Wooldridge tree beyond what's presented, as there's not enough paper in this world.

Endnotes

BOOK I

Chapter 7

27. From John Thomas Scharf, History of Maryland from the Earliest Period to the Present Day. Published by J. B. Piet, 1879; and Daughters of the American Revolution Magazine. Daughters of the American Revolution, Published by R..R. Bowker Co., 1916 v. 50 1917 Jan–Jun.

28. From Gatton Coat of Arms / Gatton Family Crest (4crests.com).

Chapter 8

Joseph Henry and Elizabeth Kolker

Above photo: Joseph Henry Kolker family, taken c. 1918.
Bottom row, L-R: Joseph Henry; a small boy with a wide,
white collar: Charles John (Sr.); behind him, Walter; in front:
Marie; Grandma Elizabeth; far right, Frank. Top row: L-R:
Bertha (Bea); Reynold; Laura; Clara.

Sadly, I don't have as much information about Joseph Henry Kolker, or his wife, Elizabeth Wiewel Kolker, as I'd like to have. Joseph Henry died in 1939, April 23 to be exact, in Lawton, Oklahoma. He's buried in Highland Cemetery in Lawton, alongside Elizabeth.

Joseph Henry was born in Iowa City, Wright County, Iowa on May 1, 1873, so he was only 66 years old at his death. The family legend has it that he died of "cancer of the face", presumably due to prolonged exposure to the Oklahoma sun as a farmer. The legend has it that the cancer ate into his brain and finally killed him. This sounds like a horribly gruesome death. Of course, I never got to know him, as I wasn't born until November of 1940.

Census records show him living in Kniest Township, Carroll County, Iowa in 1880 and 1885 and getting married to Elizabeth M. "Lizzie" Wiewel on April 27, 1897, in Mt. Carmel, Carroll County, Iowa. The story is that Joseph was a member of a "band" and Lizzie showed up at the dance, obviously attracting Joseph enough to marry her.

About 11 months after their marriage Joseph and Lizzie had their first son, Reynold Edward Kolker, on February 20, 1898, in Mt. Carmel. The following year Laura Mary Kolker was born, on July 15, 1899. Their residence continued to be Mt. Carmel while their family grew, as Bertha ("Bea") Catherine Kolker, was born there on November 20, 1901, followed by Clara Elizabeth Kolker (later Sheetz) on October 10, 1903.

On December 18, 1904, Joseph's mother, Mary Ann Rosener, died, and the next year, his father, Johann Eberhard Kolker, died on December 7. The family continued to reside in Carroll County during 1905, but by 1907 they had relocated to Okarche, Kingfisher County, Oklahoma, where Walter Matthew Kolker was born on February 14. They were still living in Okarche when Francis Michael Kolker was born on August 8, 1910, and continued to live there when Marie Catherine Kolker was born on August 10, 1911.

Finally, number 8 and last was my father, Charles John Kolker, who was born in Oklahoma City on January 10, 1914. We don't know why Dad was born in Oklahoma City, rather than Elgin or even Lawton, but his birth was not easy on Grandma, so possibly the birth had to be at a hospital with advanced capabilities. One of the stories of that difficult birth was that Grandma was crippled by the birthing process and that Grandpa Joseph somehow blamed Dad for that. We don't know if there's any truth to that, and it's probably just a myth.

In any event, census records of 1920 and 1930 show the family in Chandler, Comanche County, Oklahoma, but at some point, the family moved to the outskirts of Elgin, Comanche County, Oklahoma, a location barely a mile and a half from where I live as I write this. That house was a two-story affair, with two bedrooms upstairs—one for the boys and one for the girls. Grandma and Grandpa had the luxury of a downstairs bedroom.

My first memories of Grandma Elizabeth were while she lived in Lawton, Oklahoma, at the home of her daughter, Bea, and her husband, Dewey, Shaw. Grandma was always in bed or sitting next to it when we visited, and she was by then wheelchair-bound. Every hard, flat surface in her bedroom was covered with photos of grandkids and great-grandkids. She frequently had a rosary in her hands, and she constantly prayed. She was blind in her last years, probably from cataracts or macular degeneration.

But Grandma was not always praying. I have a memory of a family reunion at her place, in the backyard during the summer under the shade of trees. There were hordes of her children and grandchildren around, tons of food, and a barrel of German beer. Grandma had a rather large stein of beer which she seemed to be able to handle quite well because I certainly never saw her tipsy or silly from the beer—or anything else for that matter. It's not that she wasn't friendly, or warm, as she was that. She was just not the rah-rah, massive hugging grandma-type. Grandma was "bigboned" as they said in those days, but not fat.

Grandma was born in Mt. Carmel, Iowa, on May 3, 1876, so she was about three years younger than Joseph Henry. Her mother, Mary Helena Schulte Kolker, died in February 1880, leaving young Lizzie without her birth mother at an early age. The story of her young life has her taken to a Texas town to live with a family whose head was a tavern owner, and young Lizzie was not treated well at this place. She was later rescued by a sister, who brought her back to the Mt. Carmel area to be with family. It was there in Mt. Carmel that she met Joseph Henry and married him just a few days before she was 21.

Grandma died in Lawton, Oklahoma, on September 12, 1968, at age 92. She was pre-deceased by her eldest son, Reynold, who died at age 84 on June 11, 1960. She left 7 other children surviving.

During the lives of Joseph Henry and Lizzie, there were times of strong anti-German sentiment, some left over from World War I and some preceding World War II before Joseph Henry died, just months before the Germans invaded Poland on September 1, 1939. My Dad remembered that his parents, wanting to shield their kids from this anti-German feeling, did not teach them the German language, although they spoke it to each other at night after the kids went to bed. Dad remembered hearing their voices in that language coming from down below.

Both sets of grandparents lived through terrible times. On October 29, 1929, the stock market crashed, ushering in the Great Depression and the disastrous fall of the economy, not just here in Oklahoma or the United States, but across the world. Millions lost their jobs. People starved to death. Soup lines fed hungry men and women in huge, long lines. It was a time of despair. Then, for our grandparents, came the dust storms and a drought that persisted year after year. I wanted to catch the tenor of part of that by borrowing from John Steinbeck's Grapes of Wrath:

To the red country and part of the gray country of Oklahoma, the last rains came gently, and they did not cut the scarred earth. The plows crossed and recrossed the rivulet marks. The last rains lifted the corn quickly and scattered weed colonies and grass along the sides of the road so that the gray country and the dark red country began to disappear under a green cover. In the last part of May the sky grew pale and the clouds that had hung in high puffs for so long in the spring were dissipated. The sun flared down on the growing corn day after day until a line of brown spread along the edge of each green bayonet. The clouds appeared, and went away, and in a while they did not try any more. The weeds grew darker green to protect themselves, and they did not spread any more. The surface of the earth crusted, a thin hard crust, and as the sky became pale, so the earth became pale, pink in the red country and white in the gray country.

In the water-cut gullies the earth dusted down in dry little streams. Gophers and ant lions started small avalanches. And as the sharp sun struck day after day,

the leaves of the young corn became less stiff and erect;
they bent in a curve at first, and then, as the central ribs
of strength grew weak, each leaf tilted downward. Then
it was June, and the sun shone more fiercely. The brown
lines on the corn leaves widened and moved in on the
central ribs. The weeds frayed and edged back toward
their roots. The air was thin and the sky more pale; and
every day the earth paled.

In the roads where the teams moved, where the wheels
milled the ground and the hooves of the horses beat the
ground, the dirt crust broke and the dust formed. Every
moving thing lifted the dust in the air: a walking man
lifted a thin layer as high as his waist, and a wagon lifted
the dust as high as the fence tops, and an automobile
boiled a cloud behind it. The dust was long in settling
back again.

....

A gentle wind followed the rain clouds, driving them on
northward, a wind that softly clashed the drying corn. A
day went by and the wind increased, steady, unbroken
by gusts. The dust from the roads fluffed up and spread
out on the weeds beside the fields, and fell into the fields
a little way. Now the wind grew strong and hard and it
worked at the rain crust in the corn fields. Little by little
the sky was darkened by the mixing dust, and the wind
felt over the earth, loosened the dust, and carried it
away. The wind grew stronger. The rain crust broke and
the dust lifted up out of the fields and drove gray plumes
into the air like sluggish smoke. The corn threshed the
wind and made a dry, rushing sound. The finest dust did

not settle back to earth now, but disappeared into the darkening sky.

The wind grew stronger, whisked under stones, carried up straws and old leaves, and even little clods, marking its course as it sailed across the fields. The air and the sky darkened and through them the sun shone redly, and there was a raw sting in the air. During a night the wind raced faster over the land, dug cunningly among the rootlets of the corn, and the corn fought the wind with its weakened leaves until the roots were freed by the prying wind and then each stalk settled wearily sideways toward the earth and pointed the direction of the wind.

The dawn came, but no day. In the gray sky a red sun appeared, a dim red circle that gave a little light, like dusk; and as that day advanced, the dusk slipped back toward darkness, and the wind cried and whimpered over the fallen corn.

....

The people....knew it would take a long time for the dust to settle out of the air. In the morning the dust hung like fog, and the sun was as red as ripe new blood. All day the dust sifted down from the sky, and the next day it sifted down. An even blanket covered the earth. It settled on the corn, piled up on the tops of fence posts, piled up on the wires; it settled on roofs, blanketed the weeds and trees.[29]

The Dust Bowl is thought of as occurring between 1930 and 1936, with the worst year being 1935, and the worst day, Black Sunday, being April 14 of that year.

Of course, the technical boundaries of the Dust Bowl were the panhandle of Oklahoma, the northern part of the panhandle of Texas, the southwestern part of Kansas, southeastern Colorado, and northeastern New Mexico. But the Dust Bowl was not kind enough to stay within those borders. One look at a map of our location will show that southwestern Oklahoma was on the edge of this dust, so it was here, too.

Woody Guthrie, the great balladeer who was born in Okemah, Oklahoma, also lived in Pampa, Texas, where he witnessed and wrote about the dust storms in songs such as "The Great Dust Storm", "Talking Dust Bowl Blues", "Dust Pneumonia Blues", "Dust Bowl Refugee" and "So Long, It's Been Good to Know You", and others. Here's a three-verse sample of one of those Dust Bowl songs:

Talking Dust Bowl Blues
Woody Guthrie
  I got that dust pneumony, pneumony in my lung,
  I got the dust pneumony, pneumony in my lung,
  An' I'm a-gonna sing this dust pneumony song.
  I went to the doctor, and the doctor, said, "My son, "
  I went to the doctor, and the doctor, said, "My son,
  You got that dust pneumony an' you ain't got long, not long."
  Now there ought to be some yodelin' in this song;
  Yeah, there ought to be some yodelin' in this song;
  But I can't yodel for the rattlin' in my lung.

Great exaggerations also came out of the dust storms. One of my favorites: "You can fasten a logchain to a fence post or tree, and if it isn't blowing straight out, it is a calm day." Or

Woody Guthrie's: the "dust sometimes gets so thick you can run your tractor and plows upside down."

Will Rogers, another famous Okie, had his two cents worth on the combined horrors of the Dust Bowl and the Depression on Oklahomans: "... the migration of Okies to California raised the intellectual level of both states."

Not only did Joseph Henry & Lizzie Kolker and James Lafayette & Ida Brown live through dust and abject poverty around them, all of them, except Joseph Henry, lived through two world wars. What I would give to have recordings of their thoughts on these events!

As our grandparents lived through and survived these times, they toughened. The unfortunate Joseph Henry Kolker died in 1939 before the rough times were over and suffered from a horrible cancer to boot. It's hard to fathom the strength that it took for Lizzie Kolker to make it through those times. Yet she did, as did her eight children.[30]

Endnotes

BOOK I

Chapter 8

29. Steinbeck, John, The Grapes of Wrath. Chapter 1 excerpt. New York: Viking Penguin.1939

30. A summary of the immediate family of Joseph Henry and Elizabeth Kolker:

Joseph Henry Kolker,
DoB: 1 May 1873, Mt. Carmel, Iowa
DoD: 23 April 1939, Lawton, OK
Elizabeth Wiewel
DoB: 3 May 1875, Mt Carmel, Iowa
DoD: 12 Sep 1968, Lawton, OK
> Married: April 27, 1897, Mt. Carmel, Iowa

Reynold Edward Kolker
DoB: 20 Feb 1898, Mt. Carmel, Iowa
DoD: 11 Jun 1960, Lawton, OK
Gertrude Mary Fedde
DoB: 20 Jul 1901, Estherville, Iowa
DoD: 30 Apr 1972, Irving, TX
> Married: 5 May 1919

Laura Mary Kolker
DoB: 15 Jul 1899, Mt. Carmel, Iowa
DoD: 31 Aug 1973, Richardson, Dallas Co., TX
William Charles Ballard
DoB: 11 Aug 1893, Harrisburg, AR
DoD: 9 Mar 1969, Spearman, Hansford Co., TX
> Married 15 Jul 1921

Bertha (Bea) Catharine Kolker
DoB: 20 Nov 1901, Mt. Carmel, Iowa
DoD: 13 Mar 1994, Lawton, OK
Dewey Shafter Shaw
DoB: 24 Jun 1898, Rockingham, NC
DoD: 16 Feb 1960, Lawton, OK
> Married 12 Jan 1924

Clara Elizabeth Kolker
DoB: 10 Oct 1903, Mt. Carmel, Iowa
DoD: 17 Aug 1993, Lawton, OK
Leo Bernard Sheetz
DoB: 25 May 1903, Marlow, OK
DoD: 26 Sep 1970, Lawton, OK
    Married 15 Feb 1928

Walter Matthew Kolker
DoB: 14 Feb 1907, Okarche, OK
DoD: 22 Aug 1989, Wichita, Sedgwick Co., KS
Anna Agnes Nelson
DoB: 13 Dec 1906, Onaga, KS
DoD: 8 Mar 1987, Wichita, Sedgwick Co., KS
    Married 12 Jun 1933

Francis (Frank) Michael Kolker
DoB: 8 Aug 1910, Okarche, OK
DoD: 14 Nov 1991, Elgin, OK
Mary Agnes Hayes
DoB: 5 Jul 1913, Kilgore, TX
DoD: 8 Sep 1996, Elgin, OK
    Married 10 Aug 1938

Marie Catherine Kolker
DoB: 10 Aug 1911, Okarche, OK
DoD: 02 Jan 2001, Baton Rouge, LA
Paul Edward Calaway
DoB: 21 Apr 1910, Lawton, OK
DoD: 11 Jan 1968, Baton Rouge, LA
    Married 10 Sep 1936

Charles (Carliss) John Kolker (Sr)
DoB: 10 Jan 1914, Oklahoma City, OK
DoD: 11 Oct 2001, Elgin, OK

Rose Mary Brown
DoB: 8 Dec 1915, Elgin, OK
DoD: 12 Jan 1997, Elgin, OK
Married 27 April 1938 [Note: same day and
month as Joseph Henry and Elizabeth Kolker]

Frances M. Perez
DoB: 21 Aug 1926
DoD: Living
Married 19 Mar 1997

CHAPTER 9

MOM AND DAD

CHARLES J. KOLKER (SR.) AND ROSE MARY BROWN KOLKER

Mom and Dad: Rosemary and Carliss Kolker
Wedding Day, April 27, 1938

Photo taken at Lafe and Ida Brown's house, Elgin, Oklahoma. This photo, taken in Elgin, Oklahoma, on April 27, 1938, at Lafe and Ida Brown's residence in their living room, is of Dad and Mom's (Rosemary and Carliss Kolker's) wedding reception. I sat down with Anna Lee Brown Schlitt when she was still living, and she identified most people in the photo.

DAD:
date of birth: January 10, 1914
date of death: October 11, 2001
Charles ("Carliss") John Kolker
High School Graduation Photo, 1933

We have a bit of history of Dad that he completed in his own hand on October 16, 1940, when he registered for the draft at age 26. Oddly, he gave his name as "Carliss John Kolker", even though, as he stated in his below interview, he hated that name, and it was not his given name. His address at the time was 916 C Street, Lawton, Oklahoma. He stated his employer as Lawton and Fort Sill Bus Co., 202 C Street, Lawton. He described himself as weighing 162 lbs., 5' 10 ½" in height, with gray eyes and blonde hair.

On Saturday, November 29, 1997, at "Dad's house" (where I'm now living—13730 NE 75th St., Elgin, OK) I interviewed Dad on a hand-held recorder.

Here's a mildly edited version of that:

Q: What's the earliest memory you have of your childhood?
A: About the only thing I remember is that my older brothers and sisters would call me "Roly-Poly". I was heavy for my age.

Q. How did the name "Carliss" ever come about, or do you know?
A. I was told my older brothers and sisters started that, but I don't know why. The oldest ones, like Clara, Walter, Laura, Reynold, and Bea, called me that, just for a nickname they called me "Carliss".

Q. Did you call yourself that in school?
A. All through school I was called "Carliss". But whenever I'd ask for a job or something, I'd use the name "Charles". I'd try to get people to call me "Charles" or "CJ", instead of "Carliss". I never did like the name "Carliss".

Q. At some point in your life you started to use CJ as your formal name.
A. Yeah, it was a tool I'd use. It was just shorter, using CJ rather than Carliss. As I said before, I didn't really like "Carliss".

Q. But everybody called you that whether you liked it or not.
A. Yeah. Sure did.

Q. I know, of course, that you and Mom lived here in the Elgin area in your early lives.
Was she living here when you lived here as a young child growing up?
A. Oh, yeah. See I was born on the old Kolker farm [about a mile "as the crowflies" from where Mom lived], which we have pictures of in the house, and, of course, my mother and dad lived there while we farmed that while I was going to school, grade school through high school.

Q. You went to a different elementary school than Mom, didn't you?
A. Oh, yeah. That was Happy Hollow for the first 8 grades. That was a one-room schoolhouse. They had rows of seats for first grade and second grade— a row for each grade through the eighth grade. One teacher would teach the whole bunch. She'd teach first grade for one hour then the second grade. It was a big advantage for someone sitting in the row next to the one being taught so they'd hear what was coming up. They'd be prepared.

Q. Did Mom go there (to Happy Hollow?)
A. No, she went to Elgin grade school.

Q. Then you went to Elgin for high school, right?
A. Yes. Ninth through twelfth.

Q. Do you know how many kids attended Happy Hollow School when you were there?
A. I don't. There weren't a heck of a lot. My guess would be about 25 or 30, total.

Q. That was for all eight grades?
A. Yeah, and some of the ones in the eighth grade were 17-18 years old.

Q. Really?
A. Some just didn't have the opportunity to go to school all the time. Their families would take them out of school for picking cotton and other farming things.

Q. Did those older students then go on to high school?
A. I don't remember.

Q. Gee, if they'd gone on to high school, they'd be 20-21 years old when they graduated.
A. I think they thought they were doing good to get through eighth grade.

Q. So, you lived doing those times at the Old Kolker Place?
A. Yes, through grade school, high school and when I went to Cameron [now Cameron University, then Cameron State Agricultural College[31]] I lived there until I got married.

Q. That was 1938?
A. April 1938. [Dad then scrambles to remember the day in April, finally saying "the 29th", which isn't correct—it was the 27th, the exact day in April that his mom and dad were married years before.]

Q. So then you lived here in Elgin, after your marriage?
A. Yes. We lived on the other place down there. [Meaning, I believe, the "old Brown place", at the bottom of the hill –now on what is called Watts Road—west of Grandpa Brown's "new house" at the top of the hill on what is now NE 75th St. in Elgin.]

Q. I think Mom mentioned, in the writing she did, that you farmed a quarter of land right after you got married? Does that sound right?
A. Yeah. I don't remember whether that was the "old Kolker place" — we farmed that for a while.

Q. Okay. So, at some point, you moved to California?
A. Yeah, that was during the war. [WWII] Around 1940, when we left for California.

Q. It must have been in the later part of 1940. Here, Mom says, "Daddy was driving a Lawton/Fort Sill bus while we were living in a duplex on C Street in Lawton when Charles was born in 1940. So it must not have been long after I was born that you moved to California.
A. Yeah, okay.

Q. Well, let me see, the war would not have begun until December 7, 1941, after Pearl Harbor. So sometime in that period of time you moved to California....and was your first job there in the shipyard?

A. Yeah.

Q. Can you remember the name of the shipyard?
A. Yeah. It was CalShip, and that was located on Terminal Island[32].

Q. How in the dickens did you ever get that job?
A. Well, it was kind of a hard thing for me. I didn't have much of a means to get around. I had an old, run-down car. But I did get down to Terminal Island. So, I think it was Uncle Tom Wooldridge who told me that they had a shipyard down there. I went down there to see about it. In the process, I had to join a union in order to get in.

Q. Aha! So that's where my union feelings came from.
A. [Dad chuckles.] So, they hired me as a ship fitter helper, which was holding what they called "dogs" onto the metal so that the welder could come along and weld the big sheets of metal together. After that, I got a job as a welder, which was a little higher pay. I worked at that for about a year. And then I got into the electrical field and got on the ship. So I was on ships for about a year and then I got to be the lead man of a crew. I had about 9-10 different people working for me. In those 9-10 people, I had three colored people, two men, and one woman. Out of all those workers, those colored people were the workingest and nicest people in the whole bunch. So when the war was over, I decided to go back to Oklahoma. Howard Brown, who had been in Oklahoma then came to California, wanted me to stay in California and work in the construction business with him. And I didn't do that. I came on back.

Q. That would have been after the war ended?

A. Yeah, the war ended. I thought about staying in the shipyard doing ship repair work, but I'd had my fill of shipyards by that time.

Q. So you worked in the shipyard about four years?
A. About 5 years.

Q. You must have been working in the shipyard before the war began?
A. Yeah. Well, the war was in progress (but we weren't in it, yet).

Q. Okay.
A. All I can remember is we came back and stayed at the Brown place...they were visiting California. While they were gone, we had already decided to farm that half section. So I'd go down there where I was building a cabin in that old country home so we could move there when the Browns got back from California. And it snowed while I was helping building, and I'd walk down there to get to the cabin site, and the snow was deep.... two or three feet deep. So I had it all ready by the time the Browns got back so we could move into that old house, which later burned, you know.

Q. Okay.
A. And I farmed there about a year. My brother Reynold talked me into coming to Lawton, to work in the grocery store. So we went up there and worked in the store.

Q. Were you still living in the place you'd rehabbed?
A. Yeah, for a little while, then we moved to Lawton on Lee Street in an apartment. Then I got a job driving a

bus for a little more money....40 cents an hour for a 40 (? garbled) hour week.

Q. [Laughter] Wow.
A. Of course everything was cheaper then. We could go to a show every week on Wednesday when they have two for one night and we could both get in for a quarter.

Q. You were mentioning the other night that you actually moved out of your apartment because the rent went up from $15....
A. Yeah, we were living on Columbia and the rent went from $15 a month to $17.50, so we had to move.

Q. Okay, so you came back, and you worked for Reynold at the grocery store and how long did that fly?
A. Not quite a year.

Q. Before you started driving a bus?
A. Then when I was driving a bus was when you were born. [November 1940]

Q. And then how long did you drive the bus?
A. I think, ummm. I don't remember.

[Here ensues a conversation that skips to after the war, which was out of context and repeats some of which has been covered but ends with deciding that Dad had left California and the shipyard a couple of months after the war ended, which brought us to sometime in 1946.]

Q. Dad, I have two memories of the time we lived in Compton, California (while he was working in the shipyard). The first was a fight at the apartment complex in Compton when you fought a guy whose kid was bullying me. The second memory was in our car coming back to Oklahoma. I must have been very small, but I remembered a wheel coming off the car and going out into a field.

A. Oh, yeah. That was from the trailer. It came off the trailer. We were hauling some of our furniture back with us. We had an old, rickety trailer. It had an old, Model A axle under it. The nuts came loose, and the wheel came off and went around us, jumped the fence, and went on down the field.

Q. I know it made a big impression on me.

A. Robert was a baby then. Robert was born there in California. He was in a basket in the back when we went up in the mountains on the way —where the big trees are —and during the trip.

Q. Is that the same wicker basket that was in the family for years? And was sold and David ended up bidding for it and getting it back? Okay, all right. Anyway, the wheel coming off made a great big impression on me. I also remember Bob being in the wicker basket. I can remember that the area seemed to be dry-looking.

A. It was kinda out in the desert. We ended up staying all night in the area while the wheel was being fixed. It had to be welded back on. I remember Momma was so worried about you being in that kind of environment in the area where the garage was that was doing the repair. It was a dirty cabin.

Q. I don't remember the cabin at all. The wheel made a great big impression and Bob in the basket. Okay, so you came back....so probably sometime in the first part of 1946.
A. I guess that when we moved on the old Kolker farm, and I started farming...again.

Q. Okay. That makes sense. Ummm. This is probably an unpleasant subject, but it's a matter of great curiosity among us. At some point in all this, between Robert and me, Mom lost a baby.
A. Yeah, while we were living on the old Kolker farm.

Q. Was this during her pregnancy?
A. Yeah, it was pre-born. It was not fully matured, even.

Q. Do you know if it was a boy or a girl?
A. It was a boy.

Q. I didn't know that until not too long ago.
A. It was just a miscarriage. It was while we were on the old Kolker farm, I remember that very clearly.

Q. So there would have been seven of us?
A. Right. Seven.

Q. All right, I kinda went backward here. Anyway, you came back in '46 and started farming again. According to my calculations, at some point in the late 40s, you went to Lawton and started building. So there's a period there between '46 and ...
A. Yeah. I can't remember just when I started building.

Q. I can trace some of this because of when and where I went to school. I went to the fifth and sixth grades in Lawton. [At St. Mary's Catholic School on Gore.] I was in the fourth grade in Elgin.
A. Okay. So we ought to be able to figure that out mathematically.

Q. Right, exactly. A fifth or sixth grader would be about 10-11 years old. That would mean the 50s since I was born in 1940. I would have been 10 in 1950.
A. In what grade?

Q. That would be ....it must have been ....I know we might not be able to get this exactly. We're trying to reconstruct it the best I can. I know we were living in Lawton in 1950...it's how much further back we can go.
A. How old is Debbie? 45? She was just a baby when we moved from Lawton to Elgin. We had been in Lawton about five years when we moved. So you could add about five years to their age and figure out when we moved to Lawton.

Q. Okay. We can figure that out later, then. [Note: it was later determined that the family had moved from Lawton to Elgin about 1953. 5 years before that would be 1948. The problem with that is that I was in the fourth grade in Elgin, then the fifth in Lawton. I was an "early" entrant to school, so I was about nine years old in the fourth grade, meaning we were still in Elgin in 1949. Of course, if we left in the summer before the next school year started, which is likely, I would have entered the fifth grade in Lawton at age 9, reaching 10 in November 1950. Confused, yet? In any event, it seems that the

move probably took place in the summer of 1949. I was in the eighth grade in Elgin. A typical eighth grader is 13-14. Again, I was "early", so I would have been 13 in Elgin—or in 1953. It's likely, then, that the move to Elgin was in the summer of 1953.][33]
A. All right. David might be interested in some of this, so....

Q. I think he would be. All right, Dad, I'll hold this [microphone] a little bit closer to you. We were at 1946. I guess a little later than '46...maybe '47. We were at the point where you'd moved to Lawton...trying to figure out how long you were there before moving back to Elgin. You had left Reynold's grocery store, if I have things in the right order, worked a while on the farm, and then went to Lawton. Now, from the notes I have here. You joined...and correct me if I'm wrong, with Finis Pillow.
A. Yeah, we formed a partnership when we went to Lawton. My oldest brother, Reynold, Finis Pillow, and myself formed a partnership to do building in Lawton.

Q. I can remember...I guess I would have been 11-12 years old...that there was an office building there on 31st Street ...and, uh...
A. We had a little temporary building there on 31st Street. But before that, we had an office...a three-story building, where we started first. We built 35 houses east of Cameron College, on A, B, and C in Lawton southeast of Cameron. Then later, after we filled those lots up. (We bought those lots from Mr. Pisek.) Then we talked to Jack Greer and made a deal with him to start developing his quarter of land, which was west of Lawton. It was about a mile and a half further west from any existing

structures. We had to put in our own gas lines, water line, and sewer lines in order to develop that area.

Q. My directions aren't very good, but would that have been south of Cameron?
A. The Greer Addition, which we bought from Jack Greer, was north of Cameron. Ah, in the section north of Cameron.

Q. Okay. All right. Good thing I asked. So you built there for how long? Three, four, five years?
A. A total of about 5 years, yeah.

Q. So, after building there you sold the remaining houses you had...
A. Yeah, we had several houses not sold. I made a deal with my partners to make my part out in one house, that was on Oak Street, that was built of big stone. That's before you get....about a half block east...what's the name of the next street west of Sheridan Road? ....38th Street.

Q. I know exactly which house that is! I can remember it.
A. Okay. I came out here to the Brown's house...and Strategier's owned the farm. And I traded that house in Lawton for the farm.

Q. And that would have been what, about 1953?
A. '53 or '54. [See endnote 33.]

Q. Okay.
A. Yeah. Anyway, then we moved on this farm, and I started farming it. But before we did that, I started

building the dairy barn here. I built the dairy barn, got a loan from the Farm Home Administration to buy the cows. I bought about 30 head of Holstein milk cows at a sale...and they were all milking. I didn't get home with them until midnight, and I had to run them through the barn. It was the first time for them in that barn and the first time I'd milked them. So you can imagine what the barn looked like and I looked like after that.

Q. [Much laughter by both.] Yes, I can imagine. So, then at the same time that you operated the dairy were you also doing other things?
A. Yeah, I operated the dairy for two years and I decided to get back into the building business. So I found a little place in Elgin that Frances Cremer and Florene Sanders had rented. I told them I was looking for an office, and they said, "Well, why don't you move in here?" That office wasn't much bigger than this room we're in.... maybe 12 x 14 feet. And all three of us would all sit in that thing. And I started opening up K-Lowe Addition. I bought 40 acres under contract from Mac Roll and put in the first street...K Street. And I went to the Bank of Elgin, to borrow money to build these houses and the banker there said,

"Well, Carliss, you won't sell over two houses in this town, there's not anybody buying houses in Elgin."

So I had to go to Lawton to get the money. I talked to Mr. Wolf, and he said, "How much money do you need?"

And I said, "About $20,000-$30,000."

And he said, "Well...we can fix that up." Then he asked, "You live on a farm, don't you?"

And I said, "Yeah."
And he said, "Do you need a deep freezer?"

And I said, "I guess I do. But I don't have the money to buy one. "

He said, "I didn't ask you about that. If you want one, we'll go get you one and just add it to this loan."

So, that's how I started my building business in Elgin.

Q. That would have been....
A. About two or three years after I'd moved back from Lawton.

Q. So, that would have been about 1956-57...
A. It would have been about 1958 when I started actually building there. I had to do an awful lot of things: develop that land, get it approved through the FHA and VA. I had to put in my own sewer system because Elgin didn't have a sewer system.

Q. All right. I have some memories of about that time.
A. Well, you kids were helping with the dairy.

Q. I remember some of the battles you had with the Elgin City Hall.
A. Yeah. I had an awful hard time getting anything done. They didn't believe in what I was doing. I had to put in my own water line starting about three blocks from

where I started my addition.   I had to put in my own streets, my own sewer, my own sewer lagoon to connect to. All along I had to get approval from FHA and VA.

Q. In order to put your streets and sewers in did you have to get a city council vote?
A. At that time, the city council...I didn't seem to have any success, so I didn't pay much attention to them, because they wouldn't go along with me. [Much laughter by me at this.]

Q. All right. So what did you do...you remained in the building business until you retired.
A. Yeah, that's been about 19 years ago.

Q. Well, 20 from next year would be 1978.
A. '78, right. That's when I turned it over to David.

Q. All right. Good. We have that part. I think we've covered all the places you lived and worked. Unless you can think of something we missed.
A. Well, we did miss some.

Q. I know, being fair to you, that also during my life, that while we had the dairy, you were selling insurance because you had Farmers Insurance...
A. Yeah, Farmers Union Insurance. I was building... selling the houses, handling the loans, closing on the loans.

Q. You also had the dairy, but you also ran a farm so you could operate the dairy...to feed the cows.
A. My day ended about midnight. Sure did.

Q. Well, now we know why we work like we do....we inherited it. Going back to your school time. Did you have any favorite subjects?

A. Yes. My favorite subjects were math. The subjects I hated were spelling, geography, and history. I couldn't see any reason that I needed to know things that happened in 1700. So, it took me 5 years to make it through high school. Did you know that?

Q. No, I didn't know that. Was that because of the spelling, geography, and history?

A. It was because I didn't work at it hard enough. I was doing too many things outside of the school curriculum. I was running around with [unintelligible] and Carl Wolcott...no, it was Carl Wolcott's brother.

Q. But you did go on to college.

A. I did go on to Cameron College...after staying out a year. My folks didn't have the money to send me to College, so I had to make some money so I could go to college.

Q. Okay. Any injuries you can remember? Broken bones?

A. Never. The only injury was after David, no, Ricky, was born. Coming home from the hospital, the night he was born. You kids were here. On the way home a Sergeant, who had been drinking too heavy, came across the median and hit us right in the middle of the car. I have a picture of that car. The whole side was crushed in. I was falling out of the car, holding on to the steering wheel, and that car spun around three times, going down the road, and crossed the median. When it stopped, I was on the ground still holding on to the steering wheel. That is the reason this shoulder hurts to this day.

Q. Your left shoulder.
A. Yes. Left shoulder. We took it to court but didn't get anything out of it.

Q. Wow. Well, that was fairly late in life. Tell us about your father. He's always been kind of a mystery man to us. He died, of course, before I was born.
A. I don't know much about him myself. He was born in Carroll County, Iowa. He was married in Carroll County, Iowa.

Q. Do you know when he came here?
A. Supposedly he came from Carroll County, Iowa to Okarche. Because some of the kin folks he knew...the Weevils...you know, my mother's family were Weevils, lived in Okarche. They were telling him it was new country and it was rich soil, so the family moved there and farmed for several years. Frank and Marie were born in Okarche.

Q. So you were the only one born in Elgin?
A. I was the only one born in Elgin.

Q. So Reynold and the others were born ...
A. Back in Carroll County, Iowa.

Q. There was a pretty good age difference between you and Reynold?

A. Yeah, I didn't hardly recognize Reynold he was so much older than me until I got up to college age. He was gone and I don't know where he was.

Q. I can identify with that. Rick and I didn't really get acquainted until many years later after I'd left home.
A. After we did get acquainted, we worked together. Worked good together. All three of us did. [Meaning Dad, Reynold, and Finis Pillow.] It made a good partnership.

Q. Your Dad was a farmer.
A. Yeah. A farmer all his life. His Dad and Mom came over from Germany...over here...to Iowa.

Q. What was he like? Was he a strict father?
A. Yes, well, he kinda meant what he said. So, one time my experience with him...we had these outdoor toilets that we had to clean out from time to time. Two-holers we called them. So when it was my turn I decided it would be easier to just set the paper on fire and burn it out of there...save a lot of work. But it caught the whole thing on fire and burned it to the ground. And he whipped me with a razor strap that he had, the buckle end of it. I didn't burn down any more toilets after that. [Much laughter.]

Q. Was he the disciplinarian in the family?
A. Actually, my mother was more the disciplinarian than he was. He didn't come into a situation until it was pretty serious, then he laid the law down. You know, he had a mustache, you remember that.

Q. I know he looks very German in his photographs.

A. He was a good-natured man, in the ordinary run.

Q. Was he even-tempered?
A. Even-tempered. Yeah.

Q. My memories of your mother were when she was fairly elderly.
A. I don't know if you know this about her life before she was married. I hope I'm right on this. She was adopted… by somebody other than her immediate family. He was kin, but she was adopted, and they moved to Texas somewhere, and while she was there she was treated real bad. Her relatives had to go get her and bring her back to Carroll County, Iowa. Because the adopted family kept her penned up and beat her up real bad. I wish Bea had given us a detailed description of that, but we just didn't have the details of it.

Q. How old were your Mom and Dad when they got married?
A. I think he was around 24 years old, and she was about two years younger than he. Of course, her life was different after I was born. She was crippled…pretty well crippled…all the rest of her life.

Q. How was she crippled?
A. From my birth.

Q. Oh, really?
A. Uh, huh, yeah.

Q. Well, she had a pretty good-sized family.
A. Eight. Eight of us.

Q. Did she lose any children?
A. Not that I know of. Just the four daughters and four sons.

Q. Eight kids, wow. So, not so unusual then, but sure unusual now. What about your father, did he have any brothers and sisters?
A. Yeah. I can't help you much there. He had one brother in the State of Washington. That brother, who was in the hardware business, wanted my Dad to come work with him, but Dad didn't want to. He wanted to stay farming. That's the only thing I can remember about his brothers or sisters.

Q. Did you ever go visit the folks back in Iowa?
A. I never did. I don't think anybody did until later in life. Walter and JoAnn went back there and met some of Kolkers. And they took them out to the cemetery and showed them where some of them were buried.

Q. And that's Mt. Carmel?
A. Mt. Carmel, Iowa, yeah.

Q. It seems to me that we have somewhere records of family in a particular cemetery there. But as far as you know, you only have a memory of one brother of your Dad.
A. Right. I can imagine that he might have had more, but I don't know of them.

Q. I was also curious ... whether you'd have a memory of this during your life...Here

you were from a family only one generation from Germany and Hitler was coming up in Germany. Was there any discussion of that?
A. There wasn't any discussion...other than that my folks talked German to each other. When we weren't around, particularly we noticed them talking when we were in bed, and they were in bed together we could hear them talking German to each other. The reason they didn't insist on us learning German, we found out later, was they didn't want us to be ridiculed, because of the Hitler situation.

Q. Hitler would have come to power in '33, '34, somewhere in there. So there would have been a considerable number of years while you were around the home during Hitler's time. Any memory at all as to how this affected the family, and any discussion of that?
A. I sure don't.

Q. Your father would have died about the time Hitler was beginning to get nasty—1938 I think your father died.
A. Yeah, he was 68 when he died. Did you know how he died?

Q. No, not really.
A. He got a cancer on his nose. And it ate the whole side of his nose off, and then ate into his cheek. At that time that they didn't have radiation, or at least he didn't take any. It then spread through his system, and killed him.

Q. Cancer's kinda scary in our family.
A. Yeah, we all need to keep account of that stuff.

Q. Your father died of cancer. Your mother lived a long, long life.
A. Yeah, she didn't die of cancer.

Q. Didn't Reynold die of cancer?
A. Yeah.

Q. What about Laura and Bea?
A. I don't know. But they were both old when they died.

Q. Clara?
A. She might have died of cancer.

Q. Walter?
A. Walter died of complications from sugar diabetes.

Q. Frank?
A. I think Frank died…I don't think he died of cancer… of pneumonia, or at least at the last.

Q. Wow. High incidence of cancer.
A. Yeah. Sure is. You need to keep that checked up on. I'm probably carrying it around in me now.

Q. I do get checked out. I get a prostate cancer exam at least once a year. Your mother was only a housewife?
A. Yeah, a housewife.

Q. Of course, with eight kids I don't know what else she could do. With the spread between you and Reynold, did you have any memory of him at home?
A. He'd gone before I was born. I don't have any memories of the older kids while I was living at home. Only Clara,

Walter, Frank and Marie. I don't remember Clara much; she must have got married early in life.

Q. Do you have any memory of your grandparents—your father's parents or your mother's parents?
A. No, I don't. Because I never had any contact. See, I was here, and they were in Carroll County, Iowa. I never got to see them.

Q. I guess transportation was a whole different thing then.
A. Yeah, and we were poor as church mice. All the time I was growing up we had one, two, or three [indecipherable...] "jobs", maybe around the farm. I would come home from school and work, and if I worked in the summer for someone and made some money I had to give that money to my Dad to help pay the mortgage and things.

Q. How did your mother survive after your Dad died?
A. She stayed with Bea all the time, Bea and Dewey [Shaw]. She couldn't do anything...anything...She just sat there all day, every day, praying the rosary. She prayed the rosary all the time.

Q. Yeah, that's how I remember her. I can remember going to Bea and Dewey's house, and that's what she was doing—praying the rosary.
A. Yeah, she would sit there in her rocker and pray the rosary.

Q. Well, Dad, I don't want to wear you out. Is there anything you'll like to add?

A. I wish I could. I just don't remember much. There was some discussion about how the family survived when they were in Carroll County, Iowa, that there were winters when they'd have 4-5 feet of snow, and they couldn't get the door open. They'd have to shovel out. They'd shovel a path to the barn and string a string so that if it stormed while they were out there, they could follow the string back to the house. I can remember those stories.

Q. Obviously, there must be a lot of relatives around Mt. Carmel still.
A. Probably right.

Q. One of the things I found curious, there are directories of lawyers all over the country, and Chris was researching the name Kolker —K-O-L-K-E-R, in one of those directories. They are on CD discs, and you'd be surprised at the number of Kolker lawyers there are. He found a Robert Kolker who was a Senior Partner in a huge law firm in Washington, D.C.
A. Oh?

Q. Makes you wonder where these guys came from. I wonder if any are related.
A. Was it you who said that some people spell our name KOELKER?

Q. Yeah, well we used to live in an area in southwestern Illinois that had a lot of German communities. and nearly everybody we met in those communities would say, Koelker, right? K-O-E-L-K-E-R. Robert has done some research on our family going back generations, and

there's some indication that our name might have been spelled with an "e". Pronounced "Kelker". You rarely see a German name with just an "o".
A. You know Helen Koetter, right? She said that her folks and my folks lived next to each other .....were neighbors, farming...in Okarche.

Q. Oh, really?
A. You know the Koetters used to live east of where John Lodes lived. You know where that is, right? See, one of the reasons Dad moved down here was because of John Lodes. See, Ms. Lodes was a half-sister to my mother.

Q. Half-sister?
A. Yeah, she wasn't a full sister....a half-sister.

Q. I knew the Lodeses were related, but I didn't know how.
A. And John Lodes told my Dad about the farm that was up for sale...that we bought...around when I was born. So he came down here and bought that farm and moved down here.

Q. This would have been Johnny Lodes' Dad, right? Oh, yeah, I remember John Lodes. I always thought of him as a man that reminded me of John L. Lewis.
A. John sure did like his wine and beer. I used to get amused at that. My folks and them used to play pitch together, usually on Sunday. And he'd get the biggest bang out of winning. He'd just laugh and laugh and carry on.

Q. Well, thanks, Dad, for taking the time to do this. I appreciate it.
A. I'm not much of a historian.

Q. I sure hope this thing works, because I'm really going to be mad if it didn't record all this.

-—-End of Interview-—-

Dad would probably not be happy that we've discovered his high school transcript which would have been forwarded to Cameron College before he went there. But he was a man not in the least hindered by academics; he had remarkable intelligence not shown in these grades and a drive to succeed that overcame any obstacle that he encountered. Nevertheless, here is that transcript:

HIGH SCHOOL TRANSCRIPT

	SUBJECT	DATE	GRADES	UNITS
ENGLISH	Eng. I	1928-29	77	1
	Eng. II	30-31	77	1
	Eng. III	31-32	72	1/2
	Eng. IV	32-33	75	1
	Bus. Eng.	32-33	73	1/2
MATHEMATICS	Algebra I	28-29	86	1
	Bus. Arith.	32-33	82	1/2
	Plain Geom.	30-31	84	1
SOCIAL SCIENCE	U.S. Hist.	31-32	70	1
	Eng. Hist.	32-33	77	1
	Gen. Hist.	29-30	70	1
	Civics	30-31	82	1/2
	Sociology	30-31	73	1/2
	Okla. Hist.	30-31	75	1/2
FOREIGN LANGUAGE				
NATURAL SCIENCE	Genl. Sci.	29-30	78	1
	Physics	32-33	82	1
	Biology	31-32	76	1/2
	Phys. Geog.	28-29	81	1/2
VOC. SCIENCE				
COMMERCIAL	Problems (Com. Dem.)	1931-32	73	1
	Ind. Geog.	30-31	79	1/2
MUSIC				
MISC.	Psychology	32-33	77	1/2
	Total units			16

P. R. Becker
SUPERINTENDENT

Dad was a complex character. At the dinner table, he exhibited a sense of humor that often caused laughter. He was a very hard worker and an active person all his life. In fact, the story is that he was shoveling gravel from a gravel truck onto the St. Ann's church parking lot in Elgin only a few months before his death. The yard of his home with his second wife, Frances, is webbed with irrigation lines that he dug himself, for the trees in the yard. I've run into segments of these lines many times as new trees are planted.

He did not mention in his interview that as a young man, he was a Golden Gloves boxer. It's my belief that this skill enabled him to deck the bully's equally bully dad when I was four to five years old in Compton, California. That guy was heavier and taller than Dad, but he toppled like a ton of bricks when Dad hit him in the jaw after the bully made the mistake of taking a swing. Dad never mentioned this afterward. I think he was a little ashamed that he got that angry. I know I was a very proud kid. And it stopped the bullying.

Dad and Mom were gifted with incredible tolerance and patience. The six of us were not angels. An example of parental restraint occurred when I rolled a car while I was in high school. No punishment was meted out. I was left to stew in my own guilt and make, thereby, my own punishment. You'd think I would've learned from this forgiveness, but no, I later rolled the family pickup end-over-end. After I walked the five miles home from the scene of the accident and entered the house about 3 am, I woke up my parents to admit what happened and Dad said, "Go to bed. We'll talk about it in the morning." I didn't sleep much. The only thing Dad mentioned, in a calm, measured voice the next morning, was "You know, you're going to have to pay for this one by yourself." My conscience whined and groveled, but I certainly didn't say anything. I often wondered where this parental attitude came from. My theory is that young Dad was no angel himself and thought that youthful foolishness was just a part of growing up.

One story of Dad's escapades while young was told to me by Leo Koetter, a neighbor kid then in Elgin who knew of the event somehow. Apparently, Dad and several friends were in an old car that had a fold-out windshield, so as the crew approached a truck laden with watermelons, Dad crawled out onto the hood, stood on the bumper and managed to snag a melon off the truck as they sped along.

Dad in his later life was a political conservative and Republican. But this was not his position when I was growing up. He was a liberal, enough so that in 1972 he was a Comanche County Democratic Party delegate for George McGovern, a liberal Democrat candidate for president. What happened? Well, the story is that during the Jimmy Carter administration (1977-1981), the president decided to do away with an oil depreciation allowance (which allowed oil rights owners to depreciate a significant amount of their profits from their taxes)[34]. Dad had learned from Grandpa Brown the ins and outs of buying oil royalties and leasing them out to oil companies for a profit. This was a way for him to accumulate enough money for retirement. Carter's abolition of this depletion allowance benefit made Dad very angry, and he left the Democratic Party over it. He never returned.

I don't mean by relating Dad's aggravation with President Carter that I felt Dad was not a good man. He was not only a good man, but he was an exceptional one. I idolized him—except I differed with his later life politics. I hope that when I die people can only find one flaw like this. Some would not consider his actions a flaw; after all, he was trying to build his retirement in an honest way, taking advantage of a tax benefit. He cannot be blamed for that.

Dad was widowed when Mom died in January 1997. A few months later he called each of us to let us know that he was getting married again. So Dad married a wonderful woman, Frances Perez, who provided Dad with a loving relationship until his death in 2001. Frances was not only a caring woman but also a terrific cook. I don't think I'll ever forget visiting with Dad and Frances when she served cucumbers in a salad and a few peppers with his tacos. I don't think Dad had eaten cucumbers for 40-50 years and was extremely cautious of peppers because he'd had severe ulcers a lot of his life. Yet here he was gobbling all those forbidden foods as if he loved them. Love, I think is the operative word.

Frances was born August 21, 1926, and is living now with her daughter, Nora, and her husband, Joe, in Norman, Oklahoma. After Dad's death, she has moved several times with her daughter and husband, having lived at several places in Lawton, Oklahoma, and Las Cruces, New Mexico. She's a remarkable woman. By the way, after the marriage of Dad and Frances, Dad built a new house for them at 13730 Northeast 75th St., Elgin, Oklahoma—just a few hundred feet south of the home where my siblings and I spent much of our lives, at 13786 NE 75th St. After Dad's death and Frances had decided to live with Nora and Joe, she agreed to sell the house at 13730 to Sue and me, and that's where we have lived since returning from China in 2006.

Photo of Dad and Frances shortly after their wedding in March 1997.

MOM
date of birth: December 8, 1915
date of death: January 12, 1997

One of the saddest aspects of doing this family history is the lack of information for the women of the family. At least in Mom's case, I can let the following generations know what a wonderful woman she was.

What I did find, however, was a handwritten, 16-page "autobiography" penned by Mom not long after she graduated from high school at Elgin. It's too long to recount here in detail, but there are a few tidbits that you might find interesting. It's limited to her first grade through high school life. She recounts, for example, all her fellow first-grade students, including Anna Ryan, who was Mom's lifetime best friend. She remembered that she went to Midway School in the second grade because her teacher, "who lived at our other place", took her there every morning "in a buggy". The remaining years of school at Elgin were at Elgin. She wrote about going on vacation with her family, leaving on July 8, 1925, for a trek to Arkansas. They weren't there long before receiving "a letter from home containing bad news: our house at home had burned the same morning we left". So the family trudged back home to find "our house was gone and everything with it." The family lived in a tent and slept in the barn loft. This would have been the time when the magnificent house that now still stands across the road from where we live now was built.

In the fourth grade, Mom fell ill with typhoid fever. By then the family had moved to the "new garage", so she was thankful that "I did not have to spend my sick days in a tent." She complained that during her illness she "had to live on buttermilk and orange juice". She didn't like buttermilk and felt like she "nearly starved".

Trying times weren't over, though. In the seventh grade she "missed quite a bit of school on account of an operation on March 12, 1929", which is described later in this chapter.

We often forget how fortunate we are with paved or graveled roads today. Mom described an outing when "the darned Pontiac" broke an axle in the muddy road created by rain that day. Fortunately for the group, the car was towed to a mechanic, and it was ready to go by nightfall. Imagine getting a car fixed that quickly today!

Mom (and Anna Lee) had their tonsils taken out during Mom's summer vacation following the eighth grade. Anna Lee "recovered nicely," "but I was slow recovering because my throat bled so much."

A snippet of Mom's life as a ninth grader: "Easter Sunday Anna Ryan had dinner with me. We walked to Elgin in the afternoon and purchased some Kodak films and enjoyed the afternoon taking snapshots. In the evening we spend several hours by the fireplace."

Mom recalled Elizabeth Brown from Erie, PA visiting on June 26, 1931. This triggered memories I'd long forgotten of "Cousin Elizabeth", who was an old maid school teacher who dressed and acted like one. She was a tad on the eccentric side. She smelled of mothballs and, when she retired and moved to Elgin, lived in a manner most unusual. She was a hoarder par excellence, piling newspapers and magazines on the floor to great heights so that only narrow paths were left by which to traverse her house.

Mom was delighted when she was granted an exemption from taking exams at the end of the school year. She remembered the Senior Class of 1932 —all eleven of them— giving a good program on the last day of school.

But as her Junior year in high school ended, she realized that the graduating seniors were leaving, including her good friend Anna Ryan and a man she'd get to know much better: Carliss Kolker. She made no comment about Carliss. I guess he didn't make much of an impression.

Nothing in Mom's "autobiography" sounds terribly exciting. Her later life as a wife and mother was yet to come. During those years when her children observed her in action, we noticed several things.

Mom was quiet. There were no rantings and ravings to be heard from her...ever. She was steady, calm, and unperturbable. As the mother of six very active children—five boys and a girl—she was frequently tested for her endurance and patience. She never failed these tests.

One example: when Jimmy was maybe 6 and Ricky 4 or so, the two of them were outside our house playing. Mom didn't waste any time monitoring us or hovering. So Jimmy came into the house and sort of sauntered around fiddling with things. This wasn't all that unusual, except it didn't seem to be fiddling with the usual Jimmy purpose, if there is such a thing.

At some point, Mom asked Jimmy, "Where's Ricky?"

"Outside," Jimmy said.

Mom was a detective not easily misled.

"Where outside?"

"Under the tree," Jimmy answered.

Now while we're not talking about a 100-foot-tall redwood, it was a tree of maybe 18 feet in height. Falling that distance must have been eye-opening for Ricky as he cascaded through the limbs on the way to ground zero.

This led Mom to step outside to check on the patient, who was still lying on the ground, recovering. Fortunately, he was not hurt badly, just whimpering a little. Mom got him up and he seemed to be okay but shaken. There's something to be said for young, pliable bones.

Each of us ran the gambit of youthful errors. None of these seemed to faze Mom. In this regard, she and Dad were much the same: no high drama when a catastrophe or challenge occurred.

She exhibited a stoic strength that is difficult to describe. She suffered breast cancer and had a breast removed in a radical mastectomy in June 1951, followed by massive radiation at Halstead Clinic in Kansas. I believe it was cobalt, an experimental treatment at the time for breast cancer. This did extensive tissue damage, including to the lining around the heart, which eventually hardened and tightened around the heart muscle. She must have suffered enormous pain. Whatever she endured, she did it without complaining.

Mom had a lengthy medical history recently documented from materials brother David had. For example, in a letter dated August 25, 1939, to Dr. R. M. Howard in Oklahoma City, Dr. H. M. McClure recited the following:

"Miss Rosemary Brown came to see me November 5, 1937, telling me that Dr. Livermore had operated on her on March 12, 1929, for a tumor in her left axillary area. [The 1929 tumor removal was done when she was only 13 years old.]

Dr. McClure continued:

"She had a hard, fixed mass involving the upper pectoral area and also an area just above the clavicle. This was removed by sharp dissection...This was a rather difficult mass of tissue to remove as, apparently, she had had some extensive x-ray therapy previously and, as you know, this makes sharp dissection a hard job...The tissue was sent to Dr. F. C. Helwig, St. Luke's Hospital, Kansas City, Missouri. His report...'It is my opinion that the tissue...represents an angio-endothelioma, which is probably   locally invasive only. Another pathologist who has studied it at great length calls it atypical Hodgkin's disease with irregular reaction producing the bizarre picture. You can take your choice...I looked up our records and I find that Dr. Livermore operated on this young lady on March 12, 1929, and removed a cyst from her axillary region. Dr. Turley of your city examined the tissue…His report is as follows: 'Suderiferogenic adenomatous cyst. Inflammation arises from embryonic malformed glands. Malignancy must be determined clinically.' After which I believe she was given intensive x-ray therapy."

Mom was also treated at Hertzler Clinic/Halstead Hospital in July 1942 and July 1948. The 1942 bill from Halstead, for $13.10, noted "operation July 16, 1942", with no description of that operation. The 1948 bill from Hertzler was for $30.00, including $25.00 for "operation".

In Mom's handwriting, there's a note: "June 1975 – thyroid removed. Benign."

In a letter to Mom dated October 12, 1989, Dr. Linda Orr wrote: "The MRI scan that you had done of your head recently does show very small areas of stroke, located in each side of the brain. These were located higher in the brain but may contribute some to your Parkinson's syndrome."

Later in life, when Ricky was born, the doctors discovered that her body was ridden with cancer. I vividly remember sitting in a pickup truck outside a doctor's office with a very, very somber father, who had just heard the terrible news about Mom. He was very careful to tell me not to tell what he was about to say to anyone else. I was 19 years old. The doctors told him that Mom had terminal cancer and was not expected to live long.

At some point, Mom realized that we knew of her diagnosis. But she had a small baby—brother Ricky— and she wasn't about to surrender to the idea of anything terminal. She announced that she couldn't die, she had a baby and kids to care for. And that was it. She didn't. That would have been about 1959. She didn't die until January of 1997, long after baby Ricky and the rest of us were adults and out of the nest. I will never understand how she did this, but it's a clear example of the tremendous willpower she had, powerful enough to defeat terminal cancer. During this time I don't remember her complaining. It just wasn't her to do that.

Of course, Mom had much life between her birth and her marriage to Dad in April 1938. As the older of two daughters of Lafe and Ida Brown, she absorbed much of the pioneering spirit of her parents. Her stoicism was a direct hand-me-down from her father, who was grit personified. She also learned to work hard in a household that knew hard work. She learned the domestic skills expected of a girl and young woman and later turned some of those skills to good use. She excelled in her studies and went on to college at Cameron, where she remained for two years.

While she attended Cameron Agriculture and Mechanical College (now Cameron University) in Lawton, she spent time living with Naomi and Capt. George DeSass, who had a home in Lawton not far from Cameron. The DeSasses had been a military family, as George was stationed in China with the U.S. Army during the time Chiang Kai-shek was the leader of the Kuomintang and President of the Republic of China, in the 1920s, long before Mao came into power. I still have some of the brass works from China that Mom inherited from Naomi when she died. The DeSasses were a couple with no family living. No parents, brothers, sisters, nephews or nieces, or cousins. Nobody. So Mom became their "family". She took care of Naomi for years when she was widowed, lonely, and then in poor health. I can remember going to the DeSass home when Mom visited. It always reeked of smoke, as Naomi was a chain smoker. There were military accouterments around: a cavalry sword, a painting of George in uniform, and various other items from China and a military life that were interesting.

At the risk of being accused of skipping around, I'm going to quote excerpts from an account written by Mom and mailed to me on February 29, 1996. She supplements some of the life events Dad covered in his interview.

Daddy worked in his brother Reynold's meat market on 3rd Street in Lawton when we were married. I didn't work.

Daddy was driving a Lawton/Fort Sill bus and we were living in a duplex on C Street when Charles was born in 1940.

We moved to the old Kolker farm where Daddy built a new chicken house, and we raised chickens and Daddy farmed the quarter of land.

It was while we were living in the Kolker place that we lost a three-month baby. I'm not sure of the date. Dr. Martin was our doctor. Charles was probably 1 ½ to 2 years old.

We gave up farming and moved to California where many people were flocking to get into defense work. I think Charles was about 2. We first lived in L.A. and then moved to Compton (Victory Park), which was closer to the shipyard at Terminal Island where Daddy worked. [1944 Voter Registration records show both were registered Democrats living at 548 S. Colin Ave in Compton.]

I worked half a day each day in an upholstery shop while a neighbor kept Charles. The place was called Winsor Hills Upholstery shop and they made custom furniture.

Robert was born while we lived in Victory Park, Compton near Long Beach. Charles had quite a time telling the neighbors about his new baby brother that "just came up to here" and he would stoop over and put his hand down on his leg halfway between the floor and his knee. Robert was the blondest of the bunch and had lots of white hair at birth and of course a cowlick.

Charles started in kindergarten while we were in Victory Park. We came back to Oklahoma when the war wound down. There were many people out of work when the defense work was over.

Robert was tucked into the famous wicker basket and put on the back seat with Charles. We headed north to do a little sightseeing in northern California. We saw some beautiful redwoods (Sherman tree) while Robert slept in the basket. It snowed big quiet flakes.

I believe we must have moved in with Grandma and Grandpa when we got back to Oklahoma. It was April 1946 we had a cold spring. Daddy built new cabinets, painted, and did repair work to the house on the west place, and we moved in when the weather got warmer. David was born while we were still with Grandma or soon after.

We raised gardens and chickens, milked cows, and farmed while our three little boys grew. Daddy managed to work on the farm and find time to start building houses in Lawton. We opened the Greer Addition and put in streets, water, and sewer. We were the first ones to move into the Greer Addition, 1202 N. 31st Street.

While we lived here, I learned that I had breast cancer. That was 1951. My doctor at Chickasha sent me to Hertzler Hospital in Halstead, Kansas because he had removed some benign lymph cysts several years earlier (also on the left side). I stayed in Halstead for x-ray treatment after the breast surgery. The x-ray made me feel terrible. Grandma no doubt kept the boys. I recovered rapidly.

Charles, Robert, and David were all in school before Debbie came along. The boys all wanted a boy or pretended they did, but the day I came home from the hospital with a little girl they all hurried from school and all three fell down coming up the front door.

So, I had a child to keep me company again (Sept to Oct 7).

The bottom fell out of the building business, so we moved to the farm (present location) again. Daddy traded the house in Lawton for this farm in 1952. Debbie was three months old at Christmas time and we brought her to her farm home in the wicker basket. Charles was the only one that didn't use the wicker basket.

I'll back up again to tell about Robert when he was about two and got the slug in his throat. I guess I was pregnant with David so Grandma and Daddy took him to Oklahoma City to get the nickel-sized slug out of his throat. We still have the x-ray picture of the culprit that was standing on edge in his throat.

If you want to know more about the story behind the wicker basket, I'll have to tell you about it sometime or ask David.

Jim was born in the Cyril hospital while we were living at our present address. His whole life as a little child was centered around his dog, Rex. Jimmy followed Rex across the fields and down country roads. One day the mail carrier brought him home.

Rick followed three years after Jimmy. When he was left at home with me and the other kids were at school, he followed me everywhere I went. He was a loveable child born C-section."

[Mom must have tired at this point, as she continues with only "one-liner" points.]

*"*Silver paint incident." [This recalls the time that Debbie apparently was aggravating David, Robert, or both who were painting the railings around part of the dairy barn with aluminum paint. They dunked a bucket of that paint over Debbie's very blond, long hair. Mom toiled for hours with various methods to remove the paint from Debbie's hair.]*

*"*Tractor wreck involving Mickey & Gregory Cunningham and Robert." [This refers to the time that these three were out on our small Ford tractor which went out of control backward into a barbwire fence, with some of the boys on the back of the tractor getting sliced by the wire.]*

*"*Bee sting on Robert or Charles's tongue." [I'm surprised Mom didn't remember which one of us had this problem. It was Robert, who was at Grandma Brown's house and decided to put his mouth over an outdoor faucet to get a drink. Unfortunately, a bee occupied the inner part of the faucet and didn't like the disturbance, stinging Robert's tongue. His tongue swelled to the point he had difficulty swallowing. If I remember correctly, he was taken to a hospital. For a long time afterward, Robert had to be extremely careful of bee stings, as he was severely allergic and risked dying from them.]*

*"*Sally Dee dragging David to Morris'." [I don't have the full scoop on this incident, but as I understand it, David got entangled in a rope attached to Sally Dee, a rambunctious calf, which then dragged him over the fields from our farm to a neighbor's north of us.]*

*"*Tornado which blew chicken house over cows in the holding pen." This one brings to light the vagaries of memory. I remember an occasion when the family was at the dinner table at the home at 13786 NE 75th Street in Elgin, when Mom looked up and said, "Carliss, the chicken house just left." This was her nonchalant answer to a tornado taking the chicken house visible only 75 feet outside the rear of our house. The problem is that my version doesn't seem to jibe with that of my brothers or my Mom. Apparently, the tornado did occur, but somewhere in the vicinity of the dairy barn, which would have had the "holding pen".*

*"*Robert's hives." Robert would contract the hives from something, possibly tomatoes or some other plant. These*

hives would cause his body to swell to the point of being a danger to him. This caused great consternation as to his well-being.

"*Charlie, Robert, and Debbie's wrecks." I can't speak to Robert and Debbie's wrecks, but I had several episodes with rolled cars. The first occurred when I was at Elgin High School. I was at play practice, having driven our family's relatively new Chrysler there. After play practice, it seemed like a good idea to get into a race with a fellow high schooler, so we proceeded east in our respective cars on paved Highway 17, toward Sterling. My racing opponent was winning. He turned south on Trail Road, which was graveled at the time. Driving full speed on pavement onto a gravel road is not a good idea. The car skidded on the gravel, hit the dirt at the edge, and rolled into the cemetery at the corner. It landed upside down. I remember a gurgling sound while in that position and realized it was gas coming out of the gas tank and that I'd be well-advised to get out, which I did by crawling out of the window. Later, I also rolled a Ford pickup truck coming out of Apache very late at night. There's a hill, which we called "tickle belly hill" south of Apache. It seemed like a grand idea to drive as fast as that pickup would go so as to skip the bottom of the incline, sort of like flying. Well, this might have worked except that this gravel road had just been "graded", meaning a road maintainer had scraped the gravel on half the road (meaning to come back the next day and do the other half, I suppose), leaving a ridge of gravel in the middle. When the diving pickup hit that ridge of gravel nose first, it flipped—end over end. The thing did this at least three times, landing in a field next *to the road. I walked the five miles through the fields to get home at about three a.m.*

*"*Dad's wreck at Rick's birth." Dad described this event in his interview, set forth earlier.*
*"*Dad's building experience in Elgin." Likewise, Dad explained his trials and tribulations in his building experience in Elgin in his interview.*

*"*Article in Cotton Electric paper about Robert running the dairy at such a young age." Robert achieved local fame when he was featured as a 12-year-old single-handedly running our dairy business. He rose early to milk the Holsteins and manage many other parts of the operation. Quite a feat!*

[Thus ended Mom's account.]

Mom survived all these events with her usual aplomb. When we had the dairy, she was up early and was usually the last to go to bed. She was busy all day. When we were young, she made our clothes, utilizing her considerable sewing skills. Just managing six rambunctious kids would have been enough to drive most people up the wall, but she seemed to handle us all with calmness and patience.

Mom was a mother with some inventiveness when it came to her gang of boys and their male parts. Obviously, we went through potty training and peeing all over the place without notice. Mom named our male part our "peedoddler." As a young kid, I took it for granted that that was what everybody called that part.

Unfortunately, the end of her life was not easy. She developed Parkinson's Disease, which manifested itself in ways that made her life difficult. As the disease progressed, she would stay awake at night and roam around the house, keeping Dad up worried and trying to care for her. It became impossible for him to do that, and he eventually placed her in a care facility that could deal with her. She began to imagine things. For example, she would accuse Dad of going out with one of their high school classmates, as if they were still in high school. She was in a state of agitation and mental discomfort, saying things that were just not her. The normally calm, composed self she had always been was lost in the fog of the disease.

I will never forget visiting Mom at her care facility in Lawton once when I was home from the St. Louis area. Dad, Jimmy and David and I were there. When it was time to go, she did not want us to leave, calling out, "Don't leave. Don't leave." But Dad said that no matter how long we stayed that would still be the reaction that she would have when we departed. During that visit I sat with her, trying to talk to her about how she felt and engaging her as much as possible. She broke my heart when she said, "I didn't think it would end this way."

When Mom died, on January 12, 1997, the death certificate stated the immediate cause as "Acute Myocardial Infarction," with "other significant conditions contributing to death" as "Congestive Heart Failure/Parkinson's."

But it would be a distortion of her life to think of her when Parkinson's had destroyed the real Rose Mary. I'll always remember her as the rock of the family, ready to solve any and all problems and steer us through them. She was a marvelous woman and an outstanding mother.

Our parents were remarkable people. They also had a remarkable marriage and relationship. One day, while walking with Mom and Dad I heard an example of the way their relationship worked. They were discussing an issue, the subject of which I don't remember, but it was obvious that it could have provoked discord between them. I was fascinated by how the spouse who brought up the contentious issue immediately dropped it when the other seemed sensitive to that. This "backing off" was a feature of their marriage, such that I never heard them really argue. Now, they may have had midnight battles in the bedroom (although I never heard these take place, either), but they demonstrated civility and respect for each other. For example, while Dad switched to a Republican during his later life, I always suspected that Mom retained her family's allegiance to the Democrats. Not that she voiced that; she didn't. And I don't have any proof of her party registration. Rather, it was the way she kept silent when Dad raised political subjects. They each lived tolerance, patience, and an unswerving industriousness. Hard work, patience, and commitment were embedded in the DNA of these two.

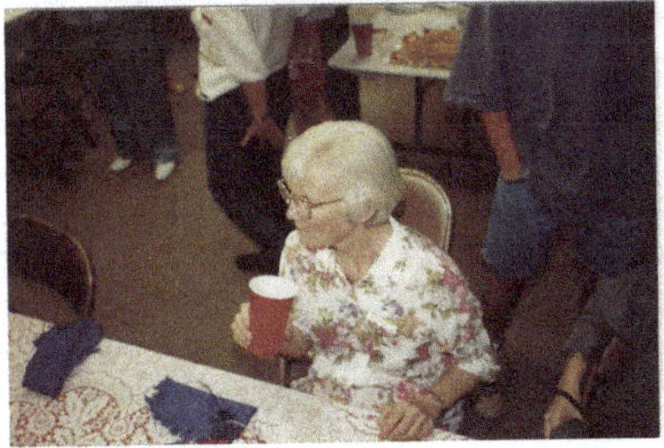

Top Left: (L-R) Rose Mary Kolker, Ricky Kolker, David Kolker, November 1991
Top right: Rose Mary Brown c. 1933, when she was in highschool, before she married my father C.J.
Bottom: Rose Mary Kolker, August 1992

Endnotes
BOOK I
Chapter 9

[31] Established as one of six district agricultural high schools by legislation passed in 1908, Cameron State School of Agriculture opened its doors in November 1909 in the First National Bank basement in downtown Lawton while a new structure was constructed just west of the fledgling community in southwestern Oklahoma. Developers named the new school for the Rev. Evan Dhu Cameron, the state's first superintendent of public instruction. J. A. Liner, an educator from Alabama, served as its first leader. The State Commission of Agriculture and Industrial Education administered Cameron and the other state agricultural schools. In the early years students studied agriculture, manual training, mathematics, English literature, and domestic science in a rigorous, six-day-a-week study program. The challenges of fund raising drove several early presidents from office despite their strong belief in the value of agricultural education. However, Cameron presidents A. C. Farley and A. E. Wickizer were energetic, vocal advocates for Cameron, and regional legislators including Jed Johnson, Sr., carried on the battle in Oklahoma City. Johnson offered legislation in 1927 giving Cameron junior college status, and the institution became known as Cameron State Agricultural College. Although its financial challenges did not end, this elevation brought long-sought respect and additional funding. From the Oklahoma Historical Society website, http://www.okhistory.org, Cameron University.

[32] Terminal Island is a largely artificial island located in Los Angeles County, California, between the neighborhoods of Wilmington and San Pedro in the city of Los Angeles, and the city of Long Beach. Terminal Island is roughly split between the Port of Los Angeles and Port of Long Beach. The island was home to about 3,500 first- and second-generation Japanese Americans prior to World War II in an area known as East San Pedro or Fish Island. On February 9, 1942, following the Japanese attack on Pearl Harbor, the FBI incarcerated all of the adult Issei males on Terminal Island. en.wikipedia.org › wiki › Terminal_Island.

[33] Just to confirm this, I checked the Abstract of Title, which provides the details of Mom and Dad buying the place where most of us grew up—now known as 13786 NE 75th St., Elgin, OK. The Joint Tenancy Deed

was dated November 27, 1953, and recorded at Book 399, Page 282 in Comanche County, OK. The conveyors were Henry R. Strategier and Helen Louis Strategier, husband and wife. The Abstract indicates that there was some mess with the title that had to be cleared up by the court, eventually landing the title in the Strategiers, before it could be conveyed to Mom and Dad, who got a Mortgage of $4,000.00 dated December 1, 1953, filed January 6, 1954, at Book 401, Page 110 in Comanche County.

[34] As Robert Bryce pointed out in his book, Cronies: Oil, the Bushes, and the Rise of Texas, America's Superstate: "Numerous studies showed that the oilmen were getting a tax break that was unprecedented in American business. While other businessmen had to pay taxes on their income regardless of what they sold, the oilmen got special treatment." Bryce gives an example in his book of how the oil depreciation allowance worked. "An oilman drills a well that costs $100,000. He finds a reservoir containing $10,000,000 worth of oil. The well produces $1 million worth of oil per year for ten years. In the very first year, thanks to the depletion allowance, the oilman could deduct 27.5 per cent, or $275,000, of that $1 million in income from his taxable income. Thus, in just one year, he's deducted nearly three times his initial investment. But the depletion allowance continues to pay off. For each of the next nine years, he gets to continue taking the $275,000 depletion deduction. By the end of the tenth year, the oilman had deducted $2.75 million from his taxable income, even though his initial investment was only $100,000."

CHAPTER 10

THE CHILDREN AND GRANDCHILDREN OF ROSE MARY AND C.J. KOLKER

Rose Mary and C.J. Kolker, Sr. had six living children, five boys and one girl — a seventh child, a boy, having been lost in a miscarriage between child numbers one and two. Just to be different, we're going to introduce them in inverse order. Each child was asked to give his or her own life story, and that is how it's set out below, each in his or her own words... except for Ricky, whose biography was captured from internet sources.

Here are the six of us, taken at our home place, 13786 NE
75th St., Elgin, Oklahoma.
November 1981.
(L-R) David, Jimmy, Charlie, Debbie, Ricky, and Bob.

Here we are again, with Dad, in January 1997 after Mom's funeral. We're arranged in birth order: (After Dad, L-R): Charlie, Bob, David, Debbie, Jimmy, Ricky.

RICHARD (RICKY) JOSEPH KOLKER

Born November 30, 1959.

Attended Elgin Public Schools, Elgin, Oklahoma, graduated from high school as class president in 1978.

Attended St. Gregory's Junior College, Shawnee, Oklahoma, 1979-1980.

Graduated from Oklahoma State University, Stillwater, Oklahoma with B.S. in 1982.

Is a retired CPA in AZ.

Has lived in multiple places, including Chandler, AZ where he presently lives, but also Sedona, AZ, Euless, Texas, Dallas, Texas, Grand Prairie, Texas, and Scottsdale, AZ.

Married Terrie D. Morris in Tarrant Co, Texas on September 14, 1991.

Terrie D. Morris was born on March 27, 1963.

Two children:

Landon Joseph Kolker, born June 17, 2000, now (2021) a junior in college in Arizona.

Madysen Marie Kolker, born May 2, 1996, now living on the east coast USA.

Ricky was unwilling to provide his life story, so the public records will have to suffice. He worked as a CPA/Auditor for the City of Phoenix until his recent retirement. Now living with his wife in Chandler, AZ.

December 2013: (L-R) Landon Kolker, age 13; Ricky Kolker; Terrie Kolker; Madysen Kolker (age 17). Taken at their home, in Chandler, Arizona.

JAMES (JIMMY) MICHAEL KOLKER

Born December 21st, 1956, at the Cyril Clinic, Cyril, Oklahoma.

Lived in Elgin most of my life. Lived in Chickasha, Oklahoma from May 1975 until November 1975.

Graduated in 1975 from Elgin High School.

Married March 19th, 1983 to Wendy Marlee Nichols at St. Ann's Catholic Church in Elgin, Oklahoma.

Wife's name: Wendy Marlee Nichols, born October 3, 1961, in Altus, Oklahoma at Jackson County Memorial Hospital.

She graduated from Lawton High School in 1979.

Two children were born of the marriage:

Eric Adam Kolker, born on April 13, 1983, at Comanche County Memorial Hospital, Lawton, Oklahoma.

Deadra Denise Kolker, born July 19th, 1986, at Comanche County Memorial Hospital, Lawton, Oklahoma.

Both are single.

Wendy worked at Warehouse Foods in Elgin from 1981 to 1984.

Worked at Warehouse Foods in Elgin from 1973-1975, and from May 1975 to November 1975 at Warehouse Foods in Chickasha, Oklahoma. From November 1975 to April 1983 I worked in the building business and construction. I helped with the development of Kolker Heights subdivision in Elgin and did some remodeling with the Farm and Home Administration.

When Dad asked me to come work with him in 1975, he wanted to make sure I was familiar with each stage of construction. It was an on-the-job training situation. He must have told the construction crews that it was up to them whether they paid me or not. Only two of the crews paid me. One was Ed Jacobi—for those who know Ed, he was one hard-working man. But he PAID ME, one of those things I will never forget.

From April 1983 until my retirement in April 2021, I worked for Goodyear Tire and Rubber Company in Lawton, Oklahoma. While at Goodyear, some of my duties were First Responder, Fire Brigade, Training Instructor, Payroll Representative, Labor Assigner, and Safety Representative. I worked with the Department of Transportation testing tires for quality, endurance, and safety. I worked in the Shipping Department managing the flow of tires to supply warehouses, keeping machinery running, and handling the logistics of semi-trailers to customers.

From 1986 to the present (2021) Wendy and I owned and operated the Storage Bins—rental of storage units, in Elgin, Oklahoma.

From 1986 to 1988 we owned and operated a t-shirt screening business in Elgin and had a little stand set up at grade school ballgames, etc.

Jimmy is the supplier of many a colorful sub-chapter in his life. With his permission, here is one of my favorites:

JIMMY AND THE BEER CAN

One hot summer day, in June or July 1976, Jimmy was coming down Trail Road from Lawton in his yellow, 1972 Ford pickup loaded with lumber for a construction job in Elgin. This pickup lacked some of the niceties: no rearview mirror and the driver's side mirror was broken off. The windows were open, it was broad daylight and it seemed, before he left Lawton, like a great day to get an ice-cold beer to drink on that ride. Being thirsty, the beer didn't last that long, and 19-year-old Jimmy needed to get rid of that empty beer can.

Now, Jimmy was a strong young man, so throwing the can out the window in a backward throw should result in the satisfying thud of metal far behind him on the road.

Nope.

Instead, there was the sound of the can skidding across the hood and onto the windshield of the County Sheriff's car directly behind Jimmy. Police lights began flashing; the siren sounded, and Jimmy shouted out, "OH, SHOOT!" (Or something like that.) Even the nearby cows stared and stopped chewing their cuds to take in the ruckus. Cows don't really get to see much excitement.

Now, the Sheriff's Deputy, straining his shirt buttons to restrain his good humor, approached Jimmy and suggested it might be an awmighty good idea to pick up that beer can so as to keep the countryside pristine. Jimmy answered he'd not only pick it up but try to eat it if that'd make the Deputy happy.

No ticket was issued. It's an example of police discretion not often seen anymore. The brothers of Jimmy have oft spoken of the many occasions that they escaped the law through the mercy of kind officers.

Jim Kolker Family: (L-R) Eric, Wendy, Jim, Deadra. Taken c. 1997.

DEBORAH (DEBBIE) ANN (KOLKER) ROLL

Born October 7, 1953.

Graduated from Elgin High School in 1971 as Salutatorian. During my time in high school, I was voted Elgin Owl yearbook queen my senior year, in 1971. I sketched a drawing of the mascot, Elgin Owl, my senior year as a class souvenir, which was used to make a mosaic tile inlay on the floor of the high school building in 1971.

Married June 16, 1979, in Elgin, Oklahoma, to Michael John Roll. Mike died on March 4, 2018. During my married life, I hand-lettered recipes and drew all the artwork for a fundraiser cookbook, compiled the pages, and had it printed for the Lawton Oklahoma Whole Food Co-operative, which was featured in the Lawton Constitution as representative of the same Co-op for my bread making. Mike and I were pro-life and Gabriel Project coordinators for St. Anthony's Catholic Church, Longview, Texas for some years in the 1990s.

I graduated from Oklahoma State University in 1978 with a Bachelor's Degree in Special Education K-12, with a minor in Art. My teacher's certificate is presently active.

I was a Special Education elementary teacher in the Elgin School District from 1978-1980. I taught Ft. Sill GED courses for soldiers in the spring and summer of 1982.

I was a substitute teacher in Lawton, Oklahoma, Longview, Texas, Spring Tree, Texas, and Pine Tree, Texas schools.

I'm now mostly retired but do occasionally substitute teaching. In 2019 I received my Texas Master Gardener's certificate after several months of study.

I lived in Elgin, Oklahoma from around 3-4 months old until approximately 1972. I lived in Oklahoma City (working); Edmond, Oklahoma (at Central State University); Stillwater, Oklahoma (while at Oklahoma State University);

Lawton (1979 married life-1992), then Longview, Texas from 1992 to the present.

Mike and I had three daughters: Emily Roll (single), Katie Roll (married), and Lucy McGoldrick (single).

My greatest joy and honor was to be a mother and homeschool all three daughters and to share close to 39 years of married life with my high school best friend and good husband, Mike. To teach them a classical arts education as well as homemaking skills, and the joys of simple life were rewarding to Mike and me. Nothing perfect here in my life, past or present, but I love my daughters with all my heart, and am proud of them.

Mike and Debbie Roll Family. Probably taken in January 1997. (L-R) Mike Roll, Katie, Emily, Lucy, and Debbie. Probably taken at Mom's funeral dinner, at St. Ann's Hall, Elgin, OK.

DAVID ALAN KOLKER

Born October 10, 1947, in Lawton, Oklahoma.

High school graduation was from Elgin High School in 1966. I was class president until impeached for getting married young. No awards that I remember.

Married to Doris Gaylene Sanders in Elgin, Oklahoma at St. Ann's Catholic Church on April 29, 1966.

Obtained an Associate's Degree from Cameron College and graduated from Oklahoma State University in 1971. Engineering and tech education.

Worked as a carpenter one summer after high school then at a convenience store night shift so I could attend college at Cameron (Lawton, Oklahoma) in the daytime.

Somewhere in here, we lived in an apartment adjoining the Red Cross where Gaylene worked and I had a janitor's job at the YMCA after school.

After the second year of college, I worked for Southwestern Book Sales selling bible reference books door to door during the summer and made enough money to pay for college. Sold in Illinois, Delaware, Georgia, and Oklahoma.

Daughter, Christy Michelle (Kolker) Fournet, was born September 19, 1969. She married William Fournet, on August 4, 1994. They have three boys and are living in Tulsa, Oklahoma as of 2021. Douglas was born on April 8, 1987; David was born on January 12, 2000; and John was born on December 12, 2001. Christy and her husband, Bill, own the Persimmon Group, a consulting firm in Tulsa.

Son, Paul Michael Kolker, was born on February 26, 1974. He married Tiffany McWhirter on April 5, 2008. They live in Moore, Oklahoma as of 2021. They have two children: a daughter, Teylor, born June 12, 2000, and a son, Logan, born November 9, 2008. Paul is a senior partner at Roberson, Kolker, Cooper, and Goeres Law Firm in Edmond, OK.

Jobs after college:

I sold over-the-counter stock for Universal Dynamics in Oklahoma City in the early 1970s.

We moved to Tulsa, and I worked with some guys that I sold books with who had a company called Arrowlite Industries....for maybe two years.

I sold mobile homes for Paul Savage Mobile Homes in Tulsa. I learned a lot about good, honest sales and service from Paul Savage. He taught me not to worry about the money, just take care of the people before and after the sale and the money will take care of itself. I used this theory my entire career and preached it to my salespeople as well. I worked here about two years.

I worked at Sherwin Williams Paint Commercial as one of their first commercial representatives. I loved this job, and the people, and learned a great deal.

Dad called in 1978 and said he had called all his kids and was going to sell Elgin Realty and Insurance and was seeing if any of us wanted to buy it. Gaylene and I had a hard decision to make. We wanted our kids to grow up around their grandparents and cousins. Gaylene's folks and relatives lived in Elgin as did my parents and some other relatives. We loved Tulsa and the job I had was going extremely well with lots of upward movement being offered at that time, but we chose Elgin. Dad told us that it was a very risky business and to have at least a year's living expenses saved up and possibly no income for a while. After moving to Elgin Dad set up a payment schedule to pay him for the business, handed me the keys, and said, "I am going to travel. Good luck." I was studying for my real estate brokers exam and my insurance license (operating under Dad's licenses) and trying to learn the business. We had $40,000.00 in savings (not bad in 1978). That money disappeared in the early 80s when interest rates shot up to 18% and we had five houses in our inventory. We eventually sold the houses at a considerable loss.

Gaylene was involved in school activities and with a hard campaign won a seat on the Elgin School Board in 1987. Gaylene was the first woman to serve on that school board in Elgin and struggled with the "good old boys club" that had prevailed for all the previous years. She served for 10 years and let the position go when grandkids in Tulsa became a stronger priority.

We survived the 1980s inflation and poor business environment and continued on as Elgin Realty and Insurance. Elgin being a small town required wearing many hats. I had five occupations within the Elgin Realty office: real estate broker, insurance agent, home building contractor, and real estate developer, and I brokered all the land auctions held by Bridges Auction. It took all five to pay the bills. The land development business finally paid off as the economy improved and we came out in fairly good shape. We sold Elgin Realty in 2006 and continued developing and running the insurance business.

As of 2021 we still have the insurance business along with a Yoga Studio that Gaylene operates, but we have retired from the others. As of 2021, we live at 904 Rock Ridge Road, Elgin, Oklahoma.

The most important and most rewarding things in our lives are our kids and our grandkids. It has been a wonderful life.

David has had published by his son, Paul Kolker, a wonderful memoir, Full Circle, that provides much more detail than given here. It is highly recommended, as it shows David's great sense of humor, his intelligence, his philosophy of life, and his deep care for his children and grandchildren.

David & Gaylene Kolker Family: (L-R) Christy, Gaylene, David, Paul.
Probably taken at Mom's funeral dinner at St. Ann's Hall, Elgin, 1997.

ROBERT (BOB) PAUL KOLKER

I am the second son of Carliss and Rosemary Kolker, Robert Paul Kolker, born January 22, 1946, in Long Beach, California. My father had been working in the shipyards at Long Beach during WWII, but when the war ended on September 2, 1945, those jobs ended. Work was hard to find, so the family moved back to Oklahoma in April 1946 when I was only about three months old. We lived on the "Old Brown Place", in an old, two-story farmhouse with no indoor plumbing and no indoor bathroom. Just a few months after returning to Oklahoma, David was born.

I have memories of going to the outhouse at night as a small child: a scary thing! It seemed really dangerous to suspend my tiny little butt over that big hole! Of course, there were no grab bars! I could fall in! I could get bit by a black widow! Who knew what could be under that seat? I remember using pages from the Sears and Roebuck catalog as toilet paper, and corn cobs when that was gone. Cistern water was available in the house at the small, red, hand pump, over the sink in the kitchen. I remember taking baths in a galvanized steel wash tub on the kitchen floor with water heated on the stove. As a recall, there was no water change between baths: Charlie (then called Johnnie) got clean water, I got seconds, and David got thirds. I have a hard time imagining Mom or Dad getting into that washtub to bathe, but they must've, since there was no bathroom and no bathtub.

I remember David and I "grazing" in the front yard. We'd walk around on our hands and knees, eat grass, and moo. Also, remember getting to look down into the cistern when Dad took off the cover one time. Lots of spiders and crickets and salamanders and such in there! The cistern was filled by runoff from the house roof. Of course, we used that water for cooking, bathing, and washing clothes and dishes, too.

When I was about five years old, I think, we moved to Lawton, to 1202 North 31st St., on the edge of the new addition. Dad had started a building business with his brother, I think. We lived in Lawton for several years. I attended first grade and half of the second grade at St. Mary's Catholic School in Lawton. We moved back to Elgin when I was in the middle of second grade, and I attended Elgin Grade School through fifth grade, then went to Our Lady of Perpetual Help School, in Sterling. I attended sixth, seventh, and eighth grade there, graduating from the eighth grade in a class of eight! All three grades were in a single room, and Sister Mildred taught all three grades. We called her "Two Gun Pete" because she used to scold us by shaking both index fingers at us! By the way, that schoolhouse had only two classrooms: first through fifth grade were in the other room. I think.

When I was about eight or so (so this must have been about 1954??), the famous chicken house event occurred. It was evening, about dusk. Mom and Dad were out milking cows, and it was really stormy. David and I were in the house standing at the back sliding glass door anxiously watching the storm, when we began to see chickens flying like bullets, horizontally, from right to left. Lots of chicken missiles! It turns out a tornado had hit the chicken house and completely destroyed it, almost as if an explosion had occurred inside it: all four walls fell outward. The tornado picked the chicken house roof up, intact, carried it about 100 yards, and deposited it on top of the cows in the dairy barn holding pen! When Dad opened the dairy barn door to let the next group of cows in to be milked, he discovered the chicken house roof on top of his cows! I don't remember much about what happened next, but I do remember wandering around in the pasture north of our house retrieving chickens, many of whom had lost most or all of their feathers. Remarkably, only one chicken was killed. And one cow had a skinned place on her back from where the chicken house roof landed on her.

Sometime around 1958, I had a Holstein heifer as a 4-H project. I planned to enter her in the Comanche County Fair in Lawton, so I had to train her to lead with a halter. This was necessary so that I could lead her around in the arena to allow the judges to look her over. At first, she didn't like the halter at all and was tough to handle. One day I was struggling to get her to cooperate when Mom called from the house that I had a phone call. Since David had been watching me, I asked if he would hold the rope while I went in to take my phone call. I didn't trust that calf (Sally Dee) wouldn't pull away from him, so I tied the rope around his waist. When I came back out of the house, neither David nor Sally Dee was to be seen! Finally, I found them out of sight over the hill and about halfway to the pond. Sally Dee had tried to pull away from David, but he had tripped, and she dragged him along the gravel road and then down the roadside ditch for about two hundred yards or so! He was a little skinned up, but my prize heifer was fine. By the way, Sally Dee won 1st prize in her class at the fair! David has hardly any scars.

After graduating from eighth grade, I went to Elgin High School until graduation from 12th grade, (as Salutatorian) in a class of 34 seniors.

Summers during my high school years meant working for a local bricklayer, hauling hay, driving a tractor, or working in Dad's "shop," where building components (trusses) were made.

After high school, I attended the University of Oklahoma for three semesters, then dropped out and joined the Army. I enlisted on January 27, 1966, just five days after my 20th birthday. In order to be assigned to the Army Security Agency, I enlisted for four years. I had basic training at Fort Leonard Wood, Missouri, secondary training at Fort Devens, Massachusetts, and specialized training in electronics communications intercept (MOS 05K20) training at Vint Hills Farms Station in Virginia, about 40 miles west of Washington, D.C.

The 05K20 specialty required a top-secret clearance. We were tasked with monitoring Soviet missile testing. Russia was testing ballistic missiles from a number of missile launch sites across Russia. Later, in Pakistan, we monitored Chinese missile launches.

My first duty assignment was to Herzogenaurach, Germany. "Herzo Base" as it was called, had been a Luftwaffe base in WWII. The base engineer, a civilian, had been ordered by the departing German Luftwaffe to blow up all the facilities before the Americans got there. He didn't. He turned the entire base over, undamaged, to the allies. He was allowed to stay there, living on the base in a beautiful house with his family. He was still living there and still in charge of keeping the base in good working order when I arrived in May 1967.

I was stationed at Herzo Base for about a year, then was sent on a temporary assignment (known as TDY) to TUSLOG Det 4, in Sinop, Turkey. It was actually a Navy base, on a tiny peninsula jutting out from the north coast of Turkey into the Black Sea. Directly across from Sinop, across the Black Sea is Sevastopol, Ukraine. While stationed at Sinop, I was able to spend several days in Istanbul and several days in Athens, Greece. In addition to exploring the area around Sinop, we could sail on the Black Sea. Sailing on the Black Sea was exciting, not least because it was notorious for sudden, violent storms.

After spending about six months in Sinop, I returned to Herzo Base in Germany for several months, then was reassigned to Peshawar, Pakistan.

I was stationed at Peshawar Air Station (PAS) in Peshawar, Pakistan, now known as the Pakistan Air Force's Camp Badaber. This is where the infamous flight of Gary Powers took off. Per Google, he "was an American pilot whose Central Intelligence Agency (CIA) U-2 spy plane was shot down while flying a reconnaissance mission in Soviet Union airspace, causing the 1960 U-2 "incident".

Peshawar is not far from the Khyber Pass, which is a mountain pass on the border with Afghanistan. The closest I ever got to Afghanistan was a trip to the village of Landi Kotal, known to the locals as "Thieves Village". It is just a couple of miles from the Afghan border. There was a huge, bizarre, outdoor market that was well-known for selling stolen goods from all over that part of the world, as well as a variety of illicit drugs. This place was right out of Indiana Jones. I was told that it was possible to buy a pair of shoes with a thick slab of hashish, or whatever you wanted, built into the sole. I was also told that Interpol agents were swarming all over the place, and unless you paid an enormous bribe, they would arrest you as soon as you made the buy. I didn't even try. Very interesting place.

The base in Peshawar was a modern (at the time) air base, built by the U.S. and leased to the U.S. While I was there, the Pakistan government terminated the lease and the Americans had to leave, so I left and was discharged from the Army. This was in September 1969.

While stationed at Peshawar, I was able to take a two-week leave to Bangkok, Thailand. I was able to explore the city and even took a trip down to the Gulf of Siam, as it was called then, now the Gulf of Thailand. I had a really good time in Bangkok. While there I stayed in a house on stilts, on a khlong, the name for a canal in Bangkok. The floor of the small house where I stayed had gaps about ¾ inch wide between the planks of the flooring. Kitchen scraps, and who knows what else just got dropped down into the water through those cracks. I had such a good time in Bangkok I forgot what day it was, so when I got to the airport, which was very small, and about 20 miles from the city, my flight had left the previous day! The flight back to Pakistan only flew every other day, so I had to wait until the next day to return to base. Unfortunately, there were no accommodations at the airport; it was open air, with big steel "curtains" that closed it off at night. The staff said I couldn't sleep there, so I had to go back to the city. But I had no money left! I'd paid for my flight to Pakistan but didn't even have enough money to take a taxi back to Bangkok. A taxi driver overheard me pleading with the airport staff and proposed a scheme to allow me to make enough money to return to Bangkok, have a meal, and a place to sleep, then he'd take me back to the airport the next day. Here was the plan: In Bangkok, taxi drivers are given a kickback by jewelry dealers if they bring in a tourist who buys something. This taxi driver ("Rick") proposed that I go into a jewelry store and act like I was going to buy something, and, at the last second, back out. In the meantime, he would be at the back door getting his kickback—he would then split his "take" with me. We went to perhaps a dozen places, and each time I convinced the proprietor that I was going to buy an expensive stone, and each time Rick collected his kickback. After we'd collected enough money, Rick drove me to a very poor area of Bangkok and led me to a tiny, three-table restaurant. On each table was what looked, to my eyes, like an angel food cake pan, filled with soup; the middle tube (where the hole in the angel food cake would be) was filled with hot coals. We paid one fee for a bowl. Later, Rick told me it was water buffalo intestine and penis soup! Maybe he was trying to shock me? After eating, he led me to a closet just outside this little restaurant. Barely fitting in this closet was a cot, very similar to those old canvas and wood folding cots that were at one time Army issue. I was to sleep in this closet. No blanket, no pillow, no guarantee that anyone would unlock the door or take me to the airport. So, having no choice, I got in the closet, climbed onto the cot, and Rick locked the door and left. The next morning I was greatly relieved when Rick unlocked the door and drove me the 20 miles to the airport. When I got back to base in Pakistan, of course I was AWOL, but my commanding officer didn't seem to care…it was never reported.

My discharge from the Army actually happened in New York. After flying back from Pakistan by way of Germany, I was mustered out in New York, then headed home to Oklahoma. The first leg of the trip was a short hop from New York to Philadelphia. As we were taxiing out to take off the alarm bells sounded, the plane came to an abrupt halt, and we were told to keep calm and exit the plane via the emergency chute. Guess who was the first off the plane? No, not me. The stewardess nearest the exit went sailing down the chute first, then went screaming down the runway. The rest of us slid down the chute and were told to get off the runway into a grassy area and lie down flat and keep our heads down. The remaining stewardess told us before we slid down the chute to take off our shoes. One lady, perhaps twenty passengers behind me failed to take off her high heels, which caught in the heavy canvas of the emergency chute, ripped it, and several unfortunate passengers following her fell through the rip and fell directly onto the runway, a distance of perhaps 10-12 feet. Several ambulances arrived to take the injured to local hospitals. It turned out that the emergency was a report of a bomb on the plane, but it was a false alarm.

Since I already had the appropriate security clearances, I was able to get a job with Sylvania Electronic Defense Laboratories (EDL) in Mountain View, California, and moved there when I was discharged. I worked at EDL full-time for a while, then part-time for another year or two while going to school at a local junior college, Foothill College. I later transferred to U.C. Berkeley and graduated from there in April 1973.

In June 1973, I married Jeanne Brady at South Lake Tahoe, California.

After graduation from Berkeley, I worked for several months as an ambulance driver, then entered the nursing program at Sacramento State University.

In 1976, my son Brian was born in Sacramento. As of this writing (2021), Brian lives in Los Angeles.

I graduated from Sacramento State University program with a BSN in May 1977.

We moved to Napa, California in June 1977, and I started work at Napa State Hospital in June 1977.

In February 1987 Jeanne Kolker and I divorced.

In 1990, Brian and I went to Europe, visiting Amsterdam, Luxembourg, Switzerland (including Zurich), Germany (including Munich, Berlin, and the tiny town of Merzen (near Osnabrück), the birthplace of our Kolker ancestors.

I married Denise Joy Stephenson (née Hodkinson) in April 2003, in Maui, Hawaii.

Vacation trips of various durations: to Paris, France (1999), and in 2006, Joy and I joined Charlie and Sue in China, along with David and Gaylene, Rick and his daughter, Madysen, and Jimmy and his daughter, DeeDee. We had a grand tour of parts of China organized by Charlie and Sue. It included the island of Cheung Chau, Hong Kong, Shenzhen, Guilin, and the Li River area, Xi'An (including the Terracotta Army), and Beijing (including the Great Wall and the worst air pollution I've ever seen). Everywhere we went the food was wonderful, and the people were very friendly and helpful.

Italy (2013) mostly in Tuscany, including Florence, Lucca, Siena, and Cinque Terre; Dublin, Ireland, including Newgrange (2015), another trip to Italy (2016), mostly Umbria, including Rome and Venice. In 2019, a cruise visiting Venice again, Croatia, Montenegro, and back to Italy: Sicily, Sorrento (with a side trip to Herculaneum), and Rome again.

I retired from Napa State Hospital, and worked part-time for three years, finally retiring for good after 38 years.

I have had a life-long love of reading. I also enjoy bird watching, and in years past I loved to scuba dive and free dive for abalone off the coast of northern California.

Robert Kolker (L) and his son, Brian. Probably taken at Mom's funeral dinner, St. Ann's Hall, January 1997.

Joy Stephenson and Bob Kolker, holding a photo of Brian Kolker, Oct. 15, 2001

CHARLES (CHARLIE) JOHN KOLKER, JR.
Charles, Jr., later known as Charlie, was the oldest of the six siblings. Because he's such a blabbermouth, the following Book II is the autobiography of Charles John Kolker, Jr.

BOOK II

The Autobiography of Charles John Kolker, Jr.

CHAPTER 11

Early Life

I apologize in advance for this overly lengthy personal history. For many decades I have accumulated boxes upon boxes of records, memorabilia, written notes, and gobs of other nearly useless stuff.

Born November 8, 1940.

I was born at Angus Hospital in Lawton, Oklahoma, and delivered home by what was then Becker Funeral Home in an ambulance as its very first customer, as the company was founded that day.

For some deranged reason, I ordered a beautifully hardbound book from the New York Times called "Your Special Day, Charles John Kolker, Jr., November 8, 1940." I can't imagine why. Did I think my birth would be on the front page of the Times? Headlines included, "Italians Launch Offensive; Drive Back Greeks on Coast; British Raid Berlin Suburb." A fairly large ad touted the "Sackville Suit— with handsomely stitched edges", for $32.50, causing the imagined boss to say to his decked-out employee, "Boy, are you in the chips! A custom-made suit!" There were ads for Chesterfield cigarettes, "Cooler...Milder...Better Tasting". And movie ads for "The Mark of Zorro", with Tyrone Power. What really struck me as nostalgic was a dance recital with the famous Katherine Dunham, which was sold out. I actually represented Ms. Dunham as a very young attorney with Rex Carr's office, which would have been about 1970. She was pretty old then but retained the air of an accomplished star. The sports section headlined, "Injury-Ridden Yale Team Prepares to Meet Mighty Cornell." All this, and much more, but not a word about that birth in Lawton, Oklahoma.

Charles John Kolker, Jr. when he was cute. Three years old.

Very early in my life Mom and Dad moved to California and Dad worked in a shipyard during the war. I have two memories of this time: First, my illustrious career as a violinist debuted on a kindergarten stage playing "Twinkle, Twinkle Little Star." Perhaps you've read the rave reviews. That career ended when I bashed the violin over the head of my pesky little brother, Robert, a few years later (when we lived at the "Old Brown Place" in Elgin). I still have that battered violin; Bob seems to have weathered the experience better than the instrument. Second, when we lived in an apartment complex in Compton, California, I was a shrimpy kid bullied by another, larger kid in the complex square. Dad witnessed the bullying and got fed up with it, stopping the kid from beating up on me. But the kid's Dad, another bully, saw this and came roaring out of his apartment to attack Dad. This was not a wise move. Dad exercised his Golden Gloves skills and decked the guy, thus becoming my hero. Neither the bully kid nor his bully father ever bothered me, or Dad, again.

Another very early, but sketchy memory was of a party that my parents attended while in California. I was probably 4-5 years old. I was the only kid wandering around watching the adults having a good time. There was a table of snacks and some opened wine bottles. From what I remember everyone was having a good time, some of which I related to that red stuff in bottles. So I had some, and then a little more, and some more. I must have felt pretty good, as I staggered into the crowd of partygoers attracting considerable attention as I was unable to walk a straight line. After considerable wobbling around somebody picked me up and took me to a bed to sleep it off. I don't remember having a hangover. It's funny what little kids remember. This would have been during the WWII years and I remember that there was at least one sailor in the crowd. I believe it was a relative serving in the Navy, but I can't be sure. In any event, this was an embarrassing event for my parents. For me, not so much.

Actually, there was a third memory, mentioned in Dad's interview. After the war, when the shipyard was paring down and Dad had his fill of the place, we headed back to Oklahoma in an old car pulling an old trailer. One of the trailer's wheels came off as we traveled down the highway and it actually passed us on the right, went over or through a fence, and into a field. I thought this was terrific to see, but it wasn't viewed so fondly by my parents, as Dad described.

Back in Oklahoma our then family of four: Mom, Dad, Bob, and me, settled in on a farm northwest of Elgin, Oklahoma. We raised rabbits for a while, and I had the responsibility of taking care of them. This worked out great, to the point of naming each of them, petting them, and getting attached to them, until they ended up on the dinner table: my first lesson in the realities of life.

The wood-framed house we lived in was shelter, but winter and lots of snow brought another reality: heavy, blowing snow blew in through gaps in the wood walls, settling on the blankets and quilts of my bed. Mom would stack those coverings on me to a depth of great warmth, to the point getting out from under them in the morning was a struggle because they were so heavy ... and so warm. In Bob's life story, he talked about the challenges of going to the outside toilet, especially in the winter. Like him, I can also remember the Sears and Roebuck catalog pages as toilet paper. My, how spoiled we are today!

Grade school had me starting in Elgin, then to Catholic school in Sterling, and ending at St. Mary's in Lawton when we moved there as Dad took up building the Greer Addition on the west side of town. It's so odd now to remember that that was the very edge of its residences. I had a paper route delivering to these new houses, with the bags full of Lawton Constitutions slung across the front and both sides of my bike. The papers had to be picked up at a delivery site about a mile and a half from our house at 1202 North 31st Street, meaning pedaling the loaded bike from there to the slightly uphill point of the first delivery was a heart-pumping challenge. Added to that challenge were the dogs at a couple of the houses. For some reason, owners of a pack of German shepherds found it amusing to sic them on the paper boy. One owner of a particularly vicious red-haired, very large Chow dog would stand in his doorway watching it attack me, snarling and biting at my legs. I had to get up enough speed to go past this site, throw the paper onto the porch, and keep my feet and legs up high enough to avoid getting bitten. If I didn't get the paper onto the porch—not the lawn—the porch, he'd call the newspaper and complain. Each complaint called in was a charge against my measly income.

I was about 10-12 years old during this Lawton period. Dad also hired me to operate a small tractor with a blade on it to smooth out building sites after most of the new house construction was nearly completed. As a small kid, maybe 60-70 lbs., it must have been a sight to see me wheeling around construction sites with the machinery.

Then the bottom fell out. About 1952 there was a recession. The home-building business collapsed. Dad traded one of the last built houses in the Greer Addition for the farm in Elgin. (We now think of this as the "Old Kolker Place", meaning 13786 NE 75th St., Elgin, Oklahoma). I hated the farm. There are so many things that were different then, and believe me, there are some things I would not trade today for what we had then. An example was the telephone.

There was a wooden telephone box about three feet long and maybe eight inches wide with a mouthpiece on the front and a receiver on a telephone cord hanging on a hook on the left side. There was also a small crank, as we were on a party line with a lot of the neighbors, and to make a phone call that rang for everyone on the party line one turned the crank for the required ring. So, for example, our phone ring was three longs and a short. The crank would be turned for a fairly extended time to produce a "long", and a short turn for a "short". Neighbors, hearing the three longs and a short would pick up their receivers so as to listen in. But doing so reduced the power to the call. I can remember calling home, hearing all the clicks of neighbors listening in and rudely yelling, "Damnit, get off the line. I can't hear my parents." Click, click, click, click went the hang-ups, and then I could hear plainly. This is what it looked like:

CHAPTER 12

St. Gregory's and Life as a Mini-Monk

Whether it was because of my dislike for the farm, or some miraculous piety, it was my ardent desire to become a Benedictine monk—I suspect because of our raconteur cousin, Father Joseph Murphy, O.S.B. ("Fr. Joe"). So, off I went to don a miniature monk's habit at St. Gregory's preparatory seminary in Shawnee, Oklahoma. This "monastic" life meant getting up at 5:30 am for a very quick splash of water in the face at the communal bathroom, then off in a silent file to the monastic chapel for Mass. The solemnity, the silence, and the sound of the monks doing the Gregorian chant made a permanent impression on me. There was something very calming about that; it was unintentional meditation. It has stuck with me to this day. Nevertheless, I didn't pass the rigors of the monastic life. Hormones began. New ways of thinking intruded on my "holiness".

There were some things I did at St. Gregory's that I'm not too proud of, and certainly would not be on the recommended list of things to do to achieve sainthood. One of those was the adventure to a recently burned-out tavern across from the monastery. Curiosity made me wonder if there could be, perhaps, at the bottom of the beer chests, some beer cans that did not explode and were there for consumption. With a buddy, we made excursions late at night to dig around, and lo and behold, there was perfectly good beer buried down near the bottom. We bundled those cans and hauled them to a ravine not too far from the monastery. They were lip-smacking good in our minds. For some unholy reason, we were never discovered making nightly forays to a ravine in the pasture.

A fellow seminarian and I decided it would also be a good idea to make our own wine. Hey, a little grape juice, some sugar, and yeast, and what could go wrong? This production took place in my locker, one of many that formed a wall between the locker doors and the back side which was the back of the dorm area. All went well for a while, as the fermentation process took hold and our dreams of fine wine magnified. Unfortunately, wine brewing produces not only a foaming overflow from the brewing container (which leaked out of the bottom of the locker) but also a distinctive smell. Father Augustine, our rector and overlord, detected that there was locker activity in his bailiwick that was not consistent with young, aspiring monks. They say that confession is good for the soul. Baloney.

Another episode I'm even more reluctant to disclose. As cloistered young monks to be we were only let out to go into town very infrequently, once a month comes to mind. Despite this, I went to the movies in Shawnee and somehow made the acquaintance of what I thought was a pretty young damsel. I sidled up to her and engaged her in conversation. This eventually led to a hair-brained scheme that only a very stupid and very young guy would think of: what if she'd be willing to come to St. Gregory's one night and sneak into the dormitory with all those monks-to-be? Would that be an adventure or what? Amazingly, she agreed, and we picked a night of rendezvous. I had learned to pick the lock to the dorm previously, so out I went into the night, found her at the appointed place and we stealthily made our way into the building, into the dorm—to my bed. The guy in the bed next to mine, seeing sin in the making, said, "Kolker, are you out of your mind?" Probably. It'll make you feel better for my immortal soul that we just lay there, fully clothed, so we could say we had completed the mission, and we then sneaked out and she made her way back to Shawnee. Of course, this sort of thing in a monastic setting has a way of being talked about. The meeting that was had with my parents and the abbot was not pleasant. He at least filtered some of my conduct so that I actually sounded better than I was—but not good enough to be a permanent wearer of those brown robes. Decades later I attended a reunion of some of my fellow seminarians and this episode was still imprinted in their minds, now much embellished and more scandalous.

Bottom line: I was bumped out of the seminary, ending my career at St. Gregory's in the secular part until the end of that year, and then spent the last two years of high school at Elgin Public School, graduating from there in 1958. The education I got at St. Gregory's forever changed me. There were enforced study halls, meaning study periods in complete silence, with a roving monk with a nasty ruler. Classes were taught by extremely well-educated monks, many with doctorates. These classes were challenging and thought-provoking. Unfortunately for me, one of those classes was Latin, taught by that very same Fr. Joe mentioned above. On the first day, he mentioned to the class that he had a cousin in the class and that he would make sure that there would be absolutely no favoritism. I don't know why he felt the need to do that, but he sure the hell kept his word.

One monk in particular impressed me with his classroom discipline. He had been a knife-thrower in a circus, which seems like an unlikely occupation to precede the priesthood, but so it was. If a student in the back of the class thought he could act out behind the back of this monk he got a rude awakening, as he would whirl around and throw an eraser that landed square between the eyes on the forehead of the offender, leaving a rectangular chalk imprint. This was effective.

We also ate our meals in silence, with religious tracts being read to us during the meal. I don't know whether it was this that lead to late-night hunger, but I managed to sneak out of our dormitory one very late night, making my way with a buddy to the basement where the refectory was—and a large, walk-in refrigerated food storage area with a heavy door such as one you'd see on a large freezer. We opened that door with our stomachs growling, anticipating the ice cream and other goodies inside. What we saw was Brother Andrew (we called him "Brandy") seated on a stool, eating his fill. He didn't even act surprised. He just said, "Come on in, boys." We did and we ate together. None of us ever mentioned this episode to anyone.

St. Gregory's changed me in ways that persist. When I started there, I was a shrimp, weighing less than a hundred pounds. This smallness attracted bullies. I learned to fight like a wildcat, inflicting as much pain and damage as I could. This was revealing because bullies don't like this kind of confrontation. It has influenced my entire life. My hackles raise high when someone tries to take advantage of me or anyone else. It embedded in me an attitude of taking on the impossible. Fighting racism, tackling corruption in the East St. Louis School System, and being a Liberal in an Oklahoma soaked in redness, conservatism, and backwardness, all rose out of the bullying and the learned reaction to it. By the way, by the second year at St. Gregory's I had grown eight inches and added quite a few pounds. This also changed the conduct of those who chose little guys to pick on.

One of the parts of attending St. Gregory's was coming home to Elgin at Easter, Thanksgiving, and Christmas.

I would hitchhike from the front of the school to the bus station in Oklahoma City, a distance of about 45 miles. It was very easy, and I never stood by the side of the highway for more than 10-15 minutes. That's something that's just not done today, sadly.

Another oddity of life at St. Gregory's was doing laundry. It is hard to believe what we did to get our laundry done. I had a cardboard-like box the size of a suitcase that I'd pack with my dirty clothes, pull the straps on it so that they were good and tight, and mail it home. Mom would wash these, fold them nicely, pack 'em back in the box and mail it all back to me. This sounds super strange now.

CHAPTER 13

Elgin High School and Early Jobs

After the rigors of St. Gregory's the rest of high school at Elgin was pretty much a cinch. I made the honor roll without much trouble (even named to the 1958 State Honor Society) and was on the yearbook staff as Assistant Editor-in-Chief. I remember the English teacher, Elizabeth Bandy, as being especially good. She encouraged me to write and use my language skills. One of my good friends during high school at Elgin was Johnny Cremer, who was a very good-looking young man who acted as my "flypaper" for attracting girls. Another high school buddy was Ronny Wagner, a Native American, who, with me, formed "The Dragons", a two-person "gang" that made us imagine we were part of something threatening, I guess. We wore matching jackets with a colorful Dragon and "The Dragons" embroidered on them. Ronny at least had a car that could pass for something hot; I had a 1950 Plymouth, which was about as "hot" looking as a wash tub. To increase the Plymouth's prestige "flames" were painted on it, from the front fender back toward the mid-section of the car. Hanging from the rear bumper was a metal placard with an embossed dragon and "The Dragons" imprinted. How all this was to elevate us is a mystery.

Another high school era experience was with Charlie Hasenbeck, who was a very talented, well-educated man of extraordinary imagination and patience. He did farming and exercised his skills by repairing and keeping in operation what could only be described as museum pieces of farm equipment. He asked me if I'd help him cut silage, and I agreed. I drove an ancient, massive tractor with iron lugs, with the driver's seat down low between two high heavy metal fenders. Charlie kept this monstrosity running well beyond its natural life. It chugged along very slowly but also very powerfully. On my first outing with this relic, I was driving the tractor, which was pulling a silage cutter, followed by a long trailer to catch the silage once cut. At the end of the workday, I was driving this caravan out of the field, through a gate with railroad tie gate posts. I took one of the railroad ties out with me on the way through the gate, then toward a creek with a steep, twenty-foot drop to the bottom. The entire train went over the edge into the creek. How I survived is a miracle. Charlie looked this catastrophe over and said, "I'll get the truck," and that was the extent of his demonstrated aggravation. His "truck" was another creature of ancient origins, but powerful enough, with the winch, to pull the whole train of farm equipment out. Once out he checked everything over, welded a few breakages, and off we went.

Another episode occurred near Sterling. Charlie had a habit of stopping at Gertie's, a local beer joint and house of less repute in Elgin, to buy cases of beer for our workday. The beer cans were placed in a 50-gallon open barrel and iced down. We drank from this supply all day. So by the end of the day, we were more exuberant than most farm workers. At the silage field near Sterling, I would drive the entourage above described and when the trailer was full of silage Charlie would drop off an empty for me while he took the full one to a silage pit some distance off. One day we had finished most of the field and it was time to go home. So Charlie hooked up the partially full trailer, I got into the truck with him and off we headed to unload. Now, a word about this truck: it was probably 40 years old at a minimum. There was not a speck of original paint on it. It had no doors on either side. Shifting gears meant a horrible grinding sound as he forced the beast into another gear, as the clutch was long gone. He drove it at full speed at all times. Here I am, bouncing around high off the road surface on a tattered seat, hanging on for dear life. Remember, this was long before seat belts. Of course, he was unconcerned about anything. We crested a hill, and I could see Highway 65 crossing perpendicularly ahead of us. Traffic moved on it both ways. Charlie paid no heed. There was to be no slowing down for the highway. I thought about childhood prayers. I yelled to Charlie over the roar of the engine, "Charlie, there's a highway ahead. Don't you think you should stop before crossing?" His answer was, "I can't. No brakes." All my inner being knotted up as I prepared for an early death. Nope. We roared across the highway. No discernable emotion from Charlie. He had been doing this all day.

Thanks to my brother, David, here's a photo of that very same truck.

CHAPTER 14

Military Life

While in high school there was a development in the military obligation of young men. Up to that time, one could serve in the National Guard and attend 48 weekend drills and two weeks of summer camp each year acting like a soldier, thereby completing one's military duty that was required at that time. But the law was due to change. A few months after I reached 16, the military obligation was to increase. Thenceforth it would be required to serve six months of active duty at a regular Army military base, then do weekend drills and summer camp. I'll never understand how I convinced my father to help me lie about my age, but on March 25, 1957, at age 16, I enlisted in the Oklahoma National Guard in Lawton, thereby entering service under the old rules. The reason for my concern was that serving six months of active duty would mean delaying entering college, which I definitely did not want to delay.

I could type, write reasonably well, and knew English grammar. All this meant I was steered into the Personnel Section of my Guard unit. Eventually, I rose to Specialist 5th Class (Spec 5, or E5), the Spec 5 rank, which doesn't exist anymore, is the equivalent of a Staff Sergeant). This was a very privileged way to be in the military, as I served as the Personnel Sergeant for my unit. Assignments of duties were made by this person: KP, cleaning the latrines, peeling potatoes, and other such unpleasant tasks which I didn't assign myself.

Anyway, I did my 48 weekends and two weeks of summer camp at Ft. Hood, Texas until I finished my two years of college at what was then Cameron Junior College in Lawton. When I transferred to St. Louis University in St. Louis, Missouri I was told to report for duty at the Army Reserve unit in St. Louis, which I did. This was an unreal experience because when I reported for duty the officer noted that I was a Personnel Sergeant and knew that the incumbent PS wasn't about to relinquish his spot, so he told me to just have a seat in the Personnel Office. And there I sat, in uniform, for a couple of months on the designated weekends. Finally, he told me to go home, and I would be carried on their roster (without pay, of course). This is how I served the remainder of my military "career". I was issued an Honorable Discharge on 26 Nov 1962.

One of the summer camps at Ft. Hood I volunteered to be in the advance unit, which meant going to the fort a few days early, driving a "deuce and a half" (a 2 ½ ton Army truck) from Lawton to Ft. Hood with a load of soldiers, inspecting our designated area and rolling up the side flaps on the huge canvas tents we were to sleep in and then "guarding" our area. Why there was a need to guard a group of empty tents in the middle of Ft. Hood was never explained. Anyway, while I was marching around our area during the 130-degree heat, wearing the heavily starched, olive-drab fatigues we were issued—long sleeves and topped with a steel helmet and helmet liner—I apparently collapsed. I don't remember collapsing, or anything else until I woke stark naked in a huge tub filled with ice and alcohol, which decidedly shocked me awake. Nobody explained what happened or what my condition was. I was visited by Gen. Mark Clark while in the hospital there. My conclusion, years later, was that I had suffered heat exhaustion or heat stroke.

When I joined the National Guard, the unit was infantry. Not long after we were transformed into an armored reconnaissance unit. This sounded much more glamorous until the role of armored reconnaissance was described: we were to drive our light tanks full speed up to the front lines, firing our machine guns and cannon, attracting as much fire from the enemy as we could so our forces could ascertain the strength and location of the enemy, then we were to turn around and hightail it back. This did NOT sound very glamorous.

CHAPTER 15

Early College and College Jobs

During one summer "vacation" from college I worked with Lawrence Clancy near Dodge City, Kansas. I lived with Lawrence in his small, but neat home outside of town. Lawrence was a good guy, but a little eccentric. When it came to mealtime, I'd go to the pantry and stare at shelf upon shelf of canned corn. Nothing else. That's what we ate. When we had an off day from the grain elevator where we worked, I'd oil the wood floors of his house, literally applying oil with a cloth onto the wood while on my hands and knees. It seemed like a strange thing to do, but the house was kept neat and clean, even though he was a lifelong bachelor. On Saturday nights he'd drive into Dodge City in his Cadillac to play bingo. I didn't play bingo but used the opportunity to wander about this small city looking for anything, just anything, that was just a little bit exciting. It wasn't there. But the trip home was sometimes exciting. A little context here: this part of Kansas is flat, very flat. So flat that there weren't even "bar ditches" on either side of the road. There was no reason for them because if rain fell it was just like falling on a sheet of flat paper....nowhere to drain to. Roads were straight as an arrow. Maybe this lulled Lawrence into sleep because that's exactly what would happen. So there we were, 100 mph barreling down the road around midnight, when I spied ahead a barricade across the road and, miracle of miracles, a bridge out. (Why the heck was there a need for a bridge?) Lawrence was not slowing down—because he was fast asleep. I had visions of life ending and shouted out, "LAWRENCE!" He jerked awake and slammed on the brakes, skidding to a stop just a few feet from the precipice of the gap.

That wasn't the only excitement with Lawrence, though. We worked at a very busy grain elevator/mill that had several large elevators full of wheat that had to be rotated to avoid molding. A large auger ran from one of the elevators to a concrete pit maybe fifteen feet deep. On one occasion the auger clogged somewhere down in the pit. Being the youngest and dumbest I volunteered to climb down into the pit to shake the auger loose. Unfortunately, the wheat had been rotated so often that it was more flour than grain. As soon as I was into the pit I realized that I couldn't see in front of me at all; I sank into this finely ground flour like it was quicksand, holding on to the ladder on the side of the pit with one hand while grabbing at the auger with the other. The good news: the auger shook loose and functioned normally. The bad news: I caught dust pneumonia from the wheat dust. My lungs are still affected by that.

Life at Cameron Junior College meant a home-away-from-home, as I lived on campus in South Hall, assigned to a room with Sam McMichael, a guy reared as a strict southern Baptist who had no tolerance for Catholics, my then faith. Sam asked to be transferred to another room but was denied. We developed a great relationship, as college expanded our viewpoints. Our room was on the first floor, with a window that had a four to five-foot window well below it to allow sunlight into the basement level. That pit posed a challenge for us: a group of students would come to our room to play poker, often into the wee hours of the morning, and beer cans were a part of our residue, so we'd open the window and toss those cans into the pit, with the objective of filling it by the end of the semester. Sam was an excellent poker player; me, not so much. He was an early riser, the opposite of my desired habit. Despite all these differences, we became great buddies. One of our experiences was to travel to the top of Mt. Scott at night with a case of beer and philosophize. Nothing was off limits. The existence of God, religion, women, social mores, useless course work, and each other's merits and demerits. Often these sessions would last hours. We solved nearly everything. Friends that would join us included Gerald Good and Micky Kernodle. With the beer in the car, there wasn't room for any more.

Sam was an Agriculture major. He had been reared in the "Slick Hills", the foothills of the Wichita Mountains west of Apache. He espoused the South rising again and was very much the country boy. After the two of us left Cameron to go our separate ways, not to even meet each other for nearly fifty years, I was absolutely floored to learn that Sam had mastered the English language, wrote poetry, and taught English. Sam possessed a phenomenal memory, reading heavy philosophical works that he could quote without reference to the text. He became a renowned storyteller, one with exceptional skill at weaving hilarious tales created from his enormous imagination. We met again long, long after leaving Cameron when Sue and I went to a storytelling Talkathon in Apache featuring Sam. He had us laughing uncontrollably. I continued to see Sam on Zoom when our Unitarian Church met. Unfortunately for all of us, Sam's health, notably Parkinson's, has limited Sam's participation.

CHAPTER 16

St. Louis University

I switched majors several times, from Sociology to Psychology and finally Philosophy. When deciding which university would be the best for Philosophy, consulting was had with Fr. Joe, who seemed to know everything. He ranked the top three: the University of Paris, Toronto University, and St. Louis University. I would have loved to have lived and studied in Paris, but even though I had several years of French courses fluency was a far-off goal. Besides, studying abroad would be costly. Toronto was just not a good substitute for Paris, so St. Louis U was the choice. It was, and is, a Jesuit school, renowned for intellectual discipline and particularly noted for its Philosophy department. It was not going to be easy—and it wasn't. Mom and Dad did what they could, sending a hundred dollars a month to help. Nevertheless, I borrowed money through the NDEA (National Defense Education Act) to help pay tuition and costs. The classes were tough. I did not do so well with the course on ancient philosophers Plato and Aristotle but had some incredibly smart professors. Fondly remembered was Dr. James Collins, who taught Contemporary Philosophy, was wheelchair bound — extremely gifted intellectually but also an easy-to-talk-to man who welcomed student inquiries and was very open to discussions in his office or even the hallways. He wrote several books, including one on Spinoza, another on Kierkegaard, and one on the Existentialists, the latter of which we used in one of his classes. There were courses on Logic, Metaphysics, Natural Philosophy, Modern

Philosophy, Contemporary Philosophy, and others. Certain of the philosophers were real mind-benders, particularly Immanuel Kant.

To help pay for this experience I got a job at Kraft Foods in St. Louis, at night, which meant starting at 11 pm and quitting at 7 am, operating a comptometer, which has multiple rows of numbered keys. After the trucks were loaded with cheese and other Kraft products, the warehouse crew would bring me the order sheets so that the current prices and the total for each product could be entered. This would be presented by the truck deliverers to the buyers around the area so they could pay. The good news was that there were often fairly long breaks between truck loadings, so I could study. The bad news was that my first class was at 10 am, so by the time I got home, cleaned up, and tried to get an hour or two of sleep, my brain and body were tired. I lived in what can only be described as a slum near St. Louis U, in a three-story roach-infested house occupied by the owners on the first floor, a couple of alcoholics on the second, and a prostitute and another college student on my third floor. The prostitute kept fairly busy which contributed to the sounds of the building.

Kraft had an unusual policy at that time that allowed employees to take all they wanted of its products at no cost. Therefore, I lived on cheese, spaghetti dinners, macaroni and cheese dinners, and such other delicacies for the two years at SLU. My ability to supply endless cheese made me a popular guest at parties. It also required substantial beer drinking to offset the effects of the cheese.

The area I lived in was colorful. In the alley between the residence and the back of the businesses on the other side of the block were often winos, prostitutes, and assorted riffraff, who sometimes ended up as dead bodies in that alley. Gas Light Square, a popular night spot of cabarets, bars, live theatres, drug dens, etc., was only a few blocks away. It was on the second floor of one of these spots that I witnessed the first real orgy I'd ever seen. Many entertainers such as The Smothers Brothers, Lenny Bruce, Miles Davis, Barbra Streisand, Jackie Mason, Mike Nichols and Elaine May, Woody Allen, Jerry Stiller, Dick Gregory, and Jack E. Leonard gained exposure at the start of their careers in the clubs of Gaslight Square.

I became acquainted with John Carter while attending SLU. He was a partygoer but was also the son of Bolen Carter, the Assistant Superintendent of Schools in charge of personnel hiring at the East St. Louis School District, across the Mississippi River from St. Louis. When I graduated and it dawned on me that a Philosophy Degree entitled me to almost nothing that paid a salary, he introduced me to his dad, who was thrilled to have a St. Louis U grad applying for a teaching job. His decision to hire me would be one he would regret.

CHAPTER 17

Rude Awakening, First Marriage, and Teaching

My very unrealistic plan had been to go on to a doctorate in Philosophy and teach at a university. A rude awakening occurred when it was discovered that some required graduate courses in Philosophy at SLU were taught in the original languages, meaning Greek, Latin, and French, mainly. Well, that meant I'd have to take several years off to gain fluency in those before applying. Too poor to even contemplate such a thing, the teaching job looked pretty good. Besides that, I had a minor in English and had a good grasp of that, so I took the role of junior high English teacher at Clark Jr. High, on State Street in East St. Louis, Illinois.

All this took place in 1962, a big year for me. During my time at St. Louis U, I met Norma Sue Taksel, a cutie who was dating a fellow resident of the Bowery where I lived. The idea of us getting serious was not what her father, Nathan Taksel, had in mind for his daughter. Nathan was a somewhat observant Jew who didn't like a Gentile like me, especially a Catholic, being with his daughter. Fortunately, the Orthodox Jewish grandmother of Sue, Bubbe, was a wonderful woman who I enjoyed talking to, and who was a lot more tolerant. In any event, the relationship developed into plans for marriage, and since Nathan had originally refused to take part, it took place at St. Ann's Catholic Church in Elgin on December 27, 1962, with Fr. Cletus Bash, officiating. Brother Bob and Sue's sister, Sharon Taksel, acted as witnesses. Sue's mom, Ruth, was Protestant and a good, remarkable woman—and a very talented one—who remained supportive. Early in our marriage Ruth became an Aero Commander dealer, and she encouraged me to take up flying, which I did, with her providing the plane. The Aero Commander was the Cadillac of private planes, so this was an extraordinary way to learn to fly. Training flights took place at Lambert Field, now St. Louis International Airport, putting me often in line with huge airliners on the taxiways to the airstrip...something like a mouse in a queue with elephants. Learning to fly was a great experience and for years I would fly over St. Louis at night, marveling at the brilliant colors of the night lights, the streetlamp patterns, and the joy of being like a bird looking at the world below. I'll never forget those flights. Years later I made a cross-country flight from the St. Louis area to a pasture airfield that John Roll owned (he had a plane hangered there) across from his home on the east side of Elgin. Ever the ham, I donned a leather helmet, a long, flowing white scarf, and goggles so that when Dad came to greet me and drive me to the family home I'd be appropriately outfitted. Dad never said a word.

1962-63 was my first year of teaching, and it was filled with lessons. The first semester I tried teaching these junior high students using the "I'll love 'em, and they'll behave" theory. Big mistake. They nearly overthrew me as their teacher. So, at the semester break, I visited the shop teacher, who helped me make a ½" thick plexiglass paddle, that when applied briskly to any surface sounded like cannon fire. It also had several holes drilled in the paddle end. On the first day of the second semester, I showed the paddle to the class, slammed it on the desk, and said, "The first person to act up gets to be the first to feel the effects of this paddle." I know, this sounds horrible—child abuse, and all—but it took less than a minute for one of the problems to act up, so I yelled at him, "Out the door to the hallway!" He nearly had a heart attack at this sudden change of strategy, but he sheepishly obeyed. The class was stone quiet. Once in the hallway, I told him to bend over, and he got a whack on the seat of his pants that sounded like a thunderclap. It was the last time in 6 years of teaching that I had any problems with student behavior. The word got around quickly. Of course, this kind of discipline is not allowed today.

CHAPTER 18

Teacher Unionism

Clark Jr. High was a hotbed of union activity. At that time the National Education Association (NEA) had a chapter at Clark, and the East St. Louis Federation of Teachers, AFT, AFL-CIO, also had a Local, Local 1220. The 1220 Building Representative, Jim Groce, a solidly built man with a pockmarked face, very soon asked me to join the union. As a country boy reared in a household with a father who didn't think favorably on unions, I declined the offer. I soon learned why unions are needed.

There were major differences between the NEA and the AFT when I started teaching. For example, the NEA thought of itself as "professional" and therefore opposed teacher strikes or almost any other assertion against school administrators or school boards. In fact, many of their members were school administrators. The AFT, on the contrary, was very militant and advocated for the right to strike, and the threat to strike even if there were laws against it, which there were at that time.

The reasons for my conversion to unionism were many. The school atmosphere was very paternalistic. Our Principal, Carl Compton, was a martinet, a man of the old school who believed teachers should strictly follow his orders. Every day he issued a written directive which was copied and placed in our teachers' mail slots to be obeyed. These directives sometimes bordered on the absurd. One directed that our students' chairs must be in straight rows of the same number of chairs, equally spaced. The idea of having a circle of chairs was verboten. Teachers, especially new ones like me, had lunch hour duty when students were to line up without talking and politely get their allotted portions of cafeteria food. He thought it would be a great idea if they had assigned seats, negating any buddies eating together. I had a problem with this and allowed the students to talk while getting their food and sitting with their friends. I was called into his office to explain why I did this without his specific permission. I told him it worked better, and the students got finished quicker and were happier. He was unsatisfied with that answer, as for him, that was not the issue. It was whether or not I had obeyed him. I told him I was going to continue doing what worked. This, of course, went down in my record he kept.

The daily directives became so irritatingly useless that I soon just put them unread in my classroom waste basket.

I had a Civics class that had 50 students, crammed together in a much too small space. I divided them into three groups: National, State, and Local Government. Each group was divided into two, one group pro and the other con. Each sub-group was to elect its own chair. Then I asked them to contact their U.S. Senator or Representative, a state senator or representative, or a local city councilperson, as appropriate for their group, and interview them. They were then to report on what they learned and debate the pros and cons. The representatives were very cooperative, and maybe even a little flattered, to be contacted, but the word got back to Mr. Compton, who called me into his office in a rage. "Who told you that you could do this?" he yelled. I replied that I thought it was a good way for the students to be engaged with civics in a real-world way and that they were learning a lot and liked doing it. It made them feel important. He was pissed. I did it, anyway.

Another favorite of Compton's was to "evaluate" my teaching by hiding behind the opened classroom door which swung out into the hallway. When I saw him doing this, I would yell out the door, "That's okay, Mr. Compton, come right on in and have a seat. The students and I welcome you." This didn't go over very well, either.

There were dozens and dozens of incidents like these. After a while I got frustrated at the constant interference. Mr. Compton was not a teacher and knew nearly nothing about English, Civics, or History, all of which I taught. He had been, of course, a coach, which is for some inconceivable reason the national standard used for selecting many principals. It is the epitome of the Peter Principle, which elevates the incompetent to the highest possible positions. Many coaches, not all, were dumber than rocks about academics, and to have one who could barely put a sentence together evaluate my English classes was an insult.

Now all this rebellious conduct was a bit risky. A new teacher is on "probation" and can be fired for any reason, or no reason at all. Most school systems have a system of tenure, which is reached after two years or so after a successful probationary period. By some miracle, I made tenure, after which a reason had to be given to be fired and if challenged had to be proved. But other events intervened which added to my protection.

The run-ins with Mr. Compton were not the only reasons that pushed me to unionism. Unbelievably, our school board was run by organized crime. There were many schemes used by the board members to skim off the school tax money. One was to get very high bids for purchases: musical instruments, schoolbooks, supplies, etc. The "successful" bidder then paid a kickback to the board members who belonged to the syndicate. Of course, while a lot of money was corruptly used this way, it was only one of many ways. I was shocked to learn that some teachers were paying bribes to get their teaching jobs. Relatives and friends of board members got jobs and the jobholder paid money for that privilege. It was a very deep cesspool of corruption. Board members who enjoyed these benefits were not inclined to decrease their take so as to pay teachers more. We were paid miserably and treated miserably, and that was not going to change by being "professional". We sought to have our Local 1220 recognized as the bargaining agent for the teachers. That was, of course, denied even after repeated efforts and entreaties. They weren't impressed.

Just how little was I paid as a full-time teacher? In December 1962, I was paid a gross salary of about $400.00. After withholdings for income taxes and teachers' retirement, I netted $279.00. This was not a living wage. My house payment, car payment, food, and utilities exceeded my net pay. The Board of Education, the Superintendent, and other powers didn't give a damn. The struggle to make a living wage gave rise to a kind of desperation: what did we have to lose? Something had to give. I joined the union. Very soon I was active enough to be elected Treasurer of Local 1220. Rumblings of a teachers' strike began. There were very serious consequences to being a striking teacher: revocation of one's teacher's certificate; jail, as an injunction against such an action was a sure thing and violating that injunction could mean jail; fines, which could be hefty; blackballing so that future teaching would be impossible.

CHAPTER 19

Crossroad: What's Next?

As my first school year ended, I took stock of my future. I loved teaching, but it seemed headed to a dead end. I decided to take the LSAT (Law School Admission Test), and lo and behold, obtained a high enough score to be accepted to the St. Louis University School of Law night program. This program, although conducted in the evenings, used the same profs as the day program and we sat in the same room taking the same tests at the end of each semester. I chose the five-year program, putting my putative graduation to 1968. Oh, well, I thought, I'm going to be five years older in 1968 anyway, I just as well be five years older with a law degree. So law school, full-time teaching, and ever-increasing union activism were keeping me busy.

Plus, with law school came the birth of children: The first, Charles John ("Jay") Kolker, III, was born on November 15, 1963; Cynthia ("Cyndi") Lynne followed on January 6, 1965; and Christopher ("Chris") Thomas on September 2, 1966. Is there fertility in law studies? These adorable kids, and my then-wife, Norma Sue, endured my very long days away from home base. They deserve great credit for being tremendous human beings in spite of my absence. I have many memories of these children during this time. Jay, for example, as a very young child—maybe two years old—had a banana-shaped scooter that he'd sit on and zoom down our concrete driveway toward the street, at full speed. At the very last second, he'd put down his little legs and the scooter would come to a "screeching" halt just inches from the end of the driveway and the street. Watching this brought our hearts to a high thumping anxiety level, but he never seemed to mind. Cindy (now Cyndi) was our household moderator, the voice of calm and reason between her older and younger brother, Chris. Without her, our household would have been much more raucous. Cyndi had, and has, the gift of forthrightness: don't ask her a question unless you're prepared for the unvarnished truth. Cyndi, sometime in the 1990s, created a photo book of all the important places in our lives: the schools she and her brothers attended, the places we lived, and even a photo of the home where Sue and I lived in Smithton, Illinois. It's something I'll always treasure and is physical evidence of the caring that Cyndi personifies.

Chris, the youngest, was the politician of the family. I can remember when we lived in East St. Louis and his parents were actively involved in political campaigns, Chris took his little red wagon down the neighborhood streets distributing political literature that he found in our house. Neighbors called, both anxious that we knew he was out alone on the streets doing this "work" but also to comment on how adorable they thought it was.

Much later, after our divorce, I'd meet their mother in Litchfield, about halfway between Springfield, Illinois, where they lived, and East St. Louis so I could pick up the kids for my visitation with them. On one of those visits, the four of us went to Lake Lou Yaeger park in Litchfield and camped out in a tent. The kids got a kick out of tying me up with rope while in the tent. These visitations were emotionally difficult. I missed the kids terribly and loved my time with them but returning them to their mother when visitation was over was gut-wrenching. I often cried on the drive back to East St. Louis.

CHAPTER 20

Life as a Union Officer

Teacher unionism and activism were on the rise across the country. New York City teachers, members of AFT Local 2, voted to strike. Al Shanker, then its President, was an interesting man. Among other credentials, he had a Master's Degree in Philosophy. A man after my heart! Later, after our Local became the second teachers' union in the country to strike, Al and I toured other teachers' unions around the country to recount our experiences.[35]

During research for this family history, I found a 48-page, typewritten account I called "Five Years in a Teachers' Union". While too lengthy to incorporate here, it provided facts that would have been hard to remember.

One fact was that for many years Boards of Education forbade married women from teaching. This was true until 1946 in St. Louis, Missouri when the Missouri Supreme Court ordered that prohibition be dropped. Single men were told not to date or be seen having a cocktail. Teachers were disciplined for "being out too late." Another fact was that school board members were nearly all white, male, businesspeople who were patriarchal, anti-union, and anti-employee rights.

By 1963 our Board of Education deemed it was permissible to "talk" to the administration, but only after it was clearly understood that the talk was only a "discussion," and in no way binding on the Board. These "talks" ended with the Board's unilateral adoption of a salary schedule for teachers which purported to give teachers raises according to years taught and education. However, this schedule was dishonored whenever it pleased the administration. It was simply a device to make the appearance of planned raises. While Local 1220 had been elected by the teachers to act as their sole bargaining agent in 1957, this was mostly ignored by the Board. The frustration of the teachers was building so that by the spring of 1964 we'd had enough. We wanted a real collective bargaining agreement, written out and signed as a binding contract between the Board and the Union. The Board's answer to this request: that it was against the law to meet with a public employees' union, and that the Board alone had the power to decide working conditions, salaries, and justification of grievances. Therefore, the Board announced, there would never again be meetings to discuss those issues.

Our Union struck on May 18, 1964, nearly two weeks before final examinations were to be given. Pickets arrived early in the morning, and we picketed the entire day. Parents brought lemonade and sandwiches to the picketers, and a few joined us on the lines. But we were terribly disorganized. Picketers weren't distributed evenly, so while some schools operated at near normal, others were shut down. There was no one in charge of the strike operation. By the second day, I assumed the duty of strike director and began touring the schools. Teachers were told to arrive at least an hour before the scheduled opening so early arrivals couldn't sneak in, as they had the first day. A headquarters was set up and Building Representatives (the "shop stewards" of our union) were to call in and report the number of teachers out, the number of picketing, and pupil attendance as accurately as possible.

We called the media as soon as our reports came in. I conveyed the statistics honestly and thoroughly, in contrast to the Board. To prove our honesty I invited news people to tour the schools to check our figures. This proved wise; we gained the respect of many reporters. Unfortunately, the editors re-wrote the articles, slanting them to the administration. One St. Louis morning paper issued an editorial titled, "Fire the Striking Teachers!" citing grossly inaccurate "facts". But well over two-thirds of the teachers were absent. Not all picketed; some sympathized but just stayed home rather than show their face on a picket line.

The pressure mounted. On the first day of the strike, 18,500 of the students out of the 1964 enrollment of 21,000 were absent from classes. That absenteeism grew as the strike progressed. Parents began complaining; small groups of them organized and then merged. Finally, after four days of striking, the Board decided to have a meeting—without the teachers. We spread the word to the parents about the meeting. A crowd of several thousand very angry parents showed up at the 7 pm meeting and tried to jam into the second-story Board meeting room. They overflowed down the stairs, filled the building, and flooded the streets, blocking traffic, honking horns, flashing headlights, and yelling.

We had expected this. Our Salary Committee—the Union's negotiators—was close at hand to be available in the event the Board decided to negotiate. But what did happen, we hadn't expected.

The Board discussed several matters having nothing to do with the strike or the teachers. The Board President was about to bring the gavel down and adjourn the meeting when a woman in the front of the room jumped up and said,

"If that gavel strikes the table, and you adjourn, you'll never leave here alive."

He hesitated. The crowd was foaming at its collective mouth. Shouts rang out, "Why haven't you acted?"

"Don't be stupid, talk with the teachers." Horns honked, the crowd roared, and tension mounted.

The Board agreed to meet. It was almost midnight. The Board adjourned to a smaller meeting room and the Salary Committee filed in and sat down on one side of a long conference table. At last, we were at business. The meeting continued into the wee hours. Arguments ran fiercely on both sides, but we were making headway. I ran in and out of the room, reporting on the progress of the negotiations to those outside because the crowd had not left. At 4:00 AM the two sides reached a tentative agreement, giving the teachers a 4% raise and including a provision that the school year would be extended four days so that the students would get a full year's education and the striking teachers would suffer no loss of pay. (The non-strikers were to be given that time off.) That was on May 22, 1964. On May 29 the Legal Advisor to the Illinois Superintendent of Schools issued a falsely based opinion that the school extension was illegal. Then two housewives petitioned the courts for an injunction to prevent an extension of the school year. The court found in favor of the housewives and the teachers were docked the four days. Five days later, based on a complaint filed by the Union, the court modified the injunction decree to exclude the docking of pay.

Despite the modified ruling, the Board on June 12 docked the pay of the striking teachers, rescinded most of the agreements reached during the all-night session, and refused to meet further with the Union. This was timed to make any Union counter-action ineffective, as school was then out. We resumed picketing but it was obviously useless, so we stopped.

To further discourage the Union the Board, on August 13, granted a 10% wage increase to all other employees of the school district except members of the Union. This was done soon after the Board had announced that the school district was "broke" and, therefore, the teachers were "being unreasonable".

Our Union announced that schools would not open in the fall of 1964 until terms had been made with the Union. I spent three weeks preceding school opening day calling every Union member, keeping them up to date with developments. This proved effective.

By August 30 the Board declared that it would seek an injunction to stop a teachers' strike. Our attorney, Rex Carr, answered, "The courts cannot force the teachers to teach." Picketing resumed on September 8, school opening day. It was a much better-organized effort. We set up a "Marine Corps" of teachers who were to be on alert to rush to any picket site where the picketers were weakening. I established "runners" who went from site to site (44 of them) keeping up morale and transmitting the information. We had our picketers wear cameras to take photos of "scabs" (teachers who walked into school).

I had an experience with one of these "scabs" at my school. He parked in the rear of the school in an attempt to sneak in. Nope. I was there when he opened the car door. I took my camera off my neck and aimed it at him, now 30 feet away. He hid behind the car door. I kept getting closer until he fell to the ground and wriggled, suit and all, beneath his automobile. I obliged him by also dropping to the ground, snapping photos all the way. He struggled out the other side of the car, pulled his coat up and around his head, and dashed for the back school door some hundred feet away. I followed in hot pursuit, snapping away. Of course, I never had any film in the camera, but the picketers guffawed at all this to the point of stomach cramps.

Of course, the Board obtained a quick injunction. Copies of the order were posted on the doors of all the schools. Among a litany of orders, the striking teachers were "enjoined from picketing any of the premises of the plaintiff in any way." The Union officers had met with the teachers before the injunction was issued. We told the teachers that new officers had been secretly named and they would take over as soon as the present officers were jailed or otherwise incapacitated. The teachers were told to ignore any instructions by our present officers, or any others, to stop the strike.

The Board, however, triumphantly declared that the teachers would be back in school the next day after the injunction was issued. But not one additional teacher went in. We did not picket; we set up lawn chairs and sipped lemonade in plain view. Pupil attendance dropped even more. The injunction was a complete failure. Our Union officers dutifully stayed at home while the second echelon took over. We had set up an endless chain of echelons, each to name its successor. We set up headquarters not only in Illinois but also across the Mississippi River in St. Louis, MO. Our chain of telephone calling kept us in contact with the Union membership. Our officers couldn't be served for contempt for several reasons: one, they were at home not participating; two, many, including me, were in Missouri, out of reach. Our leadership had faded into nowhere. We also conferred with the Central Labor Council to make sure other unions knew we had an "invisible" picket line that truckers, carpenters, electricians, plumbers, etc., were not to cross. They didn't. Many of the parents were union members.

After four days of striking in September, the Board gave in and negotiated with us. During the strike, our teachers were formed into groups to dig into every facet of the Board's finances. We found some very interesting things. For example, an administration official was forced to admit that a nearly half-million-dollar error had been made in one item of the budget. "Mere oversight," he said. We found hundreds of such oversights and fed them to the press. Purchasing practices were patently corrupt. We published prices the Board paid for musical instruments, canned vegetables, janitorial supplies, and other items, alongside the going rate paid for the same items paid by other school districts. Some of the East St. Louis city fathers were supplying these products for the inflated prices. The public was outraged.

The Board finally negotiated. They conceded our right to negotiate with them, granted us the 10% raise it'd given others, and most importantly, reduced it all to a "Memorandum of Understanding", which the Board members signed and adopted. Our Union members then met and voted to accept. The MoU also required to Board to file for and obtain the dissolution of the injunction and guarantee no further reprisals. The MoU seems no big deal today. Then it was monumental. We had changed the entire tenor of teacher unionism. It made national news.

The rest of the 1964-65 school year was quiet. In January 1965 our annual union elections took place. I urged the membership to create a new office: Executive Secretary, who was to be the right-hand man of the President of the Union. The office was created, and I was elected to fill it. I was also appointed Salary Committee Chairman. Before this appointment, our chief negotiator was our Union attorney. I decided to do this job myself, without the attorney. Prior to any meetings, we established negotiating discipline: while negotiating no member of the Union committee was to pipe up and offer something during negotiations; rather, it would be required to signal for a recess and discuss the point in our caucus, away from the Board. This gave us a unified voice. While this sounds simple enough, the Board never figured this out. Members on their side were constantly interrupting their chief negotiator with their own viewpoints, often at odds with what they'd been stating.

I sent a letter to the Superintendent informing him that we were ready to begin negotiations. Surprisingly, or maybe not, he promptly agreed, and we began meeting. Negotiations were tough. The Superintendent repeated the worn-out mantra that the Board was "broke". That didn't fly, as we had done our research to point out, specifically, where accounting sloppiness and outright graft had skewed the Board's numbers. These details were recorded by the reporters present, who we had invited to the negotiations. The public was not pleased. The Superintendent finally conceded to substantial wage increases and eventually, we tentatively agreed, we thought, to a group insurance policy: a hospitalization plan and a group life insurance plan. However, the amount of the life insurance was reduced from $5,000 to $1,000 at the last minute. We very reluctantly agreed.

In January 1966 the local elections rolled around again. I was nominated to be President of Local 1220, now a union of 1,100 employees. After being elected I swiftly wrote a letter to the Superintendent to begin negotiations for the 1966-67 school year. We compiled a comprehensive proposal, now including many working conditions provisions, a good grievance procedure, and many other improvements, plus a wage increase. Halfway through the negotiations, despite repeated assurances that whatever he agreed to the Board would also, the Superintendent told us that we couldn't depend on his agreement being agreed to by the Board. Meanwhile, the Board was sabotaging us by promising principalships to some on our bargaining team if they'd report on our negotiating stands and tactics. It happened during these 1966-67 negotiations. We discovered the spy and outed him, over his screaming protests. Several months after he was named a principal.

We had changed our tactics somewhat. Instead of asking for specific salary increases, we negotiated for a "package" amount of money, to be distributed as we chose. We had originally asked for over a million dollars, but by two days before school was to open, we were down to $740,000.00. The Board wouldn't budge from $580,000.00. We identified sources of income for another $200,000.00. Each side threatened to walk out. A mediator was called in. The clock was ticking. During the wee hours of the morning on the eve of school opening, we called various school Board members urging them to come to terms.

Meanwhile, our teachers were preparing for a long strike. We expected to be out for more than a month. During a last-night attempt to hash out an agreement, the seven-member Board was divided three to four, with three wanting to settle. During recess, the Board President signaled me in the hallway. He was looking for a compromise. I suggested several areas of give, and he caucused with the Board. He gained a fourth vote. After midnight the Board voted to approve a $680,000.00 "package". We had split the difference between us. Remaining though, were fringe benefits, language on working conditions, and other matters. The Board voted to give the Superintendent absolute authority to settle those issues with us. The Superintendent was a broken man; he approved nearly everything we proposed. He obviously didn't care anymore. He resigned before the second semester started.

Another year of relative peace ensued. We had accomplished a lot. Our contract was the only one of such comprehensiveness in the state of Illinois, and only a few in the nation could equal it. Our starting salary for a beginning teacher with a bachelor's degree was $6,250.00. We had contract privileges enjoyed by no other teachers in the country. Our grievance procedure was without parallel. We had accomplished in three years what had not been gained in the previous fifty.

But another year of strife was ahead, one that would require more stamina, better techniques, newer ideas, and greater strain than any of the other years. Our teachers were suffering from battle fatigue. Our new Superintendent was from the old school of administrators—teachers were meant to be bull-whipped into submission. He intended to break the teachers' union forever. We prepared a massive information campaign for our teachers. Old, unmet ills were resurrected. We vacuumed the Board's financial records for every last particle of financial irresponsibility. We studied ghost hiring and over-staffing, textbook purchasing, cafeteria operations, travel expenses, building construction practices, bond buying, and more. We mailed our teachers the details of these findings on a weekly basis during the summer.

This time we expected jailing of the union leaders and other teachers. We decided to face the nastiest possible punishments up front. Other AFT leaders were being jailed around the country. We knew we would have to expect the same. The Board pre-emptively declared that if the teachers struck, they would get an injunction, and seek contempt orders and maximum penalties, including revocation of striking teachers' licenses. So, at our next Union meeting, I asked for a motion for all teachers to go to jail rather than quit the strike. Some of our members, mainly men, whined and carried on about how they had to provide for their families and other woes. After about a half hour of this a frail old lady, Veronica McGinley, stood up and made the motion, saying, "I'm ashamed of the men who don't have the courage to go to jail. I'll be the first in line at the paddy wagon. Step up and show some balls."

This was an astounding statement from this skinny, gray-haired old lady. A strong second was made by several. I said from the chair that we'd had sufficient discussion and that unless there was a strong objection, we should proceed to a vote. That vote was nearly unanimous.

Later we also had a "resignation meeting" in a park, where teachers lined up to sign resignations. Each resignation was on a separate sheet of paper. It took a lot of courage for many to sign away a lifetime job, but several hundred did. We submitted the resignations en masse. Illinois law at that time required resignations to be submitted at least 60 days in advance of school opening. On the 61st day, we took the stack of resignations to the Assistant Superintendent, who was the acting Secretary to the Board, to whom the resignations had to be given. This was the same man who was so proud of gaining me as an employee several years earlier. He was so shaken that he wouldn't sign a receipt. I asked him if he would acknowledge that he'd received them, and he said yes. The newspapers had a field day with this.

Negotiations had started prior to the end of the preceding school year that ended in June 1967. The Superintendent was feeling his oats, recommending 5% wage cuts, elimination of nearly all fringe benefits, and the return of "the principal's prerogative," ceasing teacher input on matters such as the subject matter in textbooks. The Superintendent was getting heat from other school administrations around the state; we were being blamed for "arousing" the teachers elsewhere. Our Superintendent was also meeting with the State Superintendent of Public Instruction to coordinate plans against us. Unfortunately for him, we had an insider in the State Sup's office who kept me up to date on what they did and said. That info went out in bulletins to our union members, infuriating our Superintendent.

Part of the scare tactics dreamt up by the Superintendent was his announcement to the press that the school district was so broke that it would only be able to pay the teachers in "scrip", a kind of IOU. Of course, this was a self-created "broke-ness". The Board had transferred huge sums of money from the educational fund used for teachers' salaries to other funds. Thus our source of funding was underwater while others had substantial surpluses. We pinpointed this treachery and let the media know that emptying one pocket while stuffing others didn't make one "broke". Amazingly, funds were transferred back to their proper place and the financial "crisis" was over. We called a public meeting to review with parents what the Board was doing: taking away seniority rights, severance pay, and the right of teachers to have any say in matters concerning teaching. It lengthened the school year by three days without additional pay. The Board also was against allowing the school district's financial records to be examined. It wouldn't submit matters to mediation, or binding arbitration. The public didn't take kindly to these disclosures.

On Wednesday, August 30, 1967, the school year began with an "institute day", which meant all the teachers were to report to the large senior high school auditorium to hear the Superintendent and other district officials speak. We had a counter-meeting—an "unemployed teachers' picnic". Fewer than 200 teachers showed up at the institute day, while we had over 500 at our picnic. We also had TV, radio, and newspaper people roaming through our picnic crowd. We organized baseball and football teams and told the press that we had plenty of time for an entire tournament. My biggest disappointment that day: I lost three consecutive games of horseshoes.

We had a PA system at the park so that as teachers reported the number of teachers and pupils in their respective schools those results were announced to the gathered crowd, who received each announcement with applause and cheers. We had completely closed nearly half the schools and the others had only a few teachers. Only 8,000 of the district's 24,000 students showed up on the first school attendance day, and then rapidly reduced to fewer than 2,000 in just a few days. We announced an "unemployment committee" to seek jobs for teachers and invited offers from businesses and industries to hire "people with bachelor's and master's degrees in all fields". The public began to be very uneasy; parents started picketing the Board building.

The Board declared that it would fire all teachers that didn't report to work. Our answer is, "Don't bother. We've quit. You can't fire ex-employees."

The County Superintendent of Schools sent a letter to all our teachers warning them that they were acting "illegally" and issuing a myriad of threats. However, we got wind of this so our letter to the teachers arrived on the same day. No one walked back into school.

The State Superintendent announced publicly that if the teachers didn't return to work, he would be forced to "seriously consider revoking their teachers' certificates." This was the opposition's atomic weapon, for without a certificate a teacher could not only not teach in Illinois but anywhere else.

We didn't wait long to react. The evening news that same day carried our answer: "Mr. Superintendent, we dare you." He cabled our Supt. stating that it was going to be necessary to come to East St. Louis to intervene personally. On hearing this we responded that we'd be glad to have him, and we'd meet him with a band and a parade.

When the threat of certificate revocation was made the Illinois Federation of Teachers, our parent organization in the state, responded in a press conference: if the teacher certificates of the East St. Louis union teachers were revoked the 35,000 IFT members across Illinois would walk out.

We never heard from the State Superintendent again. Our local Superintendent was beginning to get the idea that we were nowhere near crying "uncle". Negotiations began to bear fruit. All the deletions threatened were reversed. Small concessions were made by the administration. The date now was September 7, ten days after the scheduled opening of school. The Board announced that it was going to seek an injunction (again). But its ammunition was running low. The teachers were calmer than they'd ever been.

The injunction petition was filed and an injunction was granted, ordering, among other things, that the teachers were "hereby enjoined and restrained from refusing to do any work for...plaintiff." That was a negative way of saying that we had to work for the school board. Hmmm. Slavery?

Before the injunction the Board met "in secret", but we found out about it and invited a reporter to go with us to see how the Board would respond to our entreaty to meet. They wouldn't let us in—a violation of a new Illinois law requiring open meetings. We pounded on the door but were refused admission. This pissed off the reporter who wrote a scathing article for the next day's paper, citing the "secret meeting" as a violation of the law. We drove a large vehicle alongside the Board building and stood on the vehicle's roof, taking flash bulb photos of the meeting inside, revealing some surprised-looking faces. Our request to the State's Attorney to prosecute the Board members for meeting in secret was refused, admitting that he wouldn't interfere because "politics was involved".

The negotiating session the next night was joined by a furious crowd of parents who were fed up with the Board's incessant refusal to bargain in good faith. The parent-picketing outside the Board building grew and the crowd became very boisterous and loud. Finally, on September 12, 1967, the dispute was settled. We gained benefits we didn't have before, and wages were submitted to a fact-finding board.

The greatest achievement, though, had nothing to do with the terms of the new contract. The victory was in our endurance. Teachers all over the country gained from our determination. The terms of our contract began to appear in teacher contracts all over the country.

My time as a teacher was nearing an end. I had started teaching at age 21 and by age 25 was leading one of the largest and certainly most active teachers' unions in the country. There had been many challenges. When 1967 approached its end, I announced to my union that in the summer of 1968, I would graduate from law school and would resign as a teacher. I thanked the union members for their incredible strength and bravery.

There is an episode that occurred during one of these strikes that should be mentioned. While I was in law school and a full-time teacher and President of Local 1220, one of the numerous injunctions was issued and served on

me as I picketed in front of Clark Jr. High, my school. The
TV stations were there to witness me being served. I tore
up the injunction while on camera and stated I was not
about to obey it. As you might imagine, this did not go over
particularly well at St. Louis University School of Law. The
next day I was called into Dean Richard Childress' office,
where he said, "You know, a lawyer—and a law student—
are expected to honor the law and obey lawful orders. How
do you explain yourself?" I knew Dean Childress' history
as a civil rights advocate, and a marcher in defiance of
orders issued in the South against such marches. He was
in the front row of several of those acts of defiance. I tried
my best diplomatic voice: "Dean, I greatly respect you not
only as Dean, but also as a strong believer in civil rights.
You have shown great courage in those battles in engaging
in civil disobedience. I am fighting for teachers who have
been beaten down for decades, if not centuries. My civil
disobedience is meant to be for their greater good." He
looked at me and said, "Well stated. I will present this
argument to our faculty for a decision." I never heard about
the issue again. I graduated from law school on time.

During my time as President of Local 1220, I would
sometimes go the few blocks from my school to the union
office in the 4400 block of State Street in East St. Louis.
This would give me a couple of hours to do union work
before I had to be at law school. On one of those evenings,
the phone rang and Clyde Jordan , a person on the Board
given to conduct some might call criminal. He said, matter-
of-factly, "I'm going to kill you." Now, during my time as a
union leader, I had been shot at and threatened many times
by the thugs associated with the Board. But being the brash
person I was I responded to Clyde, "Clyde, you don't have
the balls. I'm here at the union office, only a matter of blocks
from your office. Come on down. I'll be waiting for you." He

never showed up or explained why he didn't. I didn't have a weapon, so it would have been an easy hit. Who knows what deterred him?

Endnotes

BOOK II

Chapter 20

[35] While our Local 1220 was an aggressive teachers' union, its Local number indicates that it was the 1,220th Local in the American Federation of Teachers, compared to New York City's Local 2. (Local 1 was, and is, Local 1, the Chicago Teachers Union.) Local 1220 was a mere mite in size in the mid-1960s, with about 1,100 members, compared to Local 2 with over 50,000 members. Local 2 was so large that it held its membership meetings in what was then Shea Stadium in NYC! Our two Locals then, represented how teachers' unions, both large and not nearly so large, could organize effectively and gain substantial improvements for teachers.

CHAPTER 21

Crime and the School Board

By the way, East St. Louis was the criminal home of Buster Wortman, the crime boss who lived in a very large castle-like home on a moated island in Collinsville, IL, not far from East St. Louis. Wikipedia describes him as "an American St. Louis-area bootlegger, gambler, criminal gang leader, and a former member of the Shelton Brothers Gang...Wortman would eventually succeed the Sheltons and take over St. Louis's gambling operations in southwest Illinois [East St. Louis] until his death." His outfit owned and operated a near monopoly on entertainment machines: slot machines, pinball machines, cigarette dispensing machines, etc. An example of the way they enforced their monopoly occurred when a tavern owner in East St. Louis decided not to allow Wortman's machines to be installed at his place. Soon after someone rolled a grenade through the doorway and blew the place to smithereens. This was the same outfit that dominated the school Board. Nice guys.

Above is a photo of Wortman's moated home.

Our union was well enough organized that during my officership we decided to run our own slate of Board candidates. We spent a lot of time sifting through possible candidates that were strong enough to resist the dominant Board members. We finally chose a Catholic nun, Sr. Annalinda Hellman; a strong, black civil rights leader, Dr. Fred Kimbrough; and a white economist, John Goss. All three were elected. We were elated! We shouldn't have been. Even the nun, Sr. Annalinda, was convicted of federal crimes related to the school board and sent to prison. John Goss remained true and honest. I was intrigued as to how the nun was convinced to play the Board's game, so I talked to her. She said that Charlie Merritts, the president of the Board, approached her after her election and told her, "Sister, I know your primary concern on the Board is education of the children. So, I'll see that every proposal you make on education matters will be passed. In return, I'll expect you to support my proposals." Stupidly, she agreed. Of course, "his proposals" were crooked, inflated sales of musical instruments and other Board-purchased items, which gave Charlie and his cohorts kickbacks, leaving her out of that. Charlie Merritts himself would finally end up indicted, too.

More than indicted. On March 10, 2010, in the internet version of St. Louis Today newspaper, to-wit: stltoday.com, in an article by Michael D. Sorkin, stated the following:

"Charles Merritts, Sr. was many things: president of the School Board in East St. Louis, owner of a thriving chain of businesses, and once the most influential political force in town.

"I'm the boss," he once boasted, and tried to prove it by arranging the murder of a political rival.

******

His parents were sharecroppers in Oklahoma who fled after boll weevils destroyed their farm. They took a train to St. Louis but got off in East St. Louis by accident. They stayed because they didn't have the money to go the rest of the way.

******

One critic was fellow School Board member and newspaper publisher Clyde Jordan. [Yep, the same Clyde Jordan that threatened to kill me as recounted earlier.]

"I ain't going to stand for any criticism," Mr. Merritts said. He conspired with a middleman to kill Jordan but failed when they tried to hire an undercover FBI agent as hitman.

Mr. Merritts pleaded guilty in the attempted murder, and of extortion with five other School Board members. He was sentenced to five years in a federal prison."

It took several years for the investigation into the Board's activities to catch up with Sr. Annalinda, but the New York Times reported on it when the indictment came down:

> EAST ST. LOUIS, Ill., April 29 (AP)—Sister Annalinda Hellman, a nun and a former member of the East St. Louis School District 189 Board of Education, and William Little, a district employe, pleaded not guilty today to Federal extortion and conspiracy charges. Both are charged with conspiracy to extort more than $2,000 from St. Louis school supply company that had contracts with the district.

So this chapter of my life was drawing to a close. It was difficult to leave the many brave and dedicated teachers who had shown such courage and determination. It was a credit to them that students looked up to the striking teachers as people who believed in strong values and who risked everything to make things right. Some might think that those teachers brought disrepute to their profession. I would argue that they stood up to organized crime and a foul system of "education" and eventually uprooted much of the corruption, while at the same time gaining a voice for teachers that benefitted all. No one else could have done it. They did.

CHAPTER 22

Bar Exams; Starting Lawyer

The summer of 1968 kept me fully occupied studying for the bar exams, which I would take in two states: Illinois and Missouri. I was also working as a law intern for Rex Carr's firm in East St. Louis and was guaranteed a position there on passing the bar. I was admitted to the Illinois Bar on October 14, 1968. The Missouri license was to follow, but my focus was to be on the practice of law in Illinois, mainly in St. Clair County, directly across from St. Louis, Missouri.

I spent two years practicing law with Rex Carr, a phenomenal lawyer with the ability to quickly identify the legal issues involved in cases and the courage to try cases to a jury to get the best value. I'll never forget sitting in his office one day when an opposing lawyer called him with a multi-million dollar offer. Rex stopped him short. "Never. Let's try it." I thought to myself, "Gee, that was an awful lot of money. What gives him the confidence to refuse it?" But he was right, a jury awarded much more than he was offered.

One day coming back from lunch Rex met me at the office with Mr. Huddleston, introduced me, handed me his file, and said the jury trial was going to start in about an hour in Madison County, about an hour's drive away. I asked Rex what the case was about, and he responded that Mr. Huddleston would tell me on the way to the courthouse. Thank god Huddleston's role was as a third party, so I got to hear the guts of the case in the courtroom before it was our turn. Talk about sink or swim! We won a dismissal from the main action, which was the objective, so Mr. Huddleston was pleased, although he must have had enormous misgivings about being turned over to a greenhorn with zero knowledge of his situation.

Because of my teachers' union experience, Rex would often assign me to teachers' union-related legal activities. As a young lawyer, my former union, the East St. Louis Federation of Teachers, Local 1220 of the AFT, went on strike again, in 1970. The Board was being very rough this time, not only getting the usual injunction but enforcing it with police arrests on the picket lines. The arrested teachers were taken to the East St. Louis police station for booking and jailing, except I was there with over $100,000.00 in bail money to make sure none were jailed. So as the arrestees were brought in, I was in their line right behind them to seek bail and post the $100.00 for each teacher. The police officers were getting very frustrated because as each teacher was bailed out, he/she went right back to the picket lines. So the officers started yelling at me, telling me to stay away from the teachers and poking me with their batons, trying to separate me from them. I wasn't about to let that happen, so I was arrested, hand-cuffed, and taken upstairs to a jail cell along with Frank Smith, a leader of the United Front, a Black Panther-like organization. As it happened, Frank's first suggestion was that he take off his t-shirt and clog up the toilet so it would run over and flood below. We didn't realize that directly below our cell was the courtroom for the area, with Judge Billy Jones, presiding. The water from the toilet dripped down from the ceiling onto Judge Jones and his desk. He wasn't happy about this and instructed the officers present to go to the overhead cell and bring the occupants before him, as they did. Once there, he looked at me and said, "Mr. Kolker? What are you doing here?" I explained how I was doing my duty as an attorney for the teachers who were being brought in off the picket lines and providing their bail money. I also described the conduct of the police officers in interfering with my duties. He flew into a rage and demanded that those officers appear in front of him, "NOW!" They did and got a royal ass-chewing. I went back to my posting bail duties and Frank Smith was let go as well. I had been active in the East St. Louis Chapter of the NAACP for some time, and represented the United Front, too. Judge Jones was a former civil rights activist familiar with my civil rights activities. I'm sure this helped a little.

I had another short experience with jail as an attorney when helping in Madison County, immediately north of our county. There was a thick picket line at one of the schools and truck drivers, all union, stopped and refused to cross to deliver school meals, supplies, etc. A few scabs tried to cross and got a chorus of boos, yelling, and cursing. This drew the police, who arrested me as one of those on a picket line. Once again, I was trotted off to a jail cell, handcuffed, and put in a cell. My one phone call was to Rex, who came in a hurry. Rex had not only a high reputation in our area of Illinois, but all over the country, so his appearance caused consternation among the officials. I was immediately released, and I went back to the picket lines.

As a new attorney, I was subjected to a "tradition" for newly admitted lawyers to be assigned by the federal courts to represent an indigent accused criminal defendant. This was a supremely stupid practice, as I had zero experience as a criminal defense attorney—and, for that matter at that point had almost no experience with any trial practice. Nevertheless, I was appointed by federal judge William Juergens, presiding judge of what was then the Southern District of Illinois, to represent a man accused of bank robbery. I call this the "pink Cadillac case". My client was supposedly the "brains" behind the scheme he and two other ex-cons dreamed up while sitting at a bar in a small southern Illinois town. Of course, the nosy bartender heard most of their brave talk. They decided to rob a small bank in a neighboring town, thinking it would be an easy hit in the rarely policed rural area. First, they stole a pink Cadillac (yeah, how else to be unnoticed, right?). Needing a new license plate they scouted a Tennessee plate on a wrecked car in a junkyard nearby. Off these geniuses went to the bank, located in what was a one-street town, directly across the street from a general store. You know, the kind in those days that sold candy for kids, horseshoes, saddles, cattle feed, groceries, soda, magazines, and other country goods. This country store had a nice, big wooden porch with rocking chairs for the locals to solve the problems of the day. On robbery day that porch had one of the locals on the porch with his notepad, drawing up his worrisome farm budget. That notepad was handy to jot down the Tennessee license plate number and the descriptions of all three robbers. So, on the day in question, the pink Caddy pulled up to the bank, one of the guys stayed in the car to be the get-away driver, and the other two went into the bank, yelling, "It's a stick-up, and we mean it." The one teller hit the alarm button and ducked behind the cage to the floor, calling out to the bank president, who showed up to face our robbers. Behind the president was one of those huge safes with an enormously heavy round door, slightly open. He was ordered to go to the safe and show the fellows the money. Instead, he walked up to the safe door and kicked it shut. It slammed closed with a loud locking noise, whereupon the bank executive declared, "It's locked and won't open for 24 hours." This caused no small amount of consternation between the two heisters, who decided that it would be best to just leave and hightail it out of town, having gained zero loot. They had previously located an abandoned farmhouse about a mile away, so that's where they headed, observed, by this time by an overhead police helicopter, who corralled all the police within miles to surround the farmhouse once our villains arrived. They shortly came out, hands up, and were taken to a lockup to think about how well this had worked.

The jury trial for my accused bank robber was a disaster. The feds had made deals with the other two ex-cons, who testified about everything. When I cross-examined them, I thought my only hope was to show what despicable people these two were—and who couldn't be trusted to tell the truth. So, I asked one of them, "You were convicted and served time in prison for taking young girls across state lines, for purposes of sex, isn't that correct?" He answered, with sincerity all over his face, "Yes, sir." I went through a very long rap sheet that included about every nasty crime you could think of. Each time he answered, forthrightly and honestly, "Yes, sir." Of course, I asked each of them if they'd made a deal with the feds. No objection was made. Each quickly and unhesitatingly admitted that, yes, they'd agreed "to tell the truth", and were told that the feds would recommend a lighter sentence than they'd normally get if tried. Other witnesses included the bartender who heard the entire scheme, the guy in the rocker on the porch with his detailed notes, the bank president and the teller, and the various police who tracked the robbers to the farmhouse. Needless to say, the jury barely had time to elect a foreperson before it came back with a guilty verdict for my guy. He got 20 years because of his lengthy record. I slinked out of the courthouse a humbler person.

CHAPTER 23

City Attorney; My Own Practice

I had enormous admiration for Rex Carr, but we had differences politically. We were both Democrats, but Rex was supporting an old-line candidate for Mayor of East St. Louis, and my then-wife, Norma Sue, was working hard for his opponent, James Williams to be the first black mayor of the town. I supported James, too, but not with the vigor that Sue did, so she must get the credit for getting the win. But the mayoral contest, and other issues, divided Rex and me to the point that I left his office to form my own practice. Fortunately, Mayor Williams appointed me as general counsel in charge of the legal department of the City of East St. Louis, so I had a modest income of $15,000.00 a year from that.

As the city's attorney, I had many hats to wear. One was to attend city council meetings and render legal advice when sought. The council was a 5-member body, all elected in a city-wide vote. Mayor Williams had a three-vote majority in the beginning, but the other two: Ed Horrigan and Elmo Bush were skilled politicians determined to bring down Jim Williams. But there were other dynamics as well. One of the 3-member majority was Bob Mays, a man of small stature but feisty disposition. He had been a boxer, among other occupations. At one council meeting, Bobby and Ed got into an argument. Bobby was not one to avoid a good fight, so he and Ed stood up, faced off and Bobby knocked Ed out with a fist blow to the jaw. Police were called in and things were calmed down after Ed regained consciousness.

My predecessor as City Attorney had been in that position for years and neglected many things, including the city ordinances. Obviously, I felt that it was necessary to refer to those in the course of rendering advice. I found that over at least two decades of the ordinances were just thrown into a closet, literally. So there was a three-foot stack with no semblance of order and no reasonable way to access them. I hired a firm to help me sort through these, revise and edit them so that they were organized into chapters and sections, with an index, so that they were usable. The final product was then submitted to the council for study and a vote to approve. There were two volumes, hard-bound. They replaced any former loose ordinance, and the two volumes were to be the sole source of city laws. It was passed.

One of my other hats was to instruct the city's police officers on constitutional and municipal law. This was an almost comical duty, since the cops had no intention of paying any attention. They routinely lied on the stand in courtrooms, planted guns and dope on people they wanted to convict, and threatened and beat arrestees. I strongly, adamantly urged them to clean up their illegal acts. I could have been talking to the pavement. We were able to fire the worst offenders but couldn't clean up the whole lot because of resistance from political forces beyond our control. We had some decent, honest, hard-working people on the force, but the rotten apples tainted the batch.

My years as a private plaintiffs' attorney were the stuff of every plaintiffs' attorney. I steadily increased my representation of union teachers' unions affiliated with the American Federation of Teachers. There were many grievance hearings, disciplinary proceedings, and, of course, negotiations for new or renewed collective bargaining contracts. Some of these developed into major events. One that has burned into my memory was the strike of the Cahokia Federation of Teachers. Cahokia was and is a community south of East St. Louis. The Local's President at the time was Edward Geppert, a man of uncommon strength, moral authority, and intelligence. He was and still is gifted with enormous patience and common sense. Unfortunately, his School Board had no such gifts. We went through the usual steps: unsuccessful negotiations for a new collective bargaining contract, a strike vote by the teachers, an injunction issued by the court, and defiance of that injunction by the teachers. The leadership, including Ed Geppert, was arrested, brought before the court, and sent to jail — BUT a sympathetic judge listened to my counter-petition for application of equity (we were, after all, in an equity court). I argued that the Board had come to court with "unclean hands", dealing not just unfairly, but even illegally, by not addressing the concerns of the teachers. The judge partially agreed. His order was that the leadership would remain in jail, with a huge exception: they were to be released to my custody for negotiations with the Board, which was compelled by his order to meet every evening from 5 pm to 10 pm...and to bargain in good faith. The jailers were unionized, so they were very sympathetic to the jailed teachers, whose jailing conditions were pretty "loose". The jail door to each cell was left open, and when I came to pick them up, they were cooperative and understanding. We would go for dinner and drinks after negotiations and return fairly late. Outside the jail, there were picket lines of teachers, plumbers, electricians, carpenters, laborers, etc. from the region's unions. They honked their horns in constant vehicle encirclement and raised quite a ruckus. This drew much media attention. Of course, the Local's teachers remained on the picket lines, especially defiant because their leaders had been incarcerated. One comical aside: Judge Jerome Lopinot, one of the long-serving Circuit Judges, pulled me aside in the courthouse one day and said jokingly, "Charlie, my wife is a strong union teacher at Cahokia. Could you make sure she gets jailed?"

I was taking snacks, sodas, and reading materials to the jailed leaders, who were getting increasing positive press coverage. We would sometimes gather in one of the cells for meetings. Eventually, the pressure built so much that the Board buckled, and a settlement was eventually reached.

By the way, Ed Geppert continued to rise through the ranks of the Illinois Federation of Teachers, soon taking the top position and keeping it for some time. He is now retired, but I still see his postings on Facebook. He is a giant among men and a colossus among teacher unionists.

We unionists had argued that the use of injunctions and other punitive measures against striking teachers were counter-productive. We believed that if Boards negotiated in good faith, truly disclosed their finances, and expressed their concerns that there would be labor peace and strikes would dramatically reduce. The day came that showed we were right. First, a candidate for Governor of Illinois, Dan Walker, promised to issue an executive order on his election that state employees would have the right to organize, to bargain collectively, and to have legally enforceable bargaining agreements. I was his organizer for volunteers for southwest Illinois, comprising several counties. His Democratic opponent, Paul Simon, was from Troy, a small town in my sector. My job was to neutralize the expected heavy vote for Simon in my part of the state. We did that, and with Dan's walking the entire state end-to-end he won the primary and then the general election. True to his word, he issued the executive order he promised. It was not long before the then-dominate Democratic legislature used his executive order to fashion legislation to create an Act, which set out requirements for recognizing educational employee unions[36], guarantying grievance procedures, requiring good faith bargaining, and granting the right to strike after going through mediation attempts and if those attempts failed, providing that a notice to strike be given several days before it was to begin. Teacher strikes plummeted in Illinois; they have in the many years since never reached the level at which they were prior to the law. The law also created a state board to receive complaints from either side of violations of the law. Decisions reached by that Board were given the status of binding precedent throughout the state. This legislation was the result of many years of suffering, brutal strikes, and nearly endless threats against teachers...that they resisted. I'm proud to have had a part in this.

When computers came into more pronounced existence my oldest son, Jay, a computer expert with an education to match, pressed me to update my law office operations with computers. My first, in 1984, was a Panasonic Sr. Partner, a suitcase-sized piece of equipment that had two "floppy" drives: one 5 ¼" disc for the operating system and one for the data to be worked with. It was "transportable" at 31 lbs. It was terribly slow compared to what we have now, but it was "the cat's meow" then.

The Panasonic Senior Partner computer, the first Japanese
computer that was completely IBM-PC compatible.
It had a built-in thermal printer using paper rolls. Had a 9"
CRT green display. First shown at the Las Vegas Comdex,
November 1983.

Jay was responsible for making me only the second attorney in our county to use computers. Jay lived in Phoenix during our early computer years, and I owed him a lot for saving us by untangling problems that we encountered. I don't think I'll ever forget the time that Jay took a "red-eye" flight from Phoenix, landing at St. Louis airport in the night, working all night at our office solving our computer problems, and returning to Phoenix to his regular job. He also wired our office so that multiple computers and printers could work together. This was no small feat.

In some ways, the practice of law was not as exciting and challenging as the teacher unionism had been. Certainly, law practice requires discipline, very hard work, and dedication. I found myself working 6-7 days a week, often 12 hours a day. There were times on a Sunday afternoon when the sun was out, and others were enjoying family time or just relaxing that I found myself in my law office poring over cases and digging into facts to support a case. My practice was incredibly varied. I wrote wills, did some probate work, did many divorces, represented many teachers' unions and, of course, took and tried to juries plaintiffs' personal injury cases. The divorce cases were tried by a judge, not a jury, but they still required much preparation and not a little emotional stress. Every divorce lawyer can tell you stories of getting nearly everything settled—except the family dog, a pickup truck, or some useless piece of furniture. I would tell clients that a trial would not necessarily mean they'd get that dog, pickup, or piece of furniture, but divorces have such an element of unreasonableness that, sometimes, logic and common sense get lost. I did a substantial amount of teacher union representation: grievance hearings, discipline proceedings, and matters before the Illinois Educational Labor Board (after the IELRA was enacted). I was a member of the East St. Louis NAACP Board, and a pro bono legal counsel for it and some civil rights cases.

One civil rights case I'll never forget. My client was an elderly black man who probably had a little too much to drink. The police picked him up and put him in the caged back of a patrol car. That was not unusual. What happened next was far out of the usual. The white cop who arrested him decided that it was not enough that the man was handcuffed behind his back and confined to the back of a patrol car. He decided he would reach inside the vehicle with his baton and beat the man severely in the face, knocking out teeth, blacking his eyes, and breaking facial bones. I was able to retrieve one of the knocked-out teeth. The trial was to a jury in federal court in Alton, IL, north of St. Clair County where I usually practiced. The man was able to testify and related what had happened to him, describing that he had not resisted arrest, had not bad-mouthed the police officer, and besides that, was unable to because of the confined area he was in when beaten and his handcuffing. Numerous photos showed the awful state of his face after the beating. At one point in his testimony, I showed him the tooth, which had a long root, and asked him to identify it and show the jury where it had been in his mouth before it was knocked out. In Closing Argument I approached the jury box with that tooth, asking if they'd pass it around. The looks of repulsion on their faces were indicative of what they were going to do. And they did. They returned a sizeable verdict, and judgment was entered upon it.

Endnotes

BOOK II

Chapter 23

[36] 115 ILCS 5/ Illinois Educational Labor Relations Act. ...."It is the purpose of this Act to regulate labor relations between educational employers and educational employees, including the designation of educational employee representatives, negotiation of wages, hours and other conditions of employment and resolution of disputes arising under collective bargaining agreements." The IELRA took effect on January 1, 1984

CHAPTER 24

The Flood Case

Probably the most consequential case I had lasted thirteen years. Some background needs laying first. East St. Louis borders the Mississippi River, with St. Louis, Missouri on the opposite side. Occasionally that river floods. To control the floods, especially on the Illinois side, which is lower in elevation than the Missouri side, the East Side Levee District, known as the Metro East Sanitary District (MESD), was created, which had the authority, equipment, and supposed knowledge to build massive dirt levees that were 15-20 feet high, interrupted by gaps in the levee that would allow traffic in and out during low-water times. These gates were multi-ton structures of heavy steel, fitted into vertical tracks that would allow them to be lowered and raised electronically. At each of these locations, there were at least two sets of these huge gates so that there would be a backup if the first gate failed for any reason. It was the explicit duty of MESD to maintain these gates, but also to inspect them regularly and correct any problems. MESD had a long history of corruption. Highly paid, but usually absent, "gopher patrollers" were hired to look for weaknesses in the levees. Other also highly paid political appointees were "inspectors" of the gates, their supporting structures, and the tunnels into which they fitted.

I could easily write an entire book on this case, but you can be thankful that that is not going to happen here. But the essentials are these: On October 4, 1986, the Mississippi River was in flood stage, threatening to come out of its banks. When the river reached flood stage, MESD was to close the huge gates in viaducts leading through the levees into East St. Louis, thereby preventing the river from surging into the city. In the diagram below, imagine the City of East St. Louis at the top and the Mississippi at the bottom. The arrows indicate the normal flow of sewage out of the city through the sewage treatment plant (the box with the ovals) and then out into the river. Note the position and number of gates. These were to enable the blocking of the tunnels normally carrying sewage so that the river would not enter those tunnels going in the opposite direction into the city. There were supposed to be three of those gates (numbered 1, 2, and 3) — so there was intended to be a triple barrier to prevent the city from being flooded.

This way to the city of East St. Louis, IL.

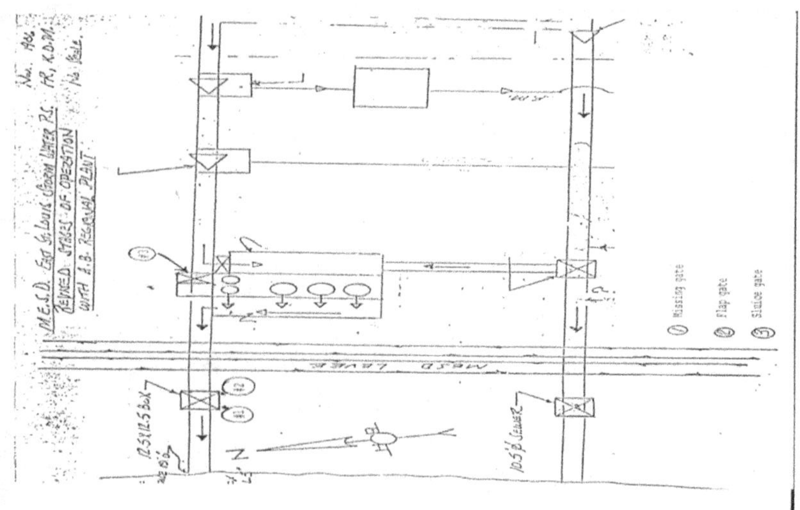

Mississippi River

Now, these gates weren't your garden-variety gates. They were massive, at 18 tons each. They fit into heavy metal frames inside the 12' tunnels. Yours truly, as he was in 1988, is standing in one of those tunnels next to a gate frame, above.

I had a professional photographer take hundreds of photos of the mangled gates that had been taken out of the tunnels and kept, under court order, in a fenced enclosure to prevent tampering. Above is a photo of one of the gates. Note the torn-off or partial rollers, which had so corroded that they were unable to withstand the force of the river coming through the tunnel.

The gate structure itself was buckled because of corrosion. Maybe one of the most remarkable discoveries was that Gate #1 (see diagram) was missing altogether! At first MESD personnel tried to deny it was missing, which it plainly was, then denied how that could possibly be. But we discovered a witness who saw the eight-story crane lift the gate out of its moorings just as the flood season was about to begin. Plus, MESD's own diagram showed the gate as gone.

Shortly after the case was filed and certified as a class action (a decision that was appealed three times) I was at a bar association meeting which was followed by a gathering at the booze bar. Soon I was surrounded by a bevy of defense lawyers who told me, "Charlie, we're going to drive you into bankruptcy before you ever get this case to trial." I replied, "We'll see."

Despite my efforts in court to restrict depositions, the defendants were able to take over 400 depositions. There was an enormous number of court hearings at which each defendant (there were four) would bring two or more lawyers. It was a defense attorneys' fee fest. By the end of the case, I had about 15 four-drawer file cabinets full of exhibits, deposition transcripts, briefs, and memoranda. In my preparations for the trial, I had prepared a truck and crew to deliver the file cabinets to the courthouse's largest courtroom.

One deposition I took—which took three days—was of the "chief engineer" of MESD. I wanted him to confirm the authenticity of the photos taken of the gates, the tunnels, the diagrams of the tunnel routes, etc. But first I wanted to check his credentials. I asked him, "Mr. Greathouse, I see on the MESD letterhead that you are listed as the "Chief Engineer". Where did you get your engineering degree?" His answer was, "I'm not an engineer. I don't have any degrees." With that came a stunned silence while I watched his attorney's mouth drop to the floor.

The 400+ depositions taken of a segment of the flood victims revealed a horrendous result of the torrent of flood waters that ripped through the MESD tunnels into the city's sewer system. Because of the theft of the heavy iron sewer lids, the city had them welded to their frames in the street pavement. The force of the water blew those lids out of their moorings, sometimes heaving a heavy sewer lid atop a 25-foot geyser in the middle of the street. With the flood waters rushing through the sewers came all the city's sewage, including not only feces and urine, but snakes, rats, and other vermin. One disabled lady, confined to her bed on the raised first story of her home, testified to the horror of seeing the sewage rising to her bedside with snakes and rats with it...and being unable to escape. Thankfully, neighbors arrived in a boat and carried her out of the house into the boat and to a rescue center. There were hundreds of these stories, telling of the loss of everything these already poor people owned: cars, furniture, clothing, toys, family photos, and the home itself, soaked in sewage or completely washed away.

I mentioned other defendants. One was Pfizer, an international company that had a large chemical company in East St. Louis, which had dumped decades of corrosive paint and other chemicals into the sewer system that made its way to those gates and tunnels of MESD. During the case, the local Pfizer attorney invited me to a "discussion of possible resolution of its involvement in the case", which took place at a large law firm in St. Louis. When I arrived for this "discussion" there were 20 attorneys from Pfizer, from all over the world. A large contingent was from its London office, so I was privileged to engage with some very proper solicitors and barristers of the English bar. In a way, it was a little comical, with all those legal forces arrayed around the table with Charlie Kolker, alone, representing the Plaintiff Class. After much hemming and hawing, the head Englishman offered a million dollars to settle their part of the case. I stared at him as if he'd thrown a dead fish on the table, then started laughing, which wasn't accepted in good humor. I asked the assemblage why they'd wasted so much money to gather everyone there to make such a ridiculous offer, which I refused, saying, "I have an obligation to convey this waste of time to my clients, but it will be accompanied by my very strong recommendation to reject it, and I would be surprised if my recommendation were not taken." They immediately jacked up the offer to a million and a half. My answer was the same. I had created a plaintiffs' class board early on in the case, assembling all known members of the class to a meeting at which they elected a broad spectrum of their group to the "board", which was voted to have the authority to hear offers, be updated on hearings, appeals and other developments and to report back to the class assembled periodically. The Board rejected the Pfizer offers.

Eventually, the defendants demanded at a hearing that the Plaintiff Class submit a list of experts, with a summary of their expected testimony. I think they were surprised at the next hearing when I placed in front of each defendants' attorney a foot-thick list of experts with summaries. The trial judge looked at his copy and blanched, realizing that this was not to be a short trial. Of course, the defendants immediately demanded to take depositions of each of the experts. I explained that would take years and reminded the court that these experts had been disclosed by each member of the class as he/she was deposed. The judge then asked that I submit a trial memorandum with the witnesses and the experts listed, an estimate of the time for each witness to testify and be cross-examined, and the total time to try the case. I told the judge that if, by some miracle, each witness took only a half hour, and taking into account the number of jury trial days in a calendar year that the trial would take a minimum of four years, but more likely five or more. He instantly told the assembled attorneys, "See me in my chambers...NOW!" At the crowded chambers, he told us, "There is no way I'm going to allow you to use this courthouse for four to five years to try this case. I very strongly am telling you, get serious, and settle this case. You won't like it if you make me try this case." Soon thereafter, he issued an order that the Plaintiff Class would try the case in groups of ten, the members of each group to be chosen by the Class, and after each group was tried and the jury rendered its decision, there would be a settlement conference.

Meanwhile, defendants were beginning to realize that they were spending millions of dollars to feed and clothe their gangs of attorneys, pay for deposition transcripts, and listen to their attorneys recount the horrific tales they heard in plaintiffs' depositions. When they realized that they might be in for 4-5 years more of $200 an hour attorneys' fees, with a possible sizable jury verdict (and punitive damages a real possibility) against them at the end, it was beginning to dawn on them that maybe talking turkey might be a good idea. They had not bankrupted me.

So, after 13 years the defendants, after many failed offers, made an offer that made sense. It was no small thing to get this offer past the Plaintiffs Class Board and then the assembled Class Members, hire an adjuster to adjust the claims of each recognized member of the class, hear objections to those adjustments, file motions and get them heard on the proposed distributions of the settlement money—all of which took another 3-4 years. But despite all this, each Plaintiff Class Member was paid 100% of his/her adjusted claim, even after attorney's fees. During the case, other attorneys tried to muscle in on the case. Some eventually withdrew and surrendered their cases and any interest in them, to me. Indeed, they were facing the financial strains of supporting the case. One attorney tried to hang on, so I filed a motion to discharge him from representation in the case, seeking an order that any and all interest he might have in the case be surrendered. The reason: he hadn't attended a single deposition, hadn't fought against a single defendant's motion, hadn't helped in the multiple appeals, appeared in court only to claim unearned attorney's fees, and even after multiple pleas from me in letters to him to help in the case, had not bothered to respond. The court ordered him to be discharged from the case, with no fees.

Before I leave this case and its part in my legal history, major credit in winning what we called "the flood case" must be given to two incredible paralegals: Geri Stallman and Beth Lenz, who marshaled the evidence in the case, managed the hundreds of telephone calls from plaintiffs, put together massive discovery documents, (including that foot tall List of Experts), organized the materials for trial, and many, many other tasks without which the case would not have successfully concluded. Additionally, my youngest son, Chris Kolker, who joined the firm after he was sworn in, contributed mightily with advice and help of both legal and practical form; in fact, without him, I'd probably still be fighting that case.

CHAPTER 25

Catherine Sue Martin

During the battles of the flood case and other legal skirmishes I had the wonderful fortune of meeting a very beautiful and very brilliant woman, Catherine Sue Martin. She helped me in so many ways it would take reams of paper to recount. She was an RN working at Belleville, Illinois, Memorial Hospital when she was introduced to me by a friend of Sue's. We were married in the St. Louis, Missouri Botanical Gardens on June 2, 1990, after nearly two years of courtship. Sue would complete her BSN (Bachelor of Science in Nursing) from McKendree College in 1990 and an MSN (Master of Science in Nursing) from St. Louis University in 1995. Sue has been the mainstay of my life. She is a patient woman to have put up with all my shenanigans; I love her with all my heart.

Sue and I at our wedding at Missouri Botanical Gardens,
St. Louis, Missouri, June 2, 1990.

On our first date, I didn't explain what we were going to do, so it was surely a surprise to her when we arrived at Bi-State Airport in Cahokia, Illinois, and approached a plane I had rented for the occasion. I was still actively flying then, and I checked out the plane with the usual checklist and helped secure her in the passenger front seat. We took off and flew south alongside the Mississippi River toward the Kentucky border. Once in the air and over the river, I told her it was the custom for new female passengers to kiss the pilot. This was, of course, an invention of the moment, but she complied, and my heart soared with the plane.

CHAPTER 26

Studying French at Cannes, France

In the late 1980s, I decided to take a month off from the practice of law to study French at a college in Cannes, France. The classes were held in the mornings from 8 a.m. to noon. The college was very close to the Mediterranean Sea. On the first day when studies ended at noon, the bell rang and everyone except an American doctor and myself stripped completely naked and ran into the sea to swim. Needless to say, seeing a group of about 15 20-somethings dash out in their youthful splendor made me forget the lesson of the day—except maybe that was the lesson.

I was able to get a room in Cannes in a quite fashionable house overlooking the Med Sea. It was owned by two widowed ladies, one of whom spoke no English and the other only a few words of English. We were a pretty good match because we had to patiently try our non-native tongues on each other, which is a good way to learn.

One day one of the ladies showed me a bulletin board in the dining room of the home that was partially filled with photos. One of the photos showed an incredibly beautiful young woman of maybe 19, standing on a beach with absolutely nothing on. It was explained that this was a niece of the hostess. Not one syllable was uttered about the nudity. I complimented my hostess for being so lucky to have such an attractive relative.

While living in Cannes with the widows one of them invited me to accompany her as she voted. Interestingly, she was a monarchist who followed the living heirs of the last

French royal head of state. I went into the polling place—
the likes of which I'd never seen before, as it was a former
palace of Baron de Rothschild. The room where she picked
up her ballot was a massive hall with 30-foot ceilings, marble
columns abounding, and a marble floor to boot. At least at
that time, voters selected from available ballots arranged
by color, so that monarchists picked a different color from
other political parties, each of which had its own distinct
color.

CHAPTER 27

A New Life: China

In 2003, with the flood case settled and the funds distributed to the victims, the file was closed and so was the end of my legal career. For about two years I had begun to suffer from burnout. 70, 80, and even 90-hour work weeks were taking a toll. I was ready to do something different. With some reluctance, my youngest son, Chris, a Magna Cum Laude law school graduate, member of an acclaimed law school debate team, and Law Journal writer who had reason to believe he'd get a high-paying job offer, accepted our negotiated transfer of my law practice to him and it was time for me to leave. Now I'd be going to an entirely new career—professor of English and other subjects at Shenzhen University in Shenzhen, China.

It really wasn't an entirely new career—professor of English and other subjects at Shenzhen University, Shenzhen, China. In fact, part of the reason I was attractive as a teaching candidate was that I had taught for 6 years, although at the junior high school level.

Not that anyone would listen, but I'd advise anyone thinking of retiring to allow at least a year, better yet, two years, to plan what retired life will be. I didn't want to just sit around and gather mold; my objective was to do something completely different. But what? Since I taught English before that seemed a good place to start, but that wasn't different enough. So the internet searches for "teaching English as a second language" produced lots of information. There were many opportunities and the first was teaching in what was then Czechoslovakia. I came very close to taking that, but the pay was so dismal that the cost of living exceeded the money earned. Back to the drawing board. Somehow China began to dominate the choices, to the point where there were 50 openings! To narrow this down I eliminated any teaching job below the university level. Then a little temperature checking led me to drop any jobs north of the Yangtze River—too cold. Finally, it was down to just a handful in southeast China. Shenzhen sounded attractive as it was just across the Shenzhen River from the Hong Kong territories, and Shenzhen University had an attractive pay and benefits package.

But I'm getting ahead of myself. The searches also identified credentialing options that I should consider before applying for a teaching position. If I obtained a Cambridge English Language Teaching Certificate that seemed a good way to up my chances of being accepted. Cambridge University had just such a course in Halifax, Nova Scotia, Canada, at the International Language Institute, so I enrolled in an intense month-long experience, from August 19, 2002, to September 13, 2002. Half the day was spent studying teaching techniques and the other half as a "practice teacher". Recent immigrants to Canada could enroll in these English language classes free of charge, with the knowledge that we weren't experienced teachers, but rookies. I had a very diverse group of students: Enio, from Cuba; Abdul Majeed, from Iraq; Victor, from Russia; Samir, from Egypt; Kais, from Lebanon; Caroline, from China; Lan, from China; Mary Ann, from Sudan; and Riyeon, from Korea. None knew any English. It was impossible to find a common language that was native to all of them. One of the techniques involved showing pictures of things and pronouncing the English word to identify it. Some of the students picked up on this quickly, others were dumb as rocks.

The Cambridge method is very rigid. A teaching hour was strictly divided into parts: warm-up activity, including encouraging students to work in pairs; presentation—elicitation techniques: body language, eye contact, monitoring, learning styles, etc.; controlled practice; freer practice activity; review/wrap-up. Each of these sections was to be conducted for a precise number of minutes per section. It was way too structured for my taste, but, hey, I signed up for this gig. To say it was challenging would be an understatement. Nevertheless, I graduated and obtained my CELTA to show off to prospective employers.

What became obvious was that there were tremendous opportunities in mainland China. But the openings were for a wide range of teaching jobs: adult education, elementary school, jobs in small villages far inland, and high school jobs. I decided I'd try only for university-level teaching. That narrowed the scope considerably. Next was deleting all openings north of the Yangtze River—too cold. Gradually the options were narrowed to southeast China—mainly Guangdong Province along the Pearl River Delta. One city especially stood out: Shenzhen.

CHAPTER 28

Intermission: Political Experiences

A huge part of my life has been omitted thus far, and that part was interspersed with all the rest of my life—my political life. Again, some context is important. At that time, and to this day, St. Clair County, Illinois, where I lived and where most of my trials occurred as a lawyer, was heavily Democratic, so much so that to be elected one was usually forced to deal with the county Democratic Party to have any success in politics. I was then, and still am, a liberal Democrat, but considered myself a reformer of sorts. I've mentioned before efforts to win school board elections in East St. Louis, which was super heavily dominated by the Democratic Party. With many others in the teachers' union, I was able to organize a precinct-by-precinct organization in the school district. We selected reform-minded Democrats to run for school board. This was unheard of at the time. We began to win. I was campaign manager for about 10-12 of those elections, all of which we won, then spread out across the rest of the county, drawing even more attention. Then I let my success as a kingmaker get to my head, so I ran for State Representative. I lost. Later, in 1988, I ran for Judge of the Illinois Supreme Court (judges in Illinois are elected by the people, not appointed). Supreme Court Judges in Illinois are elected by District, so I didn't have to campaign across the entire state, but "only" the southern part, roughly from Springfield, south to Kentucky, east of the Indiana border, and on the west the Missouri border. That's a lot of real estate. I was persuaded to make this run by Patrick Quinn, who I'd known from the Dan Walker for Governor campaign. He rounded up donors and gave advice. Pat became a friend who stayed at our house in East St. Louis several times as he ran for various offices in Illinois. He became Lt. Governor of Illinois in 2002 and became Governor when Rod Blagoevich was removed from office. Pat then ran for Governor and was elected. He became the second Governor of Illinois that I knew personally (the first was Dan Walker). But the Democratic Parties in St. Clair and Madison Counties endorsed Horace Calvo, a fine man, with judicial experience, but who was much, much older than I. I tried to argue that the Democrats should be putting a young man on the Supreme Court. (Calvo, unfortunately, proved my point once he was on the Court. He died three years into his 10-year term.)

An important race

By THOMAS L. AMBERG
Chief of the Springfield Bureau

SPRINGFIELD, ILL.—There are three things which become clear in traveling throughout southern and central Illinois in the month prior to the primary election:

1: Most voters (and that's not an understatement) don't know who the candidates are. 2: Most voters (and this certainly isn't an understatement) don't know anything about the candidates or what they stand for. 3: Most voters (no understatement here, either) vote solely on name recognition.

Despite this, the results of most elections in southern and central Illinois really don't make a whole lot of difference. The candidates for the state legislature quite often are similar in either political background, ability, or enthusiasm for the job. Give or take a few rotten apples, southern and central Illinois have elected fairly dedicated men and women.

HOWEVER, IT SHOULD BE pointed out that every once in a while there is a race for the legislature where the candidates are most certainly different in political background, ability and enthusiasm for the job, and where who is elected does make a profound difference.

This is the case this year on the East Side, where an incredibly laggard and undistinguished incumbent State Representativ is being opposed by a particularly bright, able and dynamic challenger. The incumbent legislator, with one of the poorest records in the House is Rep. James G. "Bud" Krause. The challenger is East St. Louis City Attorney Charles Kolker.

Krause, a product of a political machine, has introduced virtually nothing of importance to the East Side or the troubled city of East St. Louis in the House of Representatives. He is long remembered for his famous amendment to the Boat Registration and Safety Act, prohibiting the operation of a motorboat within 150 feet of a skin diver's buoy.

KRAUSE HAS BEEN active in only one area of legislation — insurance. When not in the legislature, he sells insurance. As for his voting record, he failed to vote on almost half the key legislation of the last session.

Kolker, on the other hand, is a candidate with specific ideas and a background of actively working for reform that lends credibility to his bid for office. He wants an end to the morally bankrupt system of squeezing "lugs" (a portion of a patronage employees' wages) out of employes who work for public office holders. He wants an Urban Homestead Act designed to help rejuvenate areas like East St. Louis. And he wants state funds for redevelopment of downtown areas in Belleville and East St. Louis.

The race in the 57th District really does make a difference. Bud Krause is a nice guy who hasn't done anything. Charlie Kolker is a nice guy who plans to do something.

Mar. 2-3, 1974   **St. Louis Globe-Democrat**   3B

VOTE
MARCH 19

☒

ON THE
DEMOCRATIC
BALLOT
VOTE FOR

COUNTY CLERK
RICHARD
ROTH

STATE
REPRESENTATIVE
CHARLES
KOLKER

HENRY
NICHOLSON

INDEPENDENT
CITIZENS FOR
POLITICAL
ACTION

P. O. BOX 973
EDGEMONT STATION
EAST ST. LOUIS
ILLINOIS 62203

Reprinted by Permission of the Globe Democrat

I did get some major newspaper endorsements for the State Representative race in 1974. The St. Louis Globe Democrat, in an editorial of March 2-3, 1974, wrote the article above.

After teaching in China from 2003-2006 Sue and I returned to Elgin, Oklahoma, a town then of about 4,000 people (while Shenzhen was about 12.5 million, or close to 18 million if one counted the "migrants"---people who came to Shenzhen to work but who were not counted as city citizens), I began attending meetings of the Comanche County, Oklahoma Democratic Party. Soon the party members elected me to be Director of Organization, followed by election to be Chair in 2013 for a two-year term. I was re-elected to a second two-year term in 2015. I remained active in that county party after retiring from the officer position in 2017. Then, in 2023 I led a revolt from that party because the new leadership was alienating volunteers, spending the party's money without much, if any, disclosure, and many other problems. We formed the Southwest Oklahoma Progressives (SWOP) and I was elected Chair.

Charles Kolker Family. Taken at Mom's funeral dinner at St. Ann's Hall, Elgin, Oklahoma, January 1997.
(L-R) Charlie, Sue Martin Kolker, Jay, Cyndi, and Chris.

CHAPTER 29

Shenzhen University

Back to Shenzhen University. Once Sue and I decided to take the adventure to China we consulted with some people who'd been to China. So we stocked up on toothpaste, hand soap, and other "essentials", packing twelve large packing cases with stuff. We landed in Hong Kong and took a bus to the border with mainland China, as Hong Kong was a separate entity then (unlike now), and that meant clearing customs leaving Hong Kong and again, a few feet later, clearing customs in China. There was much chatter by customs officials at all the cases we were taking, and more than wonderment when "Miss Pan", the foreign teacher person assigned to welcome us the next day. A van pulled up at the Holiday Inn in Shenzhen where we spent the night and we all wondered how those 12 containers were going to fit, plus us.

By the way, when we cleared Chinese customs, we were directed to a large bus, into which our belongings were placed. Besides the driver, it had only two passengers: Sue and me. Off we went into the night to a destination unknown. It was not a short drive, but finally, we arrived at the most luxurious Holiday Inn I'd ever seen or seen since. There was a grand lobby with tall marble columns and fine furnishings. After much confusion, we got checked in and taken to our room. This was a room unlike any we'd seen before: an enormous space, with a bathroom the size of a small house and a bed fit for several kings and queens. Thus began an experience that Sue and I will never forget: three academic years in China.

The next day Miss Pan, the foreign teacher coordinator, showed up and we were loaded into a van, taken to Shenzhen University, and introduced to our "residence": apartment A305 in Chao Xi Lou, the Foreign Teachers Residence on campus. It was a large apartment, with an entranceway/living room, and two large rooms in each of what was once two separate apartments, one of the rooms became a bedroom and another became the office/study. There was a fairly small kitchen with a dining table. Unfortunately, there was no water heater for the sink water (we got one later). There was a large, five-gallon, water container set on a pedestal that provided hot and "cold" water. There were two bathrooms—one on each end of the apartment. Each bathroom had a shower with a water heater for each shower. While these accommodations were not the presidential suite, they were certainly adequate. We paid a small monthly price for our apartment.

Years after we'd returned from China, I was sitting in the barber chair in Elgin's Ambrose Style Shop, owned and operated by Kevin Ambrose. He knew I'd lived and taught in China, so he remarked, "Did you know I have an aunt, Mrs. Fesler, who taught in China?" I found that remarkable—that another person in the small town of Elgin, Oklahoma, had also taught in China, so I asked, "Where in China?" "Shenzhen", he answered. Now I was intrigued. This was doubly amazing that Elgin had produced two Shenzhen residents. "What university?" I asked, knowing that the city had many universities. "Shenzhen University." Now, this was not just remarkable, but phenomenal! Later Sue and I met Mrs. Fesler at a funeral in Elgin. We were curious as to where she lived while at SZU. "Chao Xi Lou", she answered.

"Wow!" we said, "We also lived there." "Which apartment?" "A305", she responded. We were floored! The exact same apartment we lived in!

I did so many stupid things getting ready for the Shenzhen University experience. I knew I was going to be teaching English to Chinese students. Therefore, I assumed, I should load up on English grammar and basic language books. I never used them. My English majors knew English grammar backwards and forwards and had been studying it since first grade.

Soon after settling into the apartment, I went exploring for places to do grocery and sundries shopping. I will never forget standing in front of a 20-foot-long display of every imaginable toothpaste brand from the USA and many other countries. The realization that all the stuff we brought just took up a lot of space for no reason became obvious. Shenzhen had many super Walmarts and Sam's as well as their Chinese equivalents. There were huge department stores, larger than any in the entire state of Oklahoma. There were gigantic, multi-story shopping centers, with beauty shops, restaurants of every imaginable kind, electronics stores with all the gadgets one could want, hardware stores, and on and on. Every day was full of discoveries. There was the time riding on a bus as we passed car dealers: Mercedes, Lamborghini, BMW, Rolls Royce, Jaguar, etc. This was 20 years ago, and it was obvious that this city had more than my wildest imagination could have dreamed of.

A little history of Shenzhen is in order. For that I'm going to quote from The Shenzhen Experiment, by Juan Du:

The Shenzhen special economic zone [SEZ] was one of the first initiatives orchestrated as part of China's Reform and Opening Up policy under Deng Xiaoping, paramount leader of the People's Republic of China (PRC) from 1978 to 1989. To transform China's stagnant economy, which had been closed off to the world for decades, reform-minded leaders sought to learn from neighboring free market countries and regions that had achieved economic successes. Deng endorsed the creation of three SEZs in 1980 as a cautious experiment with market reforms. Shenzhen was the first, followed by Zhuhai and Shantou. The locations of the SEZs were carefully chosen for their geographic proximity to neighbors with "foreign" market economies that could also be persuaded to become trade partners. The Shenzhen SEZ was adjacent to Hong Kong, while the Zhuhai SEZ was close to Macau, and the Shantou SEZ near Taiwan. Closed to "corrupt" foreign elements, the SEZs were separated from the rest of China by secondary military-patrolled borders. Until 2006, passports and visas were necessary to enter the SEZ district of Shenzhen from anywhere in China.[37]

The story of Shenzhen is that it rose from a fishing village of about 30,000 people in 1979 to a huge metropolis today. Some authorities give the 2021 population as 12.59 million and others say it's 17.8 million. There's a reason for this discrepancy: there are millions of people who live and work in Shenzhen who aren't counted in the "official" census of the city. They are the "migrants," people who come from inner China to work in Shenzhen and stay there, but who are not registered as residents even though they may have lived in Shenzhen for 20 years. This is the result of China's Hukou system, whereby one is born and registered in his/her village and remains a resident of that village no matter where that person has moved to. This causes enormous hardships for the "migrants", as they are not entitled to use the schools or other government services of the city to which they've moved. There has been much discussion in China about reforming this system, which began in 1958, but so far, it's still in place, although there are exceptions and some people seem to be able to get registered in their new place of residence. So if one were to count the actual people in Shenzhen the bet is that the number would be closer to 17.8 million rather than 12.59. Wikipedia lists Shenzhen as China's fourth largest city, following Shanghai, Beijing, and Guangzhou, with both Shenzhen and Guangzhou being over 17 million (and both of them are in the same province: Guangdong). The two cities are only 63 miles apart and it takes only 32 minutes by bullet train to go from north Shenzhen to south Guangzhou.

I certainly will never be able to adequately describe my first walk to the classroom building where I had my first class. I was giddy with delight at this challenge. Here I was surrounded by young, vibrant college students also headed to class. The scenery on the campus was a sensory bombshell: blossoming bushes and trees, a large lake on campus to my left, tall palm trees, a few banana trees, and the scents from the blossoms wafting through the air. I can remember my thoughts: "Wow! I did it! I'm here!"

I had a variety of classes while teaching at SZU. The first semester I was assigned to teach English as a second language, among other classes, to an adult class of about 30 students of ages 25 to 50. Most had little or no English language skills. I tried projecting photos of scenic places, pointing out features, and describing them in English. For a while, I thought this worked. Eventually, I asked some of the students to describe the entire scene. Finally, a student, obviously frustrated, asked me to describe it. My version went something like this: "there are mountains in the background, with a river, and birds flying. There are also dogs and a deer." This did not fit the Chinese way of looking at things. A student spoke up with his version: "The purple mountains are lovingly arranged with swooping, blackbirds floating in the sky. The water of the river glides romantically through the area, bringing peace and joy to all." This was my first lesson in understanding another culture. We don't have to think alike to be expressive in totally different ways. The Chinese that I taught seemed to feel much more emotion about their surroundings.

Gradually I began to appreciate this new (to me) way of expressing. Much later I taught a graduate-level course in English Creative Writing and used John Steinbeck to show my students his way of using few descriptive adjectives in laying out a scenario. I wasn't asking them to change their way of expression, but only to show that it was possible to do things another way.

Languages can be so interesting. Mandarin has its own logic. Yes, it's different than the logic of English, but who's to say one is better than the other? For example, we say "northeast," but they'd say "eastnorth." Is one better than the other? The Mandarin number system builds on the first ten numbers (usually). So, "yi" (pronounce "ee") is one; "er" (pronounced "r") is two; "san" (three); ten is "shi". Thus, eleven becomes "shi yi", twelve is "shi er"; and thirteen is "shi san," etc. When one gets to the twenties, twenty-one becomes "er shi yi" and so on.

My assigned classes varied a lot. In the first year, besides that adult class, most of my classes were teaching English speaking to freshman English majors. The task was to get the students to speak. This was not the usual challenge, because Chinese students have been taught to listen to the teacher and not speak—as that is considered rude, even as challenging authority. So there was a lot of urging on my part to get very reluctant students to speak up. It was not that they weren't smart; they were very smart—and well-disciplined. Acting up just didn't happen. Gradually, a few of the best students began to speak up, and others were encouraged by this and started joining in.

I had many learning experiences teaching at SZU. I'll never forget the gross mistake I made one day in a large class. There was a good-looking young Chinese man, maybe 20-21 years old, who had located himself to be surrounded by equally good-looking young Chinese women. He couldn't resist talking and flirting, to the point of distraction for the rest of the class. I called him out, moving him to another desk and reminding him that he was not to disturb his fellow students. After class he approached me at my desk and deeply bowed again and again, obviously ashamed of himself, begging for forgiveness. I had made him "lose face," a serious offense and culturally dumb. I should have found a much subtler way; it's not that it was wrong to stop the class disruption. It was wrong to damage this young man in front of his classmates that would be difficult for him to recover. It bothers me to this day.

Later, I taught English for Tourism, which I found a little amusing, as I was to teach Chinese students to pretend to show English-speaking tourists around various famous Chinese tourist spots. The students knew those places better than I, but that wasn't the purpose—it was to get them to talk and learn to express themselves in English. They knew the English language; English grammar they had down pat. Speaking out, though, was a different matter.

By my second academic year, I was teaching Speech. I developed a list of subjects that each student was to choose from, with no two alike. They didn't like this, as it meant they couldn't copy from one another. Each student was to research the subject, create slides to project on a screen, and talk about the topic, from memory, using gestures, facial expressiveness, voice projection, and, of course, correct English. They did surprisingly well.

I also taught European History. This was a challenge, as I was not supplied with a textbook. So I wrote one. It was never published, and would now be horribly outdated, as, for example, it covered modern European history, including the EU and its government, which has considerably changed since I taught the course.

Finally, I taught Intercultural Communications. This was an interesting course for both the students and me, as there was a textbook, written by a couple of Harvard professors, which covered the cultural histories, habits, and eccentricities of peoples throughout the world. We studied negotiating tactics of Russians as contrasted to Americans and Chinese, for example.

The classrooms were large and equipped well, and some classes were large, too. For example, my Intercultural Communications class of the Spring 2006 semester had 88 students.

Nearly all of my students had been studying English since the first grade. Their early-grade teachers encouraged them to adopt English names. Because of their ages at that point, the choice of names was sometimes unusual. I had one student whose name was Tomato; another was Eagle; yet another was Auspicious. Others, supposedly because they matured, changed their names to more "traditional" English names: Edwin, Sophie, Doris, Rebecca, etc.

Sue and I have often said that each day in Shenzhen brought a totally new experience. Skyscrapers shot up on the border of the campus. When we arrived there were none; by the time we left three years later, they surrounded the place. A 40-50 story skyscraper would rise from nothing to completion in a year.

Liu Yi, my English Department head, took us to many events or arranged for us to be taken to them. We attended a concert where a large orchestra played Western music as well as Chinese music. We were taken to a huge banquet hall where perhaps 2,000 people were seated. I noticed one of our exceptionally beautiful Chinese faculty women there—a fluent English speaker—and asked her what the event was all about. "Oh", she said, "It's a meeting of the Regional Communist Party." Great, I thought. How will I explain this when I'm back home? I asked her if she was a member of the Communist Party. She said, "Yeah, I belong but I don't believe in that stuff." She explained that belonging to the Communist Party was like belonging to a country club in the U.S. "One joins to make connections and get ahead."

On Woman's Day one year, we were taken to a hotel in Shenzhen for the celebration, not knowing what was in store for us. When we entered the hotel lobby there was a double line of young women waiting. We walked between the two lines to the elevator, rode up a floor, and when the door opened there was a blaze of very bright lights from TV cameras and flashes from still cameras. Of course, all this was to spotlight Sue, the woman of the day. We were escorted to the front of the banquet hall, seated at a table with flowers and nice tableware, and fed an excellent meal while listening to a series of speakers that we couldn't understand.

Shenzhen has a wide array of parks, including "Window of the World", located in Nanshan District, which has replicas of the wonders of the world, such as the Pyramids, Angkor

Wat of Cambodia, the Eiffel Tower, the canals of Venice, the Sidney Opera House, Niagara Falls, the Grand Canyon, and many, many other sites, all built at ratios of 1:1, 1:5 or 1:15. It's so massive that we weren't able to take it all in only one day.

Shenzhen also, at least at the time we were there, had the world's largest golf area. There were 10 eighteen-hole golf courses in one very large area.

One of the professors at SZU took Sue and me to a "rooftop party" with BBQ. There were many young people, most of whom were in Edward Zeng's classes at the university. They were very friendly and welcoming. The BBQ was good, and people were obviously having a good time. When I asked what the occasion was, Edward told me it was an informal gathering of the Young Communists. Whoops. Once again, we found ourselves gathering with an unfamiliar group. Years later Edward, his wife, Echo, and his son, Chuckie, then about 12 years old, stayed with Sue and me at our home in Oklahoma for several days. We took Edward and his family to a rodeo, where they saw longhorn steers, buffalo, bucking broncos, calf roping, and the whole rodeo scene. I think Edward took a thousand miles of videos!

Shenzhen, like several Chinese cities we visited, had what I guess would be called office buildings—often 20-30 stories high, filled with little shops selling every imaginable product: cameras, computers, printers, all kinds of tech stuff, fabrics, suit makers, kitchen goods, watches and on and on. At one of these, I bought a bag of Rolexes to give away when I got back to the States. Obviously, these were fakes, but they sure looked authentic—and they all kept good time!

Liu Yi would often set me up as a judge at speech contests held throughout Shenzhen. The contestants were most often high school students, English majors, who competed for awards in English speaking. These students were very impressive. They spoke clearly and correctly in English on a variety of topics. Ordinarily, I would be part of a three or four-member judging crew of professors. We were given scoring sheets to gauge the students' skills and at the end, the top contenders would be given a prize. It was always interesting to hear students with pronounced British accents and others with pronounced American accents, reflecting their instructors' origins. By the way, Liu Yi also stayed with Sue and me at our Oklahoma home. He was amazed at the space around us, going on long walks in the morning just to soak up the environment, with its cows, farms, wide open spaces, and clear air.

The art village of Dafen, a suburb of Buji, Longgang, Shenzhen, China, is a place I never would have thought of visiting. It was established in 1989 by the painter, Huang Jiang, who was an accomplished painting copier. It soon drew over 20 artists and by 2014 there were 7,000 of them in Dafen. Both copies and originals are sold there. The village is a gated community, with a giant sculpture of a hand holding a paintbrush at the entrance.

Ed Zeng, our Chinese professor friend who was, and is, fluent in English took Sue and me there.

It's a unique section of the city, in that it's filled with both large and small art workshops. Every conceivable type of art is made here: from art to reproductions of old masters to original Chinese paintings. It's a little overwhelming, as one cannot possibly visit all the production sites.

After walking through many of these shops, Ed took us to a large, museum-like facility, stocked with hundreds, if not thousands, of artworks. My eyes lit upon two very large original paintings of scenes from the Li River near Yangshou, in southwestern China. Sue and I had been there on one of our trips and were fascinated by the karsts—needle-pointed mountains—often nestled in water and shrouded in fog. The paintings included a fisherman with his nets hung out to dry on the edge of the river. Very tranquil. One could almost hear the gentle water rippling by and the cormorants settling on the surface to fish.

I don't have the exact measurements of the paintings, but I'd guess 7-8 feet long by 4 feet wide, plus each was in its own frame of about four inches wide. The owner joined us and encouraged bids on the twin paintings. I made a few feeble attempts to no avail until Ed whispered in my ear, "ba ba ba" (eight eight eight). Eight is a good luck number in China, so Ed was clever in suggesting a triple wallop of lucky digits. Eight hundred eighty-eight yuan at that time was about $100. This seemed incredibly cheap to me for two wonderful originals, but, to my surprise, the owner accepted!

It was difficult to ask the owner to remove the paintings from the frames, which we couldn't carry on an airplane back home, and to roll them up into two hard cardboard tubes—which we could transport on the plane.

One of these I gave to my youngest son, Chris, who had taken care of our house in Smithton, Illinois, while we were in China. It now hangs in his house in Fairview Heights, Illinois. The other hangs in our home in Elgin, Oklahoma, on the northern wall of our family room. It brings back many pleasant memories every time I look at it.

Last but not least, Liu Yi, Edward Zeng, and Dr. Sima, a Chinese ophthalmologist, would take Sue and me to dinner to enjoy the many different cuisines of China. The restaurants were well-appointed, and the food was terrific!

We tried Shanghainese food, Sichuanese, and many others—all excellent. Anyone from the U.S. who thinks that the Chinese food they typically get here is representative of China's foods is vastly underestimating the very different tastes and kinds of cuisine.

The Chinese were exceptionally kind, generous, and hospitable to us. One example of this came from Dr. Sima, who was from Sichuan Province and was anxious to show us around the many sites of that province. She arranged for us to stay in a luxurious hot springs spa resort hotel—all at her expense, as was the entire trip, with meals included. We were provided with two young guides to show us around. Dr. Sima knew the mayor of the town near Chengdu where she had grown up. She had asked the mayor to treat us well. We were invited to a dinner with the mayor and some other local officials. I asked one of our guides to express our gratitude for his hospitality and generosity. The guide was terrified of the man and was visibly shaking and nearly unable to speak at all. We learned the reason for this later: he was also the head of the area Communist Party, with maximum power over the area and its residents. Anyway, the mayor and one of his aides each gave us a miniature model of a Buddhist monument that was at the top of a local mountain. The model came with its own carrying case and bright yellow cover.

While in the Chengdu area, we visited the "Chengdu Research Base of Giant Panda Breeding", or simply Chengdu Panda Base, which is a non-profit research and breeding facility for giant pandas and other rare animals. We watched a young panda chomping down on fresh bamboo shoots, which is apparently their favorite food. There was also a "maternity ward" for baby pandas, as they are delicate and need careful care to survive their youngster hood. There were large, adult pandas lounging around in trees looking about as unconcerned as drunks on a park bench.

Our Chengdu guides took us to a restaurant where the waiters were outfitted in Mao-era military uniforms. One of these came to our table to take our order, giving a vigorous military salute as he greeted us. On the walls were drawings and paintings of Mao which seemed a little mocking. In fact, the whole atmosphere suggested that nobody there was taking Mao seriously at all.

Many of the Chinese we talked to were reluctant to discuss politics or chat about the Communist Party. The longer we stayed in China the more we realized that its people had never really been involved in deciding who was to govern them. That was not a recent phenomenon, but one that was centuries and centuries old. There was an unconcerned attitude about the government and even expressions of being distanced from its actions. An oft-quoted saying was, "The mountains are high, and the emperor is far away." Yet it would be a very large mistake to think that the Chinese were not patriotic — on the contrary, my experience was the opposite: they were hyper-patriotic and proud of their country. After all, they were enjoying prosperity and increasing world power. The young Chinese college kids I taught knew their parents, grandparents and many generations before them had never had it so good. While we Americans focus on the human rights record of the Communist Party, that Party has claimed some monumental achievements. Which other country could state that it had lifted a half-billion people out of poverty?

It's difficult to pick out events that stuck in our memories. One that amused me arose out of a request to go to a recording studio to narrate lessons on English speaking. Another English professor and I agreed to the recordings and thought nothing of it. One day I was in a taxi going from our apartment to downtown. I was startled to hear my voice on the car radio, delivering one of these mini-lectures. The taxi driver was mouthing the words trying his best to learn all he could. I didn't laugh, but I wanted to. I didn't talk much as I feared he'd jump out of the vehicle in astonishment.

Another surprise was being invited to tour a water treatment plant in Shenzhen. There were journalists and photographers there, which wasn't all that uncommon, but what was different was seeing my photo on the front page of the Shenzhen Daily the next day, holding a test tube of water and being touted as an "American water treatment expert".

While we were living in Shenzhen we went "mountain climbing" up Nanshan (south mountain). Mountain climbing is often a different kind of climbing. That is, there were steps almost the whole way. Now, climbing steps is not often a cakewalk, either, and this wasn't. In any event, on the way up we stepped off the steps for a moment and it was then that Sue fell and fractured her wrist bones. We had been invited on this hike by our friend, Edward Zeng, and he offered to carry Sue down the mountain on his back. Sue felt she could position her arm so the pain wouldn't be unbearable, and we made our way down and then were taken to a hospital. We discovered that medical care was a little different—not that the hospital wasn't modern (it was), but one had to pay in advance a certain deposit in Yuan. Thank heavens for Edward, who fronted the money, and Sue was admitted. Edward felt enormous responsibility for Sue being hurt while he was "hosting" the mountain climb. We repeatedly assured him that he bore no responsibility for the fall, but I'm not sure he ever accepted that. (We did promptly pay him back for his Yuan advance.) One of the first medical persons to see Sue took her arm and tried to stretch it out, thinking that might "cure" it. She screamed in pain so he decided that might not be the best thing to try with a Westerner. The fall took place on a Sunday, and the hospital advised Sue that they'd get her to surgery on Thursday. Edward called our doctor friend, Dr. Sima, who then contacted the head of the hospital, and the surgery was scheduled almost immediately, with the hospital head leading the team. The surgery was performed in a modern surgical operating room, and she had a device installed that mounted a device into the bone of her hand and further down the arm, with a crossbar between the two. We were skeptical at first that this was appropriate, but when we researched it, the method used was precisely the one used in the USA and was state-of-the-art. She had to wear this very awkward device for several weeks while the wrist bones healed properly in place, thanks to the device.

While in the hospital, Edward arranged for his niece, Sherry Yun, to sit with her in the room. Sherry was a young girl—maybe 17—and she has remained a friend to this day. She came to the U.S. to study at Iowa State University and we picked her up at the airport and delivered her to the university. After graduation, Sherry began work at Google, where she remains today. We recently had a FaceTime session with her and her new baby, Henry Li. (By the way, I officiated at her wedding in San Mateo, California, having obtained a minister's license to do so.)

When our time in Shenzhen and at the University came to an end, Liu Yi, my English Department head, met us at our apartment in the early morning as we were loading up to head home via the Hong Kong Airport. He followed us to the gate in the walls surrounding the campus, following an ancient Chinese custom of seeing visitors off at the walls of the city. It was such a thoughtful thing to do; we were deeply touched.

Shenzhen University had a program that encouraged traveling to other countries. We profs were given a small "travel stipend" and could use the university travel bureau to arrange trips. As a consequence, Sue and I visited Australia, New Zealand, Thailand, Cambodia, Vietnam, and many different parts of China. We saw the terra cotta soldiers in Xi'An, the Great Wall outside of Beijing, stayed in Shanghai for a few days, and enjoyed every bit of it.

So, after we left China in 2006, I soon got restless again. On a whim, I applied to present lectures on a Royal Caribbean cruise ship. This resulted in a free cruise that traveled from Bangkok, Thailand, to the shores of Cambodia, Vietnam, Hainan Island on the southeastern coast of China, Shenzhen, and finally Shanghai. My lectures were on our previous travel experiences at those places. I had lots of photos, slides, and historical material to use.

I was surprised at the auditorium on the ship where the presentations were made. It had a large stage, fully equipped with sophisticated sound facilities, a sound crew to help, large video screens on each side of the stage, and a video crew situated in the back of the auditorium, adjusting lights, sound, and effects as desired. The auditorium seated around 400.

Endnotes
BOOK II
Chapter 29

[37] Du, Juan, The Shenzhen Experiment, The Story of China's Instant City, Cambridge, Massachusetts: Harvard University Press, 2020, at Introduction. 5-6.

CHAPTER 30

Elgin, Oklahoma

So we took up residence in Elgin, Oklahoma, in 2006, having bought the home that Dad and Frances had built for themselves. Frances, now widowed, was ready to live with her daughter, Nora, and her husband, Joe, so we bought the home and have lived there since. Life in Elgin, a town of maybe 4,000 souls, is a big change from living in a Chinese city of somewhere between 12-18 million, but we've adapted. It's definitely a pleasure to be near two brothers, David and Jimmy, and their families. The air is certainly cleaner. Elgin has gained considerably more amenities since we've lived here, and Lawton, only 15 minutes away, has also changed for the better. We are now both in our eighties and suffering some of the consequences of old age. But we're happy. We've seen much of the world, lived overseas, and gained an appreciation of other cultures that would have been difficult to get in a small town in Oklahoma. While we are some distance from our six accumulated children: Sue's Wayne and family in Houston, Texas; Dale and family in Plainfield, Illinois (a suburb of Chicago); and Kristi and family in Caseyville, Illinois (in the MetroEast across from St. Louis, Missouri) and my three: Jay, now in Salt Lake City, Utah; Cyndi in Phoenix, Arizona; and Chris, in Fairview Heights, Illinois, we communicate using the marvelous modern technology and thus don't feel out of touch. Life has been good to us.

BOOK III

LAURA DREWS

Comment introducing Book III: This part of the Family History is very special. You will be introduced, in her own words, to Laura Drews, a delightful addition to our family that we discovered in 2020. It's astounding that we had no knowledge of her existence before then, but we are grateful that she's now an acknowledged part of the family.

LAURA DREWS IN HER OWN WORDS

On October 25, 1974, I was born to Deborah Kolker weighing 8lbs 4 oz and 21 inches long. I was born in Fort Worth, Texas at Duncan Memorial Hospital. At two weeks old, I was given up for adoption to a married couple who lived in Lake Charles, La. As soon as my adopted mom and dad picked me up from the Edna Gladney Home, which is the adoption agency my birth mom lived in while she was pregnant with me, we flew to Oklahoma City, Oklahoma. My parents were so excited to show me off to the family!

There isn't too much I can remember at such a young age, but I do remember slamming my fingers in a sliding glass door when I was four. Thankfully, I didn't break anything. In second grade I fractured my elbow by jumping off a swing. This was rough because it was my right arm, and I am right-handed.

Sometime in my elementary years, my parents started reading a book to me. The book was called, The Little House

That Found Happiness. This book helped me understand all about adoption. I thought I was a very special little girl. Not only was I adopted, but I was also adopted by two parents who loved me very much. When I was 10 years old, I went to Europe with my parents. We went to England, Paris, and Scotland. I remember a lot about this trip. I toured everything a person could have possibly toured. My parents had this trip thought out very well. We stayed in a three-story apartment (flat) in London. This was a nice apartment, but taking groceries up to the second floor was rough! I remember riding the double-decker buses and riding the underground tube (train). In York, England, my parents bought me a bike. I remember taking that bike back on the hovercraft and the airplane back home. Whew, that was not easy! While visiting Scotland I remember I thought seeing kilts on men was a little different. Oh, Paris was beautiful! I was too scared to go all the way to the top of the Eiffel Tower, so I only went halfway up. My mom stayed with me while my dad went all the way to the top. We stayed in Europe for 5 weeks. It was so fun, so I thought!

When we got back home, my parents separated. My dad was manic-depressive and an alcoholic. This tore my parents' marriage. We all went to therapy for his alcoholism and to learn about how to cope with a manic-depressive person. After all three of us attended therapies, my parents got back together. It was a time I will never forget. The first dinner with my dad back in the house, my parents presented me with a very special gift. It was a necklace that I will always keep very close to my heart. Life was great again! Wrong! My mom filed for legal separation about a year later. My dad was mentally and physically abusive. Six months later, my mom filed for divorce. I was around 12 years old at the time. I lived with my mom, and I remember being scared to death of going to my dad's. I never knew if he was going to be drinking or if he would just leave me in my room at his condo while he went to his new girlfriend's house. His girlfriend was someone he met at a singles group at his church. It took me a long time to want to have anything to do with her. I was in such denial because my dad was seeing another lady and it wasn't my mom! I hated going to my dad's house. I remember crying and calling my mom begging her to come get me. My dad finally married her, and she ended up being a wonderful stepmom!

As I got older my dad finally got help! He quit drinking and was on medicine for his manic depression. I finally had my dad back! My dad and I were always very close, so when my dad was mentally ill it was very hard on me. I never thought I would be able to have that dad/daughter bond again. After my parents divorced my dad bought me my own phone line so he could call me. I loved it! I thought I was big stuff with my very own phone line in the house. He never missed a day of calling me! We were so close, and I loved our relationship. When I was young my dad and I always said The Lord's Prayer together at night. Another special thing we did together was on Saturday mornings the two of us went to eat donuts or he took me to McDonald's for breakfast. This was just some of the many things we did together.

A lot of fun things happened when I turned 16. I got my first car, got a cell phone installed in my car (I thought this was first class), and I was able to date! I dated a few guys before finding my high school sweetheart and the husband I have today! His name is Brian Carl Drews. He went to a different high school than me, but that didn't stop us from seeing each other almost every day. This was a great time in my life! We had so much fun together. He would meet me at my school my senior year when I got out of class, and we just hung out! It was amazing and we were inseparable. Brian and I did everything together. If he wasn't at my apartment, I was at his house. After graduating from high school, I went to college at McNeese State University. My mom made me live at home during my first semester of college before I could move out. As soon as I could move out, I did! I moved into an apartment. I thought I was SO BIG! Freedom!! I went to college for 2 years before dropping out and going back to work. I worked for five years. We dated for 6 years before getting married. We eloped to Las Vegas. Neither one of us wanted a huge wedding.

During those five years, I married Brian in June 1997. A few years after we got married, we both went back to college to finish our degrees. I graduated with a bachelor's in Psychology and a minor in Sociology. When I graduated, I was three months pregnant with twins! Needless to say, I did not pursue my degree. I was sick with this pregnancy, so I stayed at home while Brian worked.

Brian and I were married for 6 years before starting our family. On October 4, 2003, my twin daughters, Kylie Brandle Drews and Kourtney Brianna Drews, were born prematurely. They were miracles from God! Both were born perfectly healthy six weeks early!

When the girls were four, I got pregnant with a baby boy. It was during this pregnancy that I decided to contact the adoption agency where I was adopted, the Edna Gladney Home. I hired a private investigator through the adoption agency to try and find my birth mom. It was not a guarantee she would be found, but I felt it was worth a try. Within just a very short time I got word that the birth mom had been found. We started our communication through letters that the agency had to read before passing them on to the recipient. They would put the letter in a separate envelope and mail it to the recipient. We had to be very careful what we put in the letters because we could not tell each other our last names, we could say what state we lived in, but could not say the city we lived in. This was a great way to find out a little information about each other. I wanted to find out my medical history, among several other things. Most importantly, I was interested in the story my birth mom had to tell about my existence. Mainly, her story, about how I am here today and why she gave me up for adoption. We sent pictures of each other to each other. She told me she has three daughters. All three daughters, my sisters, knew nothing about me, and her husband, not my birth dad, knew about me, but it was a touchy subject with him. She tried to convert me to Catholicism in these letters. I told her I was raised Episcopal, and I wasn't converting at the time. The very next letter she told me she was closing off contact and she returned all of my pictures, but one back to me. She said she would notify Gladney if or when she decided to open the contact again. As you can imagine this was very upsetting to me, but I figured this would happen. One reason this really upset me was she knew I was pregnant, and she closed off the contact a month before I gave birth to my son, Zachary Carl Drews. A month before my twins started Pre-K, my son, Zachary, was born on July 29, 2008. He was a healthy beautiful baby boy!

After she closed the contact off between us, I really wanted to find my birth dad! She gave me a bad taste in my mouth about my birth dad, but I wanted to hear his story. Something seemed fishy about my birth moms' story and I was curious as to what my birth dad would tell me.

My adopted mom bought me a 23andMe kit. After a year of it sitting on the shelf, I finally decided to put it to good use. I sent it off and within a very short time, I had results of a first cousin! I immediately contacted this first cousin and after giving her some information she knew I was a match! It was history after this! I was in touch with two of my three sisters! Still to this day, I stay in contact with one every couple of weeks and talk to the other one on occasion. After meeting my birth moms' side, I was able to talk to my uncles and found out my birth dad's name. This information gave me clues on how to look for him online. After digging through a few findings, unfortunately, I found my birth dad's obituary. This was very upsetting to me for many reasons. My birth dad died in 2008 and this was the year I was in contact with my birth mom. A month and a half after my birth mom stopped the communication between us, my birth dad died. I couldn't believe it! My dream of meeting my birth dad was not in my future, but it did lead me to two brothers' names whom I found in my birth dad's obituary. I immediately looked up their names and found that one of my brothers was a cop in the same county where my birth mom and birth dad lived. I looked up his name online and found a telephone number that brought me straight to his desk. I left a voice message with him, and he called me back! We had a great conversation and he proceeded to give me my other brother's number. My other brother called me shortly after my phone call with the first brother. We have talked or texted pretty much every day since December 14, 2020. It has been a great experience.

I had a lot of fear to reach out to the cousin I found on 23andme, but I knew if I didn't make the move then I would never have the opportunity to meet any of my birth family. I still hope to meet my mom's brothers one day, but because of COVID, we have not made any attempts, yet. I have met two of my sisters and both brothers! My lifelong dream of having siblings really did come true. I was raised as an only child and always wanted to know if I had siblings in my birth family. I am very blessed that all of my birth family was very accepting and loving. I now have my birth family as part of my life!

[End of Laura's own words.]

Laura gave permission to supplement the above with information about her birth father, as follows:

Detlev "Ted" Werner Mason was born November 28, 1952, in Giessen, Landkreiss Giessen, Hesse, Germany. His mother was Elfriede Klingelhoefer-Schmidt Mason, born in the same place and died in Lawton on June 14, 2019. His father was Sgt. Eugene Mason, who Elfriede met while working at the Rivers Barracks USA Army Base in Giessen, Germany, and they were thereafter married. Brother Jimmy remembers Debbie introducing Ted to our parents at the family home at 13786 NE 75th Street, Elgin, and remembered him as a tall man. Ted has a brother, Terry L. Mason, born in 1961, who is still living in Lawton, married to Nancy Mason.

Laura Drews and her family.
Top to Bottom: Laura; her husband, Brian; twin daughters,
Kylie and Kourtney; Zachary.